Colección Tamesis

SERIE A: MONOGRAFÍAS, 338

THE RECEPTION OF MACHIAVELLI IN EARLY MODERN SPAIN

KEITH DAVID HOWARD

THE RECEPTION OF MACHIAVELLI IN EARLY MODERN SPAIN

TAMESIS

First published 2014 by Tamesis, Woodbridge

ISBN 978 1 85566 282 7

Tamesis is an imprint of Boydell & Brewer Ltd
PO Box 9, Woodbridge, Suffolk IP12 3DF, UK
and of Boydell & Brewer Inc.
668 Mt Hope Avenue, Rochester, NY 14620–2731, USA
website: www.boydellandbrewer.com

A CIP catalogue record for this book is available from the British Library

Printed on acid-free paper

Typeset by

The Word Service, 1 Oxford Street, Hungerford, RG17 0ET

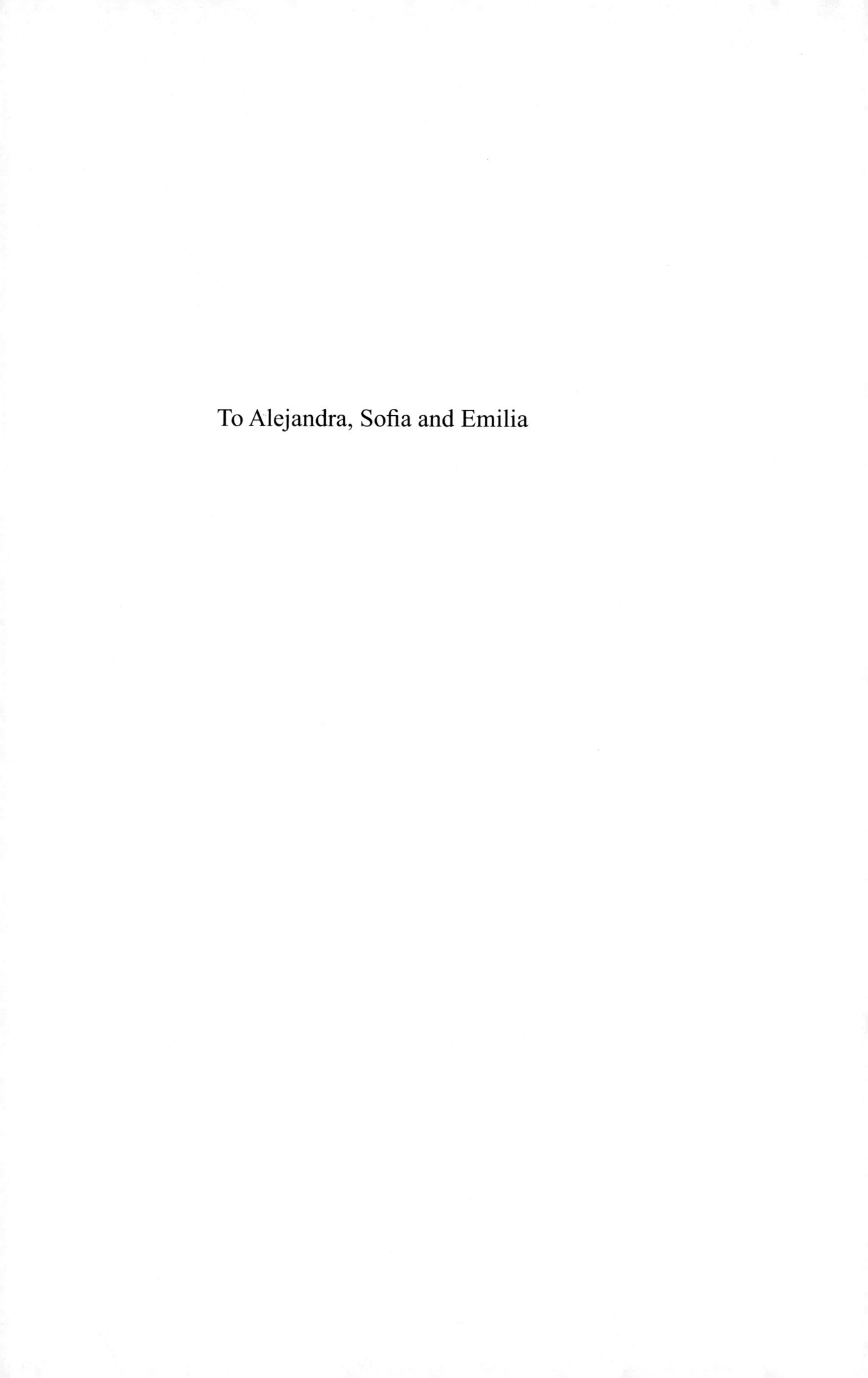

To Alejandra, Sofia and Emilia

Contents

Acknowledgements ix

Introduction 1

1. Medieval and Renaissance Humanist Political Discourse and Machiavelli 13

2. Machiavelli and Spanish Imperialist Discourse in the Sixteenth Century 41

3. Machiavelli and the Foundations of the Spanish Reason-of-State Tradition: Giovanni Botero and Pedro de Ribadeneyra 69

4. Machiavellian Discourse in the Hispanic Baroque Reason-of-State Tradition 97

5. Juan Pablo Mártir Rizo's Rereading of the *Prince* 129

Conclusion 155

Bibliography 159

Index 167

Acknowledgements

I would like to offer a special thanks to E. Michael Gerli for his generous guidance at all stages of this project, and to Alison Weber, Deborah Parker and John Lyons, for their helpful comments. I would also like to thank the readers at Tamesis for their constructive suggestions.

This project would not have been possible without the financial support of the First Year Assistant Professor Summer Grant as well as the Office of the Vice President for Research and the College of Arts and Sciences at Florida State University.

Chapter 2 contains a slightly revised version of "Fadrique Furió Ceriol's Machiavellian Vocabulary of Contingency," *Renaissance Studies* 26, no. 5 (2012): 641–57, reprinted with the permission of the Society for Renaissance Studies and Blackwell Publishing. Chapters 3 and 4 contain revised sections of "The Anti-Machiavellians of the Spanish Baroque: A Reassessment," *LATCH: A Journal for the Study of the Literary Artifact in Theory, Culture and History* 5 (2012): 106–19, reprinted with the permission of the editor of *LATCH*.

Introduction

In 1637, Claudio Clemente published his *Machiavelismo degollado por la Christiana Sabiduria de España y Austria* in Alcalá de Henares. In it, after a brief introduction to the "Politicos," whom he characterizes as members of a religious sect, Clemente takes his readers on an imaginary expedition in which he infiltrates their temple and witnesses an induction ceremony for a young noble.[1] It is worthwhile to recount this narration, because its overtly fictitious nature illustrates very well to what extent the anti-Machiavellians of the reason-of-state tradition had been utilizing an invented characterization (or, in this case, a caricature) of Machiavelli and a group of his supposed devotees for rhetorical ends.

He begins by explaining that it was difficult to enter the temples of the "Idolatras de la Policia": "porque ninguno puede alcançar los negocios que alli se tratan, las palabras que se dizen, los mysterios que se celebran, si no es que en primer lugar se aya el tambien consagrado por Sacerdote de los mismos mysterios, y jurado aquel tan sagrado y inuiolable juramento."[2]

This insistence on the secrecy, of the "mystery," of the *políticos*' rites and knowledge brings new dramatic life to the tradition of *arcana imperii*.[3] Clemente declares his intention was to expose the *políticos* for what they were: "para que auiendo descubierto sus secretos, vengan todos en aborrecimiento deste contagio mortal del comercio y trato de vnos hombres con otros."[4] His method was to approach a man whom he suspected of being "el Sacristan y Guarda de la Capilla de aquel templo,"[5] who responded that he could not possibly admit him into the ceremony: "por estar juramentado con vn inuiolable juramento que auia hecho por la vida del Monarca, y por la dicha de la Republica."[6] Nevertheless, after much begging and insistence, the guard acquiesced.

1 Claudio Clemente, *El machiavelismo degollado por la Christiana Sabiduria de España y Austria* (Alcalá: Antonio Vázquez, 1637), 1–30.

2 Ibid., 7.

3 For the association between Machiavelli and the *arcana imperii* in the early modern period, see Peter S. Donaldson, *Machiavelli and Mystery of State* (Cambridge: Cambridge University Press, 1988).

4 Clemente, *Machiavelismo degollado*, 9.

5 Ibid., 9.

6 Ibid., 10.

Clemente provides a detailed description of the temple, whose walls were lined with portraits of the most illustrious *políticos*: "Eteocles, Euripides, Iulio Cesar, Seneca, Cornelio Tacito, Cricias, Tiberio, Arnaldo de Brixia, Pedro Cugnerio, Nicolas Machiauelo, Carlos Molineo, Iuan Bodino, Philipo Plesio Morneo, Lanueo, y otros muchos,"[7] most of whose names had been repeatedly listed as dangerous writers and men of action throughout the Spanish anti-Machiavellian tradition, as we shall see. At one point in the ceremony, all the attendees recited out loud in both Latin and Spanish their fundamental rule: "*El creer en Dios, el guardar la ley que cada vno quisiere, y quanto le pareciere, el guardar la justicia, cometer maldades, se ha de obseruar en quanto se estuuiere bien a la comodidad de la vida, y al vtil del gouierno.*"[8] For the *políticos*, the common good of the political community is the only goal, and all religious and moral considerations may be disregarded in order to achieve it.

Clemente then introduces the *Orador*, a character who serves as the cult's priest. After providing a detailed commentary on their fundamental rule and enumerating in chronological order all of the best *políticos* and their specific contributions, the Orador arrives at the master of them all:

> Pero todos aquestos que he ido contando a la larga, cuan grandes ellos son (y son en la verdad grandissimos) si se comparan en la ciencia politica con *Nicolas Machiavelo* (a la inuocacion de cuyo nombre todos nos leuantamos, haziendole reuerencia) sin dificultad le dan y conceden la palma. Ninguno comprehendio esta facultad mas diuinamente; ninguno la dispuso con mas cuidado; ninguno escriuio della con mas claridad y ornato; ninguno la sacò a luz con mas aliento; ninguno la enseñò con mas fruto. Y para que no parezca, que aquesta es solamente amplificacion retorica, veanse sus escritos, que todos traemos en las manos aquestas inmortales memorias de su sabiduria, a pesar del Vaticano de Roma, que tantas vezes se ha embrauecido contra ellas.[9]

Machiavelli is revered by the *políticos* like a religious prophet. They carry his collected writings to the ceremony as if they were the Bible. And despite his appeal to the contrary, the Orador's portrait of Machiavelli that follows is precisely a rhetorical amplification of a specific enumeration of aphorisms attributed to Machiavelli that Clemente has drawn from the Spanish anti-Machiavellian tradition:

> Aqui imploro tu fee, Pretendiente Ilustre; dime, de quan adelantada policia es determinar, que el derecho y justicia de la guerra se ha de medir con sola la voluntad del Principe. Pues esto determinò Machiavelo: de quan diuino

7 Ibid., 12.
8 Ibid., 17.
9 Ibid., 26.

> consejo es serle autor al Principe, de que en la administracion de su Imperio se ponga delante de los ojos para imitar a vno de los mas insignes Tiranos, y que fixe en el su atencion; porque juzga que es fuerça, ayan sido hombres de excelente ingenio, adelantado valor, los que solo a sus fuerças y a su industria debieron la conquista de sus Imperios? Desto fue autor Machiavelo. De quanta sagacidad es el persuadir al Principe, que si quiere tomar vengança de alguna Ciudad, ò Prouincia, sin que le cueste mouer guerra contra ella, la procure viciar con corrompidas costumbres; y que si quiere cortar a sus enemigos todas las esperanças y deseos de venir a paces, los haga grandes injurias: y si pretende tener absoluto señorio de las Prouincias sugetas, disponga de tal suerte las poblaciones y colonias, que sean excluidos los antiguos moradoradores [*sic*]; y a los que mostraren sentimiento desto, los destruya y acabe con sus casas y familias? Esto persuadio Machiavelo. De quanta prudencia es conocer, que los antiguos agrauios no se pueden borrar con nueuos y crecidos beneficios; que no ai que fiar de nadie, aunque sea del amigo mas del alma: que si quiere el Principe executar algun castigo, le ponga siempre titulo y pretexto lustroso; que la crueldad se ha de derramar de vn golpe, los beneficios se han de destilar a gotas; que se han de fomentar facciones, y parcialidades entre sus mismos subditos; que han de ser entresacados de la Republica los que tienen zelo de su bien; que por la causa de reinar, ni se ha de ir a la mano en sus maldades, ni poner limite a sus engaños, ni tener compassion de las haziendas, y vidas de sus vassallos? Todo esto conocio Machiavelo. De quanta confiança, y magnanima seguridad es atribuir a los consejos, y prudencia de Moyses los loores de sus hazañas; y aunque mas se alboroten los supersticiosos, y mas contradiga aquessa que llaman sagrada Escritura, quitarle de las manos a Dios la gloria de tan felices sucessos, y gloriosos triunfos? Esto supo quitar a Dios, esto supo ofrecer a Moyses nuestro Machiavelo.[10]

The Orador gives Machiavelli credit for the separation between politics and religious ethics: "De quan grande capacidad es el que en la materia de Imperio, y Estado aya apartado de los coraçones tan de raiz todos los escrupulos que se pueden ofrecer, auyentado los miedos, y rezelos de la justicia diuina, que amenaza a los malhechores; y quitado la congoxosa eleccion de la Religion verdadera, ò falsa; y otras mas de mil cosas, que no sin aduertencia callo?"[11] The Orador concludes by comparing Machiavelli's sect with those of Luther and Calvin, further underlining its religious nature:

> Todos aquellos executò Machiavelo, porque arrancò los escrupulos con generosidad, y anchura de coraçon; auyentò los miedos con fortaleza, quitò las congoxosas elecciones con felicidad: y digo con felicidad, porque pues es cosa muy assentada, y que aun los mismos contrarios la confiessan, que

10 Ibid., 26–28.

11 Ibid., 28.

> se ha esparcido, y dilatado tanto la dotrina de aqueste sabio Principe de los Politicos, que si se comparan con los que ella ha tenido los sequaces de Luthero, y Caluino, y otros autores de semejantes sectas, sin dificultad les vence en numero, en lustre, en autoridad, y riquezas.[12]

As the readers may infer when they take a position of ironic distance from the Orador, Machiavelli's sect is even worse than Luther's and Calvin's, because it enjoys many more followers.

The ceremony ends when the young initiate makes his pledge:

> *Yo Poliphilo juro por la deidad de la Diosa Policia, y por vida del Monarca, en cuyas sagradas estatuas con crecida veneracion pongo la mano, que tengo de viuir, y acomodarme en todo a la formula y modo de viuir de los Politicos: y que en el creer que ay Dios, en la obseruancia de la Religion, en la guarda de la justicia; ò por el contrario, en resoluerme a qualquier mal hecho, solamente tengo de atender a los interesses de la vida, y al bien del Estado.*[13]

When the ceremony is over, Clemente describes the horror that the spectacle has produced in him and he proceeds to attack the supposed beliefs of the *políticos*. He simply cannot believe that there could exist a people so barbarous that they would treat piety and religion as a toy. Nor can he believe that they could be so idiotic that they do not see that, "en quitando la Religion, y dando licencia a los vicios, se destruyen y acaban las Republicas."[14] This thought leads Clemente to point out how the *políticos* themselves recognize that religion is necessary to control the people. In order for this to work, it would need to remain a secret that they are using religion in this way. Why then, Clemente asks, do the *políticos* reveal this secret all the time by publishing it in their works for the public to read? Clemente can think of only one answer: "Es por ventura, para que sabiendolo el vulgo, nos perdamos todos, y se deshaga la vnion y vinculo, con que vnas naciones y otras se vnen, y se alian?"[15]

To answer the question of how it was possible, in the first half of the seventeenth century, for a Spaniard to publish such an obviously fictional characterization of Machiavelli and his supposed disciples is only one aim of this book. In fact, Clemente is an extreme example that appeared toward the end of a tradition that gradually made this kind of mischaracterization widespread. At the same time, he is an exception to the rule that Spaniards throughout the early modern period did incorporate Machiavelli's ideas into their own treatises. The purpose of this study is to demonstrate that a real Machiavellism

12 Ibid., 28–29.
13 Ibid., 30.
14 Ibid., 32–33.
15 Ibid., 34.

was present in Spain throughout the early modern period. In order to do this it is necessary to distinguish between this real Machiavellism, defined as the observable appropriation of key Machiavellian concepts carried out by an individual or group of writers, and a rhetorical pretense of anti-Machiavellism, which was only pervasive during and after the Spanish Counter-Reformation Baroque. The mischaracterization of the historical person called Niccolò Machiavelli served a twofold rhetorical purpose: first, much like what we have seen in the extreme example of Clemente, Spanish political writers used an invented, secular "doctrine" founded by "Maquiavelo" as a rhetorical tool that allowed them to define their own Catholic political ideas by opposition; second, their ostensible opposition to Machiavelli distracted their readers, especially those readers who were not directly familiar with Machiavelli's works, from the fact that they had adapted specific Machiavellian discourses to their own worldview. In this way it will be possible to bring to light the early modern reception of Machiavelli in Spain, a subject which unfortunately has been either neglected or misunderstood by previous scholars of European political thought.

The Early Reception of Machiavelli in Europe

Giuliano Procacci has laid out a general outline of the European reception of Machiavelli, focusing on those writers who read Machiavelli directly and avoiding those who express an interpretation of "Machiavellismo" as the theory and practice of "ragion di stato."[16] The first readers of Machiavelli admired and imitated his method of searching for general rules of politics in both history and contemporary experience. As Rodolfo De Mattei has shown, many of Machiavelli's first readers approached Machiavelli's works in a markedly non-polemical way, agreeing with Machiavelli's method but pointing out what they considered minor errors of judgment.[17] According to Procacci, the European reception of Machiavelli is best understood as part of the reception of the Italian Renaissance in general.[18] As writers continued to confront modernity with antiquity, Machiavelli was read in association with other writers, both ancient and modern.

Above all, Machiavelli's works were read in conjunction with Aristotle's. In 1523, Agostino Nifo da Sessa published his *De regnandi peritia ad Carolum V Imper. Caesarem semper Augustum*, which constitutes a reworking in Latin of Machiavelli's *Prince*. Essentially, Nifo transforms Machiavelli's *Prince* into

16 Giuliano Procacci, *Machiavelli nella cultura europea dell'età moderna* (Rome: Editori Laterza, 1995), vi.

17 Rodolfo De Mattei. *Dal premachiavellismo all'antimachiavellismo* (Florence: Sansoni, 1969), 123–62.

18 Procacci, *Machiavelli*, 141.

a work that more closely resembles a traditional *De regimine principum*. Structurally, Nifo reorganizes his work into five thematically unified books. The first eleven chapters were divided among books 1 and 3, dedicated respectively to the acquisition of states and to their maintenance with respect to internal problems or threats. Chapters 12 through 14 become book 2, dedicated to the conservation of one's state against external enemies. Chapters 16 and 17 become book 4. Book 5, which discusses honest means of governing and the best prince, is Nifo's own. In terms of content, Aristotle's *Politics* is the key with which Nifo interprets Machiavelli, repeatedly citing especially book 5 of the classical work of "nostro peripatetico."[19] Machiavelli's *principe* becomes either *re* or *tiranno* depending on the specific case. Ferdinand the Catholic, for example, is a *re*, but Nifo leaves out how he uses religion for political ends and how he used a "pietosa crudeltà"[20] when he expelled the Jews from Spain. For Nifo, who only two years earlier had published a *Libellus de his que ad optimis principibus agenda sunt*, the good prince was a Christian prince: this explains why, in his re-elaboration of Machiavelli, he left out or modified anything that might have sounded irreverent.[21]

As Procacci has pointed out, Nifo initiated a long line of reception of Machiavelli, lasting throughout the sixteenth century, characterized by an interpretation of his works through Aristotle.[22] In Francesco Sansovino's *Dialogo della pratica della ragione*, composed between 1538 and 1542, Aristotle's *Politics* and Machiavelli's *Prince* are considered a group in opposition to Castiglione and Plato. In his 1549 Tuscan translation and commentary of Aristotle's *Politics*, Bernardo Segni refers his readers to the *Prince* in his gloss of chapter 10 of book 5, where Aristotle discusses political corruption. Likewise, in his commentary to chapter 1 of book 4 of his 1550 translation of Aristotle's *Ethics*, he summarizes Machiavelli's treatment of liberality. Girolamo Cardano, in his *De sapientia* of 1544, offers the examples of Moses, Cirus, Romulus, Teseus, Edipus and Castruccio Castracani of how wisdom can overcome fortune, in a way that resembles chapter 6 of the *Prince* and the *Vita di Castruccio*. Similarly, when he turns to human wisdom Cardano's portraits of Nabide, Agatocle, Oliverotto da Fermo, Francesco Sforza, Castruccio and especially Cesare Borgia all resemble Machiavelli's own treatment of these same figures. Besides these similar portraits, Cardano found many of his political precepts in the *Prince* and *Discourses on Livy*: to give just a few examples, the prince should only use his own arms; he should prefer to be feared rather than loved; and he should make his behavior conform to the times.[23]

19 Ibid., 68.
20 Ibid., 69.
21 Ibid., 65–70.
22 Ibid., 70–71.
23 Ibid., 70–78.

In Italy evidence of this association disappeared, understandably, when Machiavelli was included on the Roman Index of 1559; the same did not happen in other countries. For example, Louis Le Roy, in his 1568 French translation and commentary of Aristotle's *Politics*, in his notes on book 5 (that is, the same passages that had led Segni to make the same association), we find a similar reference to Machiavelli's works. Continuing the humanistic tradition of comparing ancients to moderns, part of how Le Roy uses Machiavelli is to update Aristotle. He not only cites the *Prince* and the *Discourses*, but the *Florentine Histories* and the *Art of War* as well. Le Roy was interested in Aristotle and Machiavelli because he wanted to study the universal rules of politics. In fact, in his *De l'origine, antiquité, progrès, excellence et utilitè de l'art politique* of 1567, Le Roy considers himself and Machiavelli as exceptions to the general negligence of the study of politics in comparison to other sciences, such as grammar, mathematics and astrology, because in their writings they both combined knowledge with experience.[24]

Spain is conspicuously neglected in Procacci's and others' general studies of the early, direct reception of Machiavelli. Perhaps this is due to the traditional view that the Spanish Inquisition prevented Spaniards from reading Machiavelli's works early on. However, over two decades ago Helena Puigdomenech Forcada demonstrated that Niccolò Machiavelli's political treatises circulated widely in Spain soon after they were first published in Rome, Florence and Venice in the 1530s and 1540s. From indirect evidence, we know that Charles V often read Machiavelli's *Discourses*. In 1552, a Castilian translation of this treatise entitled *Discursos de Nicolas Machiavelo* was published with the approval of Charles and dedicated to his son, the future Philip II. Machiavelli's works are among the many books in Italian that Spanish nobles and clergymen collected throughout the sixteenth and seventeenth centuries. In the second half of the sixteenth century alone, don Francisco de Mendoza Bobadilla, cardinal of Burgos, don Francisco de Zúñiga Guzmán y Sotomayor, duke of Béjar, the famous writer, soldier and diplomat don Diego Hurtado de Mendoza, don Iñigo López de Mendoza, duke of the Infantado in Guadalajara, and don Juan de la Cerda, duke of Medinaceli, all owned at least one of Machiavelli's works. Furthermore, despite the Roman Index of 1559, Machiavelli was not prohibited in Spain until Inquisitor General Gaspar Quiroga's Index of 1583–84.[25]

Despite this abundant evidence of the material circulation of Machiavelli in Spain, the question of what Spaniards took out of their reading of Machiavelli has continued largely unanswered until now. José Antonio Maravall dedicated a chapter of his *Estudios de historia del pensamiento español* to a vast but thus necessarily superficial consideration of Machiavelli and Machiavellism in Spain,

24 Ibid., 141–50.

25 Helena Puigdomenech Forcada, *Maquiavelo en España: Presencia de sus obras en los siglos XVI y XVII* (Madrid: Fundación Universitaria Española, 1988), 39–79, 140–62.

touching very briefly on many writers in whose works he found similarities with the Florentine.[26] Since then only a handful of studies have made an attempt to pinpoint specific Machiavellian readings by Spanish political writers in the sixteenth century. Francisco Castilla Urbano has recently noted several similarities in the political thought of Machiavelli and the humanist Juan Ginés de Sepúlveda, which do not, however, suggest a direct influence of one over the other.[27] In his exhaustive study of Spanish political treatises written during Philip II's reign, R. W. Truman has shown that both Sebastián Fox Morcillo and Fadrique Furió Ceriol must have been familiar with *Il Principe*, even though they do not cite Machiavelli by name, and that Tomás Cerdán de Tallada agreed with one passage that he cites in the *Discourses*.[28] Finally, Sydney Anglo has recently pointed out that Balthazar Ayala borrowed extensively from the *Discourses*.[29] Building on this line of research, the aim of Chapter 2 is to demonstrate that in the second half of the sixteenth century many Spaniards incorporated Machiavellian discourse into their own fashioning of an aggressive, Catholic Hispanic imperial ideology.

Machiavelli and Reason of State

Our understanding of the general European reception of Machiavelli is even less clear during the Counter-Reformation. Although his name is commonly associated with the term *reason of state*, Machiavelli never once employed this term. Giovanni della Casa first employed the phrase *ragione degli stati* in 1547 in contrast to *ragione civile*.[30] But it was not until the publication of Giovanni Botero's *Della ragion di stato libri dieci* (1589) that the phrase became popular among Counter-Reformation Catholics, thus initiating a long tradition of treatises that focus on this subject, which would last throughout the Baroque. Our understanding of the relationship between Machiavelli and this tradition has been refined since the publication of Friedrich Meinecke's *Die Idee der Staatsräson*

26 José Antonio Maravall, "Maquiavelo y maquiavelismo en España," in *Estudios de historia del pensamiento español* (Madrid: Ediciones Cultura Hispánica, 1983), 39–72.

27 Francisco Castilla Urbano, "Rasgos maquiavélicos en un pensador antimaquiavélico: Juan Ginés de Sepúlveda," in *Maquiavelo y España: Maquiavelismo y antimaquiavelismo en la cultura española de los siglos XVI y XVII*, ed. Juan Manuel Forte and Pablo López Álvarez (Madrid: Biblioteca Nueva, 2008), 111–33.

28 R. W. Truman, *Spanish Treatises on Government, Society, and Religion in the Time of Philip II: The* De regimine principum *and Associated Traditions* (Leiden: Brill, 1999), 39–66, 89–114, 194.

29 Sydney Anglo, *Machiavelli—The First Century: Studies in Enthusiasm, Hostility, and Irrelevance* (Oxford: Oxford University Press, 2005), 551–52.

30 Peter Burke, "Tacitism, Scepticism, and Reason of State," in *The Cambridge History of Political Thought: 1450–1700*, ed. J. H. Burns (Cambridge: Cambridge University Press, 1991), 479–80.

in der neueren Geschichte (1924). Meinecke, who was interested in the implications of Machiavelli's ideas for the development of the modern state, over-generalizes when he gives Machiavelli the credit for the presence of political realism in all subsequent political writers. For him, Counter-Reformation thinkers took Machiavelli's political realism and "rendered it far more effective in influence, by making it into a well-reasoned, compact, and elegantly polished system."[31] Meinecke distinguishes between two kinds of Machiavellian reception: those who fought against Machiavelli as completely evil, and those who fought him only on the surface, but borrowed from him freely.[32] Meinecke considered Giovanni Botero one of the latter, concluding that he learned from Machiavelli that political action was based on the "selfish interest of ruler or State" and that "state interest and self-interest were in essence identical."[33] In this way, in addition to the over-generalization noted above, Meinecke essentially perpetuates the same error that he had noticed in the writers he analyzes: like them, he ignores or misinterpreted what he calls Machiavelli's republican ideals.[34]

In an effort to correct Meinecke's over-generalization, De Mattei argues that in many instances, Meinecke's interpretation of Botero as Machiavellian is the result of confusing the distinction between the bad reason of state about which Botero warns his prince, and the good, Catholic reason of state that he advises him to follow. For example, when Botero says that reason of state is reason of interest, he is alluding to the bad reason of state.[35] Robert Bireley also disagrees with Meinecke, maintaining that Botero was fundamentally anti-Machiavellian.[36]

More recently, however, historians have moved beyond this debate, pointing out specific similarities between Machiavelli and the Counter-Reformation writers of the reason-of-state tradition. For example, Maurizio Viroli contends that both Machiavelli and Botero employ language typical of the art of the state of the Florentine Quattrocento, which dealt with how a private person or faction could maintain power within an ostensibly republican regime, adapting it to the public institution of the principality.[37] Similarly, at a conference dedicated to Botero in 1990, Kenneth C. Schellhase argued that essentially Botero made Machiavellian political language acceptable for Catholic princes: "In effect,

31 Friedrich Meinecke, *Machiavellism: The Doctrine of Raison d'État and its Place in Modern History*, trans. Douglas Scott (New Haven, CT: Yale University Press, 1957), 45.

32 Ibid., 50.

33 Ibid., 68.

34 Ibid., 44–45.

35 Rodolfo De Mattei, *Il problema della "ragion di stato" nell'età della Controriforma* (Milan: Riccardo Ricciardi Editore, 1979), 57–59.

36 Robert Bireley, *The Counter-Reformation Prince: Anti-Machiavellianism or Catholic Statecraft in Early Modern Europe* (Chapel Hill: University of North Carolina Press, 1990), 46.

37 Maurizio Viroli, *From Politics to Reason of State* (Cambridge: Cambridge University Press, 1992), 131, 253.

Botero disguised Machiavelli in priestly vestments and thereby made him welcome in the courts of Catholic princes."[38]

Spain figures prominently in histories of the anti-Machiavellian reason-of-state tradition. Beginning with Maravall's fundamental 1944 monograph study of seventeenth-century Spanish political thought, historians have tended to begin their account of the Spanish reception of Machiavelli at the end of the sixteenth century, with the first and most important Spanish anti-Machiavellian, Pedro de Ribadeneyra, whose *Tratado de la Religion y Virtudes que deue tener el Principe Christiano* was first published in 1595. Since then, there have been two tendencies regarding the early modern Spanish reception of Machiavelli. On the one hand, Maravall himself argued that Spanish Baroque political writers, even those who attack specific maxims taken out of context from the *Prince* or *Discourses on Livy*, in general accept Machiavelli's practical treatment of politics.[39] Similar to Meinecke's, recently Maravall's definition of Machiavellism has been criticized as too broad, so that he runs the risk of over-generalizing the Florentine's influence.[40]

On the other hand, the historians J. A. Fernández-Santamaría and Robert Bireley have argued that the anti-Machiavellians' perspective on politics was diametrically opposed to Machiavelli's, suggesting that Machiavelli's influence was very limited in Spain.[41] Unfortunately, these historians do not deal adequately with Machiavelli's texts themselves. For example, toward the beginning of his book, Bireley asserts that "many Christians were unwilling to accept Machiavelli's vision of politics and his claim that a Christian could not participate in politics effectively."[42] Bireley's summary of Machiavelli's thoughts on religion, a complex problem to which we will return, is cursory at best. From the outset of his study, he simply accepts, as a given, the anti-Machiavellians' own characterizations of themselves as such.[43] Similarly, Fernández-Santamaría admits that his study of the anti-Machiavellians in reality has little or nothing to do with Machiavelli's writings: "No es mi intención hablar aquí de Maquia-

38 Kenneth C. Schellhase, "Botero, Reason of State, and Tacitus," in *Botero e la "ragion di stato": Atti del convengo in memoria di Luigi Firpo (Torino 8–10 marzo 1990)*, ed. A. Enzo Baldini (Florence: L. S. Olschki, 1992), 243.

39 José Antonio Maravall, *La teoría española del Estado en el siglo XVII* (Madrid: Instituto de Estudios Políticos, 1944), 365–87; idem, "Maquiavelo y maquiavelismo," 39–72.

40 See, for example, Juan Manuel Forte and Pablo López Álvarez, eds, *Maquiavelo y España: Maquiavelismo y antimaquiavelismo en la cultura española de los siglos XVI y XVII* (Madrid: Biblioteca Nueva, 2008), 22.

41 J. A. Fernández-Santamaría, *Razón de estado y política en el pensamiento español del barroco (1595–1640)* (Madrid: Centro de Estudios Constitucionales, 1986), 14–18; idem, *Natural Law, Constitutionalism, Reason of State, and War* (New York: Peter Lang, 2006), 2:21–159; Bireley, *Counter-Reformation Prince*, 3, 25.

42 Bireley, *Counter-Reformation Prince*, 3. Cf. ibid., 11.

43 Ibid., 25.

velo. Mi interés, por el contrario, se centra sobre un grupo de pensadores, bien definido en términos del tiempo y del espacio, y en cómo sus miembros interpretan lo que creen ser el pensamiento de Maquiavelo."[44] Yet throughout his study, next to phrases like "como la época interpretaba haber sido la intención de Maquiavelo," we find in addition simply, "la doctrina de Maquiavelo," as if this represented something intrinsic, something that anyone who read Machiavelli's writings would understand.[45] The problem with these histories is that their method is the result of an insufficient treatment of the problems of interpretation. First, they do not take into account the complexity and diversity of interpretations of Machiavelli's texts. They do not define adequately their own interpretation of Machiavelli, or even recognize it as such, assuming instead that their reading of the Florentine is somehow universal, at least for their readers. Second, they accept implicitly the premise that what the anti-Machiavellians say about Machiavelli and his supposed followers may be considered a genuine or honest interpretation of Machiavelli. In other words, they assume that what the anti-Machiavellians say about Machiavelli is what they truly believed and that their observations are based on a close and direct reading of Machiavelli's texts. As a result, they overlook ways in which Machiavelli's influence may be observed in the same anti-Machiavellians.

In order to correct these histories, the aim of Chapters 3, 4 and 5 of this study is twofold: first, to trace the history of the anti-Machiavellian tradition in an effort to demonstrate that its characterization of Machiavelli is in fact a mischaracterization; second, to carry out a close comparative reading of the anti-Machiavellians' and Machiavelli's texts themselves. For too long we have accepted uncritically the anti-Machiavellians' descriptions of the so-called "doctrine" and "school" of Machiavelli and his supposed followers and of their own self-characterization by contrast to this doctrine. As the extreme example of Clemente makes clear, this diabolical "school," this "doctrine," did not really exist at all. It is a fiction based on a mischaracterization of Machiavelli that has an observable history, and which the anti-Machiavellians exploited in order to define themselves by opposition. The Spanish anti-Machiavellians' "Maquiavelo" was a convenient scapegoat. These writers' goal was not to describe accurately Machiavelli's thought, but always to condemn the opposite of their own advice based on a worldview shaped by Catholic doctrine. This is a rhetorical operation, not a historiographical one. At the same time, when we recognize the rhetorical and ideological nature of the anti-Machiavellians' characterizations of both Machiavelli and themselves, it is possible to notice that, almost without exception, these same Spanish political writers incorporated key aspects of Machiavelli's discourse into their own advice, whether they had read Machiavelli directly or not.

44 Fernández-Santamaría, *Razón de estado*, 18.

45 Ibid., 111.

1

Medieval and Renaissance Humanist Political Discourse and Machiavelli

Machiavellians and Anti-Machiavellians, Past and Present

The European reception of Machiavelli is an extremely complex subject and much work remains to be done. Perhaps the most important obstacle to an accurate understanding of the reception of Machiavelli in Spain and elsewhere is that today there exists a daunting number of different scholarly readings of Machiavelli. This problem is compounded by our current, popular usage of the term "Machiavellian," which I argue ultimately derives from the anti-Machiavellian mischaracterization of Machiavelli popularized during the Counter-Reformation Baroque. Perhaps surprisingly, it is possible to find traces of this mischaracterization of Machiavelli in twentieth- and twenty-first-century scholarship, most notably in the writings of Leo Strauss and, more recently, Sydney Anglo. In his otherwise deeply penetrating analysis of Machiavelli's works, Strauss himself recognizes that he agrees with what he calls the "noble," "old-fashioned" and "simple" reading of Machiavelli as opposed to the "sophisticated" and "up-to-date" interpretation, arguing that Machiavelli was waging a war that "can be described, with the somewhat free use of Christian terms, as a war of the Anti-Christ or of the Devil who recruits his army while fighting or through fighting against the army led by God or Christ."[1] For Strauss, "Machiavelli's teaching is immoral and irreligious," and he disagrees with those who say otherwise simply because Machiavelli points out the usefulness of religion: these "pupils of Machiavelli" ignore "his complete indifference to the truth of religion."[2] This accusation may very well contain some truth: as is well known, political thought suffered a profound and widespread shift in the wake of Machiavelli and his early readers. Nevertheless, it is equally legitimate to say that Strauss is a pupil of the Counter-Reformation anti-Machiavellians, who intentionally misrepresented or exaggerated Machiavelli's ideas.

1 Leo Strauss, *Thoughts on Machiavelli* (Chicago: University of Chicago Press, 1984), 10, 171.

2 Ibid., 12.

Anglo, for his part, in his two books on Machiavelli, consistently dismisses the Florentine's thought. In his *Dissection*, he calls Machiavelli's critique of the Catholic Church, found in *Discourses* 2.2, an "extraordinary farrago," concluding that "the whole argument is one of Machiavelli's most shapeless."[3] Similarly, in his otherwise meticulous scholarly and critical review of the early modern reception of Machiavelli in Europe, Anglo reductively characterizes Machiavelli's thought using dismissive phrases, such as when he refers to the *Prince* 16–19 as Machiavelli's "topsy-turvy catalogue of virtues."[4]

In contrast to these somewhat anti-Machiavellian readings, scholars such as Felix Gilbert, Mario Santoro, J. G. A. Pocock, Quentin Skinner and subsequently others have developed an ideological reading of Machiavelli that attempts to pinpoint the contribution Machiavelli made to the tradition of political language as it existed up to his own lifetime. In their view, Machiavelli carried out a fundamental reorganization of Renaissance humanist discourses into a new vocabulary of contingency which could take into account the unpredictable in political life.[5] This ideological reading is in turn useful for understanding the reception of Machiavelli, because it allows us to draw conclusions about the political discourse written after Machiavelli: assuming a given political writer had access to both the medieval political tradition and Machiavellian discourse, either directly or indirectly, it is possible to categorize some specific aspects of their own discourse as traditional, and others as Machiavellian. In this study, I will carry out this method for determining whether or not early modern Spanish political writers should be considered Machiavellian, based on the observable appropriation of Machiavelli's vocabulary and theoretical framework used to deal with the unpredictable, the contingent in political life. Before turning to the reception of Machiavelli in Spain, this chapter lays down the groundwork necessary to achieve this goal, which consists of two steps: first, to establish what traditions of political thought were available to Spaniards before the arrival of Machiavelli; second, to review in detail the ideological reading mentioned above to highlight the ways in which Machiavelli reorganized traditional political thought.

3 Sydney Anglo, *Machiavelli: A Dissection* (New York: Harcourt, Brace & World, 1969), 112.

4 Anglo, *Machiavelli—The First Century*, 61.

5 See, especially, Felix Gilbert, *Niccolò Machiavelli e la vita culturale del suo tempo* (Bologna: Mulino, 1964), 47–58; idem, *Machiavelli and Guicciardini: Politics and History in Sixteenth Century Florence* (Princeton, NJ: Princeton University Press, 1965), 153–200; Mario Santoro, *Fortuna, ragione e prudenza nella civiltà letteraria del Cinquecento* (Naples: Liguori, 1967), 179–231; J. G. A. Pocock, *The Machiavellian Moment: Florentine Political Thought and the Atlantic Republican Tradition*, 2nd ed. (Princeton, NJ: Princeton University Press, 2003), 156–58; Quentin Skinner, *The Foundations of Modern Political Thought* (Cambridge: Cambridge University Press, 1978), 1:113–89; idem, *Machiavelli* (New York: Hill and Wang, 1981), 21–77.

Aristotle, Kingship and the Common Good in the Middle Ages

The medieval concept of kingship, based on a Christian adaptation of Aristotle, was universalist in character. The *corpus mysticum*, which allegorically imagines the king as the head of the body politic, was originally a theological trope. As Ernst H. Kantorowicz has shown, this phrase was originally used exclusively to designate the Eucharist, the Host on the altar. When the idea of transubstantiation was introduced and finally made dogma in 1215, the term *corpus verum* replaced *corpus mysticum* to designate the Host. Around the same time, writers began to apply the term *corpus mysticum* in a new way to refer to the body of the Church, meaning the collection of believers in Christ, past, present and future. By transference, writers soon began to borrow this same term to refer to secular kingdoms, whose head was the king.[6] This theological imagery permeated European political thought from the thirteenth century onward, lasting throughout the early modern period, even as monarchical and republican writers alike increasingly explored secular, juridical means of legitimation. The idea that the king derives his worldly power from God implies a situation of mutual obligation: while the subjects are morally compelled to obey, the king is equally duty-bound to be virtuous in every way. This explains in part the abundant presence of the word *speculum* in titles of medieval manuals for princes: the king's image is reflected in these books, to be sure; but also, his own behavior should be a reflection of God. For the medieval mind, this divine character attributed to the monarch underlies one of his most important responsibilities: to look after the common good of his kingdom.[7]

Reference to the concept of the common good may be traced at least as far back as Aristotle, if not before. In his famous discussion of the three kinds of regimes, rule by one, the few or the many, Aristotle divides all three into just or unjust, according to whether their aim is the "common advantage" or the "private advantage."[8] Saint Thomas Aquinas, drawing from Aristotle's notion of politics as natural to man, declares at the very beginning of his *De regimine principum ad regem Cypri* that the role of the king, as opposed to the tyrant, in a society is to guide his community toward the common good: "If, therefore, the one governing ordains a multitude of the free to the common good of the multitude, the government will be right and just, as is suitable for the free. But if the government is ordained to the private good of the one governing, the government

6 Ernst H. Kantorowicz, *The King's Two Bodies: A Study of Mediaeval Political Theology* (Princeton, NJ: Princeton University Press, 1957), 193–232.

7 José Manuel Nieto Soria, *Fundamentos ideológicos del poder real en Castilla (siglos XIII–XVI)* (Madrid: Eudema, 1988), 54–55.

8 Aristotle, *The Politics*, trans. Carnes Lord (Chicago: University of Chicago Press, 1984), 95–96.

will be unjust and perverse."[9] For Thomas Aquinas, the best form of government is the kingdom, because it most resembles both nature and God's kingdom in Heaven. In this way, the king's obligation to rule according to the common good is intimately linked to his image of a virtuous ruler who dutifully carries out God's divine will on earth.[10] At the same time, the "good" which is pursued in the Middle Ages is not earthly, but rather salvation in the next life. This goal is located outside of the passage of time: it is static and universal with respect to historical events. For this reason, according to the medieval mind, the king's virtue should not and does not depend on particular situations on earth.

This theological underpinning of the medieval idea of the common good is observable in the thought of one of Aquinas's students, Giles of Rome, whose *De regimine principum* (1285) was one of the most widely read political treatises in late medieval Europe. Giles of Rome applies Aristotelian concepts to the rule of a hereditary monarch. The prince is God's representative on earth: therefore, he ultimately must look to God to find happiness in the next life. In addition, following his teacher Aquinas, Giles used an Aristotelian conception of *civitas* to argue, against the republican writers on the *podestà*, that political life (*vivere politicum*) is not attained in the republican, political regime (*regimen politicum*) but only in a hereditary monarchy. The rule of one is not only more natural, Giles argues, it is more peaceful, as the history of the Italian republican city-states attests.[11] In Spain various translations of this work were created, most notably the glossed version commissioned from Juan García de Castrojeriz by the Bishop of Osma around the time he was designated major chancellor of prince Pedro in 1344, during the reign of Alfonso XI. This moment in the history of Spanish political thought is significant because Alfonso XI was continuing the program of his predecessor, Alfonso X, to further consolidate royal power, a process which would culminate in the *Ordenamiento de Alcalá* of 1348, which made the *Fuero Real* and the *Siete Partidas* effective in cases not pertinent to the new laws promulgated. Furthermore, García de Castrojeriz's *Glosa castellana al "Regimiento de príncipes" de Egidio Romano* would soon become the most widely read rendering of this political treatise in late medieval and early modern Spain, being printed as early as 1494 in Seville.[12]

The image of the *corpus mysticum* appears toward the very beginning of book 1 of the treatise, in García de Castrojeriz's gloss of chapter 5, a discussion of

9 Ptolemy of Lucca, *On the Government of Rulers:* De regimine principum*; With Portions attributed to Thomas Aquinas*, ed. and trans. James M. Blythe (Philadelphia: University of Pennsylvania Press, 1997), 63.

10 Nieto Soria, *Fundamentos ideológicos*, 54–55.

11 Viroli, *From Politics to Reason of State*, 36–44.

12 Juan García de Castrojeriz, *Glosa castellana al "Regimiento de príncipes" de Egidio Romano*, ed. Juan Beneyto Pérez, 2nd. ed. (Madrid: Centro de Estudios Políticos y Constitucionales, 2005), xx–xxvi.

the king's purpose and justification: "E así como la cabeza es mejor que todos los otros miembros, porque los guía e les da governamiento, así el rey deve ser el mejor que todos los otros ommes."[13] To confirm this proposition, García de Castrojeriz refers to Saint Ambrose, who in his *Hexaemeron* declares that "no sin razón sirven todos los miembros a la cabeza así como a su sennor e a su Dios" and that the prince "debe ser tal como la cabeza en el cuerpo del omme, ca es semejanza de la majestad de Dios."[14] Soon after, in chapters 12 and 13 of book 1, which explain that the king must put all of his hope in God, García de Castrojeriz's translation reaffirms the image of the king as a reflection of God: "entre todos los ommes el rey deve más semejar a Dios, porque especialmente trae en sí la imagen de Dios en governar al pueblo, así como Dios govierna el mundo todo; e por ende, si bien e derechamente govierna su pueblo, muy gran galardón rescibe de Dios."[15]

In these same chapters, it becomes clear that the way in which the king can imitate God is by looking after the common good of his subjects:

> el rey es governador del pueblo, e por ende deve entender en el bien común del pueblo; e este tal bien es divinal; e por ende en él deve poner toda su bienandanza, e este bien avrá cuando bien governare su pueblo e amare a Dios sobre todas las cosas e guardare los sus santos mandamientos e los ficiere bien guardar a sus súbditos.[16]

In this passage, the common good itself is defined as divine, because it directs both the king and his subjects toward God. Giles repeats Aristotle's classic division between king and tyrant, which, as we have seen already, was based on a distinction between the common and a particular good: "ca los unos principados entienden siempre en salvar el bien común, c los malos, posponiendo el bien común, entienden siempre en el bien propio."[17] However, following Aquinas's example, Giles couches this distinction in theological terms: "mayor es el bien común e más divinal que ningún bien personal; e por ende, si el rey más ama el bien del reyno todo que el bien de ninguna persona singular e más face por ello, gran galardón e gran gloria rescibirá de Dios por ello."[18] If the king looks after the common good of his kingdom, he will not only be a good king, but also receive God's glory and eternal happiness.

Medieval manuals provided kings with a fixed set of virtues to have and vices to avoid in order to carry out God's divine plan on earth, providing for the

13 Ibid., 28–29.
14 Ibid., 29.
15 Ibid., 65.
16 Ibid., 62.
17 Ibid., 761.
18 Ibid., 66.

common good of their subjects in both this life and the next. As such, the rules for good governing did not depend on specific situations on earth. The idea that the common good could be contingent upon each individual situation would not arise until the Florentines incorporated this goal within their republican ideology at the end of the fourteenth and the beginning of the fifteenth century.

Civic Humanism in Spain

Hans Baron's description of the development of "civic humanism" in Republican Florence at the turn of the fifteenth century as an ideological attack directed at its enemy, Giangaleazzo's Milan, is well known and has stood the test of time, despite minor objections.[19] Salutati is normally given more credit than Petrarch for originating this more social, political kind of humanism. In fact, according to Baron, a comparison between Petrarch's and Salutati's reception of Cicero's letters anticipates a difference between Trecento and Quattrocento historiography: while Petrarch condemns Cicero's desire to be active in political life, preferring the Roman's forced solitude of his later life, Salutati, an active politician, praises the active life in public politics, dedicated to serving the common good.[20] In his *History of the Florentine People*, one of Salutati's students, Leonardo Bruni, divided history into distinct epochs characterized by a political community whose origins, growth and decline could be observed. This political community in turn could be evaluated according to the extent to which it achieved two goals, internal tranquillity and individual creativity. In the past, the Roman republic had come close to achieving these two goals in its last two hundred years. But Florence had become the only kind of state that could possibly fully realize them, a cross between a medieval community and a Greek polis. Following his teacher, Bruni suggests that virtue always accom-

19 Hans Baron, *The Crisis of the Early Italian Renaissance: Civic Humanism and Republican Liberty in an Age of Classicism and Tyranny* (Princeton, NJ: Princeton University Press, 1955). See Albert Rabil Jr., "The Significance of 'Civic Humanism' in the Interpretation of the Italian Renaissance," in idem, ed., *Renaissance Humanism: Foundations, Forms, and Legacy* (Philadelphia: University of Pennsylvania Press, 1988), 1:141–74; Paul Oskar Kristeller, "Studies on Renaissance Humanism During the Last Twenty Years," *Studies in the Renaissance* 9 (1962): 7–30, acknowledges as valid Baron's account of Florentine civic humanism of the first half of the fifteenth century, but does not believe it encompasses Renaissance humanism as a whole, which began long before and continued long after, but rather that it constituted an episode, which even in the same period was opposed by a despotic humanism of Milan and other centers. Cf. Jerrold E. Seigel, "'Civic Humanism' or Ciceronian Rhetoric?" *Past and Present* 34 (1966): 3–48; and Baron's response in "Leonardo Bruni: 'Professional Rhetorician' or Civic Humanist?" *Past and Present* 36 (1967): 21–37. Seigel develops his point of view more amply in *Rhetoric and Philosophy in Renaissance Humanism: The Union of Eloquence and Wisdom, Petrarch to Valla* (Princeton, NJ: Princeton University Press, 1968).

20 Baron, *Crisis*, 97–100.

panies liberty.[21] In addition, in his *Dialogues*, Bruni is the first to substitute Dante's praise for Caesar with praise for Brutus and the others who killed him. Moreover, in his *History*, he moved back in time the foundation of Florence, which had been attributed to Caesar, to Sulla in Republican times.

This revisionist historiography was intended to portray Florence as the heir and defender of the Roman "Respublica" and civic freedom.[22] The very word, *respublica*, originally simply referred to public affairs in general, the "public thing," and this original meaning was not lost to medieval and Renaissance readers. In this way, Florentines such as Leonardo Bruni and later Matteo Palmieri, Alamanno Rinuccini and Donato Acciaiuoli considered the public or common good as etymologically linked to their own form of government: only the free republic considers the common good of all its citizens.[23] From all this, as Florentines divided up history into distinct periods characterized by more or less republican freedom, they tended to replace the universal, monarchical vision of history with a more secular, political one, in which human beings, by collaborating as a community, determine their own future.

In Spain the fifteenth century was also witness to a shift toward more secular considerations of the common good, but for different ideological reasons. The rise of the Trastámara in the mid-fourteenth century marked an intensification of a long struggle between monarchical and aristocratic factions, brought on first by the succession crisis which concluded with the regicide of Pedro I (1350–69) by the hand of his half-brother, Enrique of Trastámara. After the brief reigns of Enrique II (1369–79) and Juan I (1379–90), Enrique III (1390–1406) ruled without handing power to any favorite. However, his death in 1406 marked the beginning of a long regency in the name of his son, Juan II (1406–54), shared by Fernando de Antequera and Catalina de Lancaster. In 1412, Fernando became king of Aragon, not without leaving a great deal of inheritance and power in Castile to his sons, the Infantes de Aragón, who would be a source of civil strife throughout Juan II's reign. This crisis reached a pinnacle during the reign of Enrique IV (1454–74), and concluded in 1479 after Isabel and Ferdinand finally defeated opposition after five years of civil war.[24] In the face of this continual civil unrest, throughout the fifteenth century Castilian royalists never abandoned their use of theological imagery to legitimize their monarchs' pretensions to power; on the contrary, the idea

21 B. L. Ullman, *Studies in the Italian Renaissance* (Rome: Edizioni di storia e letteratura, 1955), 339–43; Eric W. Cochrane, *Historians and Historiography in the Italian Renaissance* (Chicago: University of Chicago Press, 1981), 7–9.

22 Baron, *Crisis*, 38–68.

23 Viroli, *From Politics to Reason of State*, 77–91.

24 Mario Penna, ed., *Prosistas castellanos del siglo XV*, vol. 1 (Madrid: Ediciones Atlas, 1959), xxiii–xxix; John Edwards, *Ferdinand and Isabella* (New York: Pearson, 2005).

of the divine origin of the king intensified with the arrival of the Trastámara.[25] At the same time, the presence of secular modes of political thought in Castilian monarchical treatises increased steadily.

It is in this context, during the reigns of Juan II and Enrique IV, that Castilians, as well as Aragonese, Navarese and Portuguese, first came into contact with Italian humanists and their methods.[26] Alfonso de Cartagena, Bishop of Burgos, is probably the most important figure for understanding the early Spanish reception of Quattrocento humanism, especially regarding his theory and practice of translation. He was instrumental in setting in motion a movement which has come to be called "vernacular humanism," characterized by the study of ethics and politics in vernacular translations of ancient, pagan literature, on the part of a relatively new and quickly growing group of lay readers made up primarily of noblemen and courtiers, but not excluding the monarchs themselves.[27] Although Castilians were not as interested in philological rigor as the Italian humanists, at least not until the arrival of Antonio de Nebrija,[28] many of them treat the same moral and political themes as a result of a similar return to the classics, but for different ideological motives: while the Quattrocentro Florentines' exploration of republican forms of government led them to analyze the contingent nature of politics throughout history, in Castile the crisis of monarchical power increasingly forced writers to complement the universal, theological characteristics of royal imagery with secular, contingent concerns. While Rodrigo Sánchez de Arévalo and Alfonso de Palencia, just to give two examples, both continue to refer to the divine and universal origin of monarchy, at the same time they explore the contingency of political life through reference to the common good.

Rodrigo Sánchez de Arévalo and Alfonso de Palencia were disciples of Alfonso de Cartagena and accompanied him, as part of the Castilian delegation, to the Council of Basel (1431–38), where Cartagena and Leonardo Bruni initiated their debate regarding Bruni's Ciceronian translation of Aristotle's *Ethics*, an important moment in the history of Spanish humanism. Upon his return to Castile, Sánchez de Arévalo actively participated in the courts of

25 Nieto Soria, *Fundamentos ideológicos*, 54.

26 Jeremy Lawrance, "Humanism in the Iberian Peninsula," in *The Impact of Humanism on Western Europe*, ed. Anthony Goodman and Angus MacKay (London: Longman, 1990), 220–58.

27 Ottavio Di Camillo, *El humanismo castellano del siglo XV* (Valencia: F. Torres, 1976), 41–66; Jeremy Lawrance, *Un tratado de Alonso de Cartagena sobre la educación y los estudios literarios* (Barcelona: Universidad Autónoma de Barcelona, Facultad de Letras Bellaterra, 1979), 7–26; idem, "The Spread of Lay Literacy in Late Medieval Castile," *Bulletin of Hispanic Studies* 62, no. 1 (1985): 79–94; idem, "On Fifteenth-Century Spanish Vernacular Humanism," in *Medieval and Renaissance Studies in Honour of Robert Brian Tate*, ed. Ian Michael and Richard A. Cardwell (Oxford: Dolphin, 1986), 63–79.

28 See Francisco Rico, *Nebrija frente a los bárbaros: El canon de gramáticos nefastos en las polémicas del humanismo* (Salamanca: Universidad de Salamanca, 1978).

both Juan II and Enrique IV, who both sent him on several diplomatic missions, until he finally settled in Rome, where he was designated Castellano of Sant'Angelo until the end of his life. There he was involved in an interesting episode in which he exchanged letters with a group of Italian humanists, including Platina and Pomponio Leto, imprisoned in the castle because they were accused of plotting against the pope. In these letters, Sánchez de Arévalo expresses reservations with regard to ancient, pagan literature, which in his view should always be subordinated to biblical and Patristic literature.[29] Nevertheless, in his writings he reveals extensive classical learning, especially in his familiarity with Aristotle.

Sánchez de Arévalo's most important political treatise, the *Suma de la política*, was written between the fall of 1454 and the spring of 1455, just at the beginning of Enrique IV's reign. His focus on peace and stability throughout this treatise reveals his hope that the new king will be able to end the civil strife that had plagued the entirety of Juan II's reign. This goal perhaps explains the emphasis on secular concerns which characterizes his treatise. The *Suma* is divided into two books: book 1 discusses the foundation of a city, focusing on material concerns like "cómo toda cibdad deve ser fundada en sitio y lugar temprado,"[30] and "cómo la cibdad deve ser habundante de muchas y sanas aguas";[31] book 2 centers on the government of the city or kingdom. Throughout book 1 Sánchez de Arévalo repeatedly refers to the common good of the citizens, following the medieval tradition of advice books for princes, with which he was most certainly familiar. However, while the medieval notion of the common good was primarily theological in character, deriving its basis from God and aimed toward the afterlife, as we have seen in the treatises of Thomas Aquinas and Giles of Rome, Sánchez de Arévalo's notion of the common good focuses more on this life.

At the beginning of book 1 Sánchez de Arévalo states the end for which cities and kingdoms were established: "Primeramente pertenece a todo buen político endereçar y disponer a los cibdadanos para que puedan conseguir su fin desseado, que es bien y virtuosamente bivir."[32] His conception of political life has a dual nature: the goal of everyone involved in political life should be to live virtuously, according to Christian morals, and well, according to the necessities of this life. This dual nature is visible in his treatment of the duties of the king. On the one hand, he continues the medieval tradition of insisting that the king be virtuous according to Christian values: "Pues, entre todas las virtudes que al rey convienen, la principal es que tema a Dios, y sea úmil y devoto de la

29 Karl Kohut, "Sánchez de Arévalo (1404–1470) frente al humanismo italiano," *Actas del VI Congreso de la Asociación Internacional de Hispanistas* (1980): 431–34.

30 Penna, *Prosistas castellanos*, 256–58.

31 Ibid., 261–62.

32 Ibid., 281.

Iglesia y onrrador della."[33] Similarly, following the same medieval tradition, Sánchez de Arévalo dedicates much space to the king's particular responsibilities to his people, contrasting him with the tyrant.[34] On the other hand, Castile's constant civil strife has made him aware of the necessity to take into account the contingent nature of political affairs, as is evident in his *Compendiosa Historia Hispánica*, where he constantly demonstrates how political stability is threatened when the monarch does not maintain his virtue.[35] As he puts it in his *Suma*, "en los negocios morales no son provechosas las doctrinas generales, mas conviene dar particulares documentos."[36]

As we saw in García de Castrojeriz's translation of Giles of Rome's *De regimine principum*, the common good in the Middle Ages was intimately associated with the *corpus mysticum*, which itself was invested with a mythical, theological conception to politics, giving the king a divine character. Sánchez de Arévalo does refer to the *corpus mysticum*; however, he places this reference within a long discussion of how the king can bring about peace in this life. In this context, Sánchez de Arévalo's *corpus mysticum*, except for its name, is stripped of any theological implication. He dedicates the entirety of chapter 9 of book 2 to "cómo toda cibdad o reino deve ser mucho uno en concordia."[37] In reality, however, this discussion on peace begins in the previous chapter dedicated to "el pueblo" made up of citizens or subjects, where he insisted that "es necessario que los tales cibdadanos y súbditos sean bien amadores de sus cibdadanos y repúblicas, reputando el daño de sus vezinos por propio."[38] In this way Sánchez de Arévalo's ideal kingdom would be a civil community, reminiscent of those theorized by the Florentine civil humanists of the early Quattrocento, in which each citizen considers his own good to coincide with the good of every other citizen in the community. Following this assertion, in chapter 9 Sánchez de Arévalo refers to the *corpus mysticum* in his plea for peace:

> Pues, todo buen político deve concordar a los cibdadanos y a los poderosos discordantes, de guisa que todos sean conformes al bien común, tomando enxemplo en el cuerpo humano … Assí deven hazer los miembros de toda cibdad e de todo reino, pues es un cuerpo místico, e, por tanto, dévese ayudar porqu'el bien común se augmente por su concordia y unidad.[39]

33 Ibid., 283–84.

34 Rodrigo Sánchez de Arévalo, *Suma de la política*, ed. Juan Beneyto Pérez (Madrid: Consejo Superior de Investigaciones Científicas, 1944), 19.

35 Robert Brian Tate, *Ensayos sobre la historiografía peninsular del siglo XV* (Madrid: Editorial Gredos, 1970), 85–92.

36 Penna, *Prosistas castellanos*, 284–85.

37 Ibid., 295.

38 Ibid.

39 Ibid., 296.

In his discussion of the *corpus mysticum*, the analogy Sánchez de Arévalo creates, drawing from John of Salisbury's *Policratus*,[40] is not one between the body of the kingdom and the body of the Church, whose head is God, but one between the body of the kingdom and a human body. The common good in this passage refers to peace and unity among the citizens of the kingdom in this life. Sánchez de Arévalo's message to Enrique IV is that he must reconcile the factious Castilian nobles, the "poderosos discordantes" in order to bring peace and stability to his kingdom.

A similarly secular conception of the common good, and for similar reasons, is found in Alfonso de Palencia's *Tratado de la perfección del triunfo militar*. After accompanying Cartagena to the Council of Basel, Palencia lived and studied in Florence for about six years, toward the end of the 1440s and the beginning of the 1450s, where he met Cardinal Bessarion, George of Trebizond and other humanists. In a series of articles, Robert Brian Tate has convincingly demonstrated the important influence Italian humanism exerted on Palencia's work, especially the civic humanism of the early Quattrocento.[41] Palencia's *Batalla campal de los perros contra los lobos* and his *Tratado de la perfección del triunfo militar* both treat the civil strife in which Castile was engulfed during the reigns of Juan II and Enrique IV. Regarding the *Batalla*, Tate establishes several coincidences between this allegorical treatise and the account, provided in Palencia's own *Crónica de Enrique IV*, of the conflict between the Infantes de Aragón (the wolves) and don Álvaro de Luna and his supporters (the dogs), although the connections are not absolutely without exceptions. The biggest problem with this interpretation is the difference in endings: while everyone, including Palencia himself, agreed that the Battle of Olmedo resulted in victory for the pro-Álvaro faction, in the *Batalla* the conflict results in a draw or in any case a loss for everyone. Tate explains this by showing how Palencia brings history up-to-date by suggesting that the same factions continued to "bleed" each other, but in a different setting, in Andalusia, alluding to an attempt by some of Seville's burghers, led first by Fadrique de Aragón, conde de Luna, and later by Alfonso de Fonseca the Younger, to create a commune.[42]

40 Kantorowicz, *King's Two Bodies*, 207–8.

41 Robert Brian Tate and Anscari M. Mundo, "The *Compendiolum* of Alfonso de Palencia: A Humanist Treatise on the Geography of the Iberian Peninsula," *Journal of Medieval and Renaissance Studies* 5 (1975): 253–78; Tate, "Political Allegory in Fifteenth-Century Spain: A Study of the *Batalla campal de los perros contra los lobos* by Alfonso de Palencia (1423–92)," *Journal of Hispanic Philology* 1, no. 3 (1977): 169–86; idem, "The Civic Humanism of Alfonso de Palencia," *Renaissance & Modern Studies* 23 (1979): 25–44; idem, "*El tratado de la perfección militar* de Alfonso de Palencia (1459): la Villa de Discreción y la arquitectura humanista," in *Essays on Narrative Fiction in the Iberian Peninsula in Honour of Frank Pierce*, ed. Robert Brian Tate (Oxford: Dolphin, 1982), 163–76.

42 Tate, "Political Allegory," 179–83.

With respect to the *Tratado del triumfo de la perfeccion militar*, Tate shows how Palencia describes *Exercicio*'s vision of Rome in terms similar to Poggio Bracciolini's famous *De varietate fortune*: although one cannot establish a direct dependence between the two, both Palencia and Bracciolini express the same sentiment contrasting ancient glory with the present corruption. Palencia was profoundly influenced by the Florentine architectural splendor, conceived of as an expression of civic glory, as is evident in his description of Barcelona in the *Tratado* as well as in the unpublished epistle *De laudibus Hispalis*, a description of Seville which, although it follows typically medieval patterns of the genre, also emphasizes the abundance of international trade, especially by Italians, and explains the wealth of Seville solely through the virtue of its citizens. In all likelihood, Palencia was a frustrated civic humanist, who was not necessarily republican, but who had admired the civic virtue of the Florentines and who always expressed his aversion to the nobility and courtiers, who in his opinion were selfish and never took into consideration the common good of the kingdom.[43]

This aversion to the nobility is expressed at the very beginning of the *Tratado*, in the prologue to his own Spanish translation, dedicated to don Fernando de Guzmán, in which he explains the allegory: *Exercicio* is Spanish because Spaniards are prone to exercise arms without *Orden* or *Obediencia*. So he will have *Discreción* teach him the necessity that all three accompany each other so that *Triunfo* could visit his province.[44] In essence, Palencia is laying the blame for Castilian civil strife on the nobility, who are traditionally the warrior class. It is for this reason that he wrote the *Tratado* in the form of a fable, so that he could avoid offending "los ánimos de los grandes."[45] *Exercicio*'s association with the nobles is established at the very beginning of the narrative, when he comes upon a pair of *labradores* engaged in hunting and proceeds to accuse them of carrying out an activity that he had only given to nobles so that they might exercise their souls while they are not fulfilling their primary function: "conservar con diligente cuidado el cuerpo de la cosa pública…"[46] Palencia's rather literal translation of the term *respublica* reveals a close link between the body politic and the common or public good. Just like Sánchez de Arévalo, Palencia's use of the *corpus mysticum* is primarily secular: the function of the nobility is to protect the common good of the kingdom in this life. In the context of the political crisis of Castile, caused by a factious nobility led by the Infantes de Aragón, this statement on the part of *Exercicio* must have smacked of ironic naivety to the readers. In fact, one of the rustics, who turns out to be a learned citizen who has fled from the corruption of the city, responds by providing

43 Tate, "Civic Humanism," 30–43.

44 Penna, *Prosistas castellanos*, 346.

45 Ibid., 346–47.

46 Ibid., 349.

Exercicio with a contingent history of nobility, showing how the original virtue which through time gives a group of people the honor associated with noblemen always becomes corrupt, as many examples throughout history show. Through the villager's words, Palencia undermines the traditional timeless notion of nobility through a keen historical sense of circularity. The rustic concludes by showing how throughout history, truly great men were not the ones who practiced hunting, but rather the nobles who had already become corrupt.[47] In this way, Palencia borrows the contingent and circular sense of history developed by the Florentines of the early Quattrocento in order to bring forth a biting criticism of the Spanish nobility, accused of betraying over time their function of protecting the common good of the kingdom.

Virtue and Fortune

Toward the end of the fifteenth century, Charles VIII of France's descent into Italy and capture of Naples in 1494 shocked the Italian spectators, as their histories, memories, letters and poems recall ten to twenty years later. This event upset the diplomatic balance of power associated with Lorenzo the Magnificent and caused an intellectual crisis among the humanists. This crisis is most visible in the way they re-examined the theme of fortune, especially in the way their faith in virtue seemed to vacillate. This crisis is noticeable in the later writings of Giovanni Pontano, *De fortuna*, *De prudentia*, *Aegidius* and *De immanitate*. In his analysis of the fortuitous Pontano develops a new meaning for prudence: no longer the faculty of choosing between things to avoid or follow, prudence now carries out this function in a changing and unpredictable world, constantly adapting and altering behavior according to circumstances.[48]

The idea of chance, that certain events occur at random, is practically inevitable for human beings, who cannot perceive the causes of everything that they observe happening around them. In any case, this idea must be older than the goddess Fortune herself.[49] In fact, the Latin word *fortuna* was not originally associated with chance. As the Romans' general perception of the universe changed, so too did their conception of the goddess Fortune: one period was marked by the belief that order ruled the universe and that Fortune was the equivalent of Fate; later, those who rejected order conceived of Fortune as capricious. Whether or not she was worshipped, during the Empire her popularity flourished. At the same time, however, the Romans made intellectual

47 Ibid., 350–53.

48 Santoro, *Fortuna, ragione e prudenza*, 11–21; idem, "Humanism in Naples," in Rabil, ed., *Renaissance Humanism*, 1:323–24.

49 Howard Rollin Patch, *The Goddess Fortuna in Mediaeval Literature* (New York: Octagon Books, 1967), 4.

attempts to limit her powers.[50] Perhaps for this reason, throughout this period the Romans regularly paired virtue and fortune as opposites. To have virtue meant one of two possibilities: first, to have a good command of fortune, to be able to demand good luck; second, what has come to be associated with the philosophical point of view of Stoicism, to be able to deal nobly with whatever fortune might bring you. This opposition between virtue and fortune was often defined along the lines of gender, such that having virtue was about being an active man, as its etymology suggests (*vir*), as opposed to a feminine, passive unpredictability.[51]

After the spread of Christianity, and following the Euhemeristic tradition, writers denied Fortune's existence as a goddess while they simultaneously alluded to her as a literary figure to continue to express the idea of unaccountable chance.[52] Beginning with Boethius' *De Consolatione Philosophiae* and for the rest of the Middle Ages, fortune came to be closely associated with providence: for those with good faith, fortune was our imperfect perception of God's divine will, or providence, which would in the end lead to our redemption. As a result, the active sense of virtue in ancient Rome gradually disappeared in favor of a more passive Christian virtue, expressed as philosophical faith. Dante may serve here as an example: in *Inferno* 7.25–99, he writes that God made fortune "general misistro et duce" of "gli splendor mondani," and whose "giudicio … sta occulto chome in erba l'angue." Here Dante uses figures to represent in the readers' imagination the idea that fortune is our human, imperfect perception of God's will or providence.[53]

Petrarch was the first to return to a classical conception of the goddess, urging his readers, in his *De remediis utriusque fortunae*, to oppose her with wisdom and spiritual devotion. Interestingly, in one of his *lettere senili* he felt it necessary to declare that he did not actually believe she existed, that he had simply referred to her as a literary figure he had read so much about in literature. Likewise, in Boccaccio's early works, Fortune appears abundantly, frequently associated with the travails of love. Later in life, on the other hand, he falls back on the medieval Christian conception of the goddess, referring to her in his *Commento sopra Dante* as a poetic fiction.[54]

It was not until the turn of the fifteenth century that it became advantageous for the republican ideology, especially in contrast to the monarchical ideology of Giangaleazzo Visconti of Milan, for Florentine humanist scholars to try to

50 Ibid., 10–13.

51 Pocock, *Machiavellian Moment*, 37.

52 For an account of the Euhemeristic tradition, see Jean Seznec, *The Survival of the Pagan Gods: The Mythological Tradition and its Place in Renaissance Humanism and Art*, trans. Barbara F. Sessions (Princeton, NJ: Princeton University Press, 1972), 84–121.

53 Pocock, *Machiavellian Moment*, 36–40; Patch, *Goddess Fortuna*, 14–20.

54 Patch, *Goddess Fortuna*, 20–22.

recover the ancient, active meaning of virtue. In this context, the change from passive, Christian virtue to active, civic virtue led humanists to a new conception of fortune as well. Pocock explains it thus:

> The operations of fortune were no longer external to one's virtue, but intrinsically part of it; if, that is to say, one's virtue depended on cooperation with others and could be lost by others' failure to cooperate with one, it depended on the maintenance of the polis in a perfection which was perpetually prey to human failures and circumstantial variations. The citizen's virtue was in a special sense hostage to fortune, and it became of urgent moral importance to examine the polis as a structure of particulars seeking to maintain its stability—and its universality—in time.[55]

In order to deal with the potential for this kind of chaos in a political community, represented in the figure of fortune, the Italian humanists began to refer to prudence, one of the four cardinal virtues, but with a new, secular meaning.

Aristotle defined prudence, or *phronesis*, as practical wisdom used to make ethical decisions. Later on, in the Middle Ages, prudence was closely associated with providence. In fact, the two words derive from the Latin *provideo*. For the medieval mind, prudence was one of the four cardinal virtues: the individual's ability to distinguish between right and wrong, good and evil, which would lead him or her to salvation. In the fourteenth and fifteenth centuries, however, as more and more Italian humanists read Cicero and Aristotle directly, they developed a new usage of the word *prudence* as the ability to decide when to and when not to be sincere, depending on one's goals in each unique situation.[56]

In his *De officiis*, Cicero defines prudence as decorum in the political realm and argues that it is superior to theoretical wisdom because it involves action rather than contemplation.[57] Italian humanists such as Coluccio Salutati and Giovanni Pontano wrote that readers might learn prudence by reading examples in history because these examples help them deliberate about actions.[58] In his *De nobilitate legum et medicine* (1399), Salutati replies to a treatise by a Florentine doctor named Bernardus, which claimed that medicine was superior to law. Salutati defends law by saying that it operates in the active rather than the contemplative life, and that it helps men bring about the common good, a goal which is both human, because it differentiates us from animals, and divine, because it is associated with charity. Instead of universal

55 Pocock, *Machiavellian Moment*, 76.

56 John Martin, "Inventing Sincerity, Refashioning Prudence: The Discovery of the Individual in Renaissance Europe," *The American Historical Review* 102, no. 5 (1997): 1323–24.

57 Victoria Kahn, *Rhetoric, Prudence, and Skepticism in the Renaissance* (Ithaca, NY: Cornell University Press, 1985), 35.

58 Ibid., 39–40, 55–67.

truths, which medicine claims to have but does not, law deals in the realm of usage, decorum, practical reason, prudence and probability: that is, the idea that the truth depends on individual situations. In this way, Salutati's defense of law is an indirect defense of rhetoric and its virtues. If human affairs are contingent upon practical considerations, then only orators have authority in politics, because they take into consideration usage or *consuetudo*, "the social and linguistic manifestation of prudence."[59]

Even before the crisis of 1494, in his *De Principe* (1468), Pontano places more emphasis on reputation than previous writers of the mirror-of-princes tradition. The Ciceronian advice to found government on the love of the citizens is narrowed to the prince's relatives and entourage. His concern should be with avoiding the reputation of being greedy and cruel, rather than gaining the reputation of being liberal and humane. On the other hand, the prince has the duty to seek the happiness of the whole population and he should not imitate the example of tyrants.[60]

Pontano was the first, following the crisis of 1494, to give fortune a much more volatile and unpredictable character, turning the classical contrast between virtue and fortune into a constant struggle for dominance. Victoria Kahn understands Pontano's two treatises, *De prudentia* and *De fortuna*, as exercises in rhetorical exposition *in utramque partem*: they contain contradictions because Pontano offers the various opinions which he has read regarding the nature of prudence and fortune. Readers are supposed to develop their own prudence by deciding for themselves what to conclude. Prudence and fortune struggle with each other for control of the contingent realm of human affairs. Fortune is presented as a rhetorician who can argue for and against without regard for ethical decorum; prudence depends on usage and action.[61]

Pontano emphasizes the part of prudence called *versatilitas*, the ability to know how to adapt to changing circumstances and occasions. So, for example, in some cases it is best to wait (*cunctatio*), while in others it is best to act quickly (*celeritas*). For Pontano, prudence is the faculty used to make these kinds of decisions. Pontano also suggests the need, in certain circumstances when necessity leaves no other option, and when the desired end is just, to extend this versatility or flexibility to morals. However, he carefully distinguishes *versatilitas* from *versutia*, or fraud, which he condemns. Another term Pontano discusses is *ingenium*, one's natural inclination, for which he gives several examples from recent history such as Alfonso and Ferrante of Aragon, Lorenzo de' Medici, Ludovico Maria Sforza and Alessandro VI. The prudent man knows how to adapt to circumstances according to reason, despite one's natural inclination. Reason is, in fact, the guide for the prudent man according

59 Ibid., 64.

60 Viroli, *From Politics to Reason of State*, 111–13.

61 Kahn, *Rhetoric, Prudence, and Skepticism*, 73–74.

to Pontano, and this aspect of his thought leads Mario Santoro to conclude that although Pontano paid close attention to reality, he was nevertheless proposing an ideal for humanity, as he himself appears to admit when he asks how many people actually follow his model of a prudent man.[62]

As these writers understood increasingly, because human beings were not perfect like God, while some desired to bring about the common good, others sought only personal gain: according to Aristotle's classic division, the former were considered virtuous; the latter, tyrannical. To be more specific, prudence could be used for the common good or for a particular tyranny.

Diego de Valera

Diego de Valera was a unique and important figure in fifteenth-century Castile, distinguishing himself in both arms and letters. He traveled Europe extensively as a knight-errant, visiting courts and participating in battles in Burgundy, France and Bohemia, and his writings reveal an openness with respect to the new, humanist vocabulary of contingency emerging from Italy. Eventually, he became the Castilian authority on nobility and his influence on this matter was far-reaching both geographically and chronologically. As E. Michael Gerli has shown, his letters and treatises represent an interesting and unique example of "performing nobility," characterized by Valera's constant concern with legitimizing his own noble status, despite his *converso* origins.[63] Over the course of his life he gave advice, whether solicited or not, in the form of epistles and treatises to three Castilian monarchs, Juan II, Enrique IV and Ferdinand the Catholic. In times of shifting alliances, Valera always portrayed himself as a defender of monarchical government, although he was a declared enemy of don Alvaro de Luna, Juan II's *valido*, whom he arranged to have captured and imprisoned. Valera's various writings contain an interesting mix between traditional and innovative ways of considering political life, as is shown in his use of the vocabulary under examination in this chapter.

Throughout his works, his treatment of kingship is predominantly traditional in character, repeating the virtues a Christian monarch must live by in order to fulfill his obligation to God. Likewise, Valera's conception of the common good is intimately associated with the king's divine role on earth. At the very beginning of his *Doctrinal de príncipes*, he refers to the traditional contrast between king and tyrant: "Así rey—según santo Thomás, en el primero libro del Regimiento de los príncipes, al rey Johán de Chipre—es uno que por bien común de la tierra o provincia, rige o govierna … E Santo Thomás,

62 Santoro, *Fortuna, ragione e prudenza*, 23–65.

63 E. Michael Gerli, "Performing Nobility: Mosén Diego de Valera and the Poetics of Converso Identity," *La Coronica: A Journal of Medieval Spanish Language and Literature* 25, no. 1 (1996): 19–36.

en el libro cerca alegado, que el rey que rige a provecho suyo e dapño de los súditos, es tirano injusto e malo e indigno del regimiento."[64] This traditional contrast, which forms the backbone of the first chapter, is closely followed by chapter 2, a long demonstration of "Cómo el rey deve ser muy temeroso e amador de Dios."[65] Thus, the king's obligation to provide for the common good of his kingdom is associated with his obligation to God. Valera explains this divine obligation by referring to the *corpus mysticum*: "E, así como el rey es cabeça, alma e coraçón de su reino … así ha de sostener mayores cuidados e fatigas que todos los de su señorío, de los quales a Dios ha de dar cuenta."[66] As the head of the kingdom, the king is obligated to God, because God alone gave him his right to rule. In this same chapter, Valera further reinforces the association between the king and God as he begins to enumerate the virtues which the king must have: "Deve ser el rey gracioso, benigno, tenprado, modesto, siguiendo los pasos de Aquel, cuyo lugar en la tierra posee; trabajando por le parescer quanto la humana natura consiente, tomando enxenplo de los claros varones pasados."[67] In this way, the king must possess all of the many virtues listed in this long chapter in order to best reflect God's image on earth. In sum, Valera's conception of virtue and the common good is traditional because it is intimately linked to the king's divine origins.

On the other hand, this same chapter also reveals a practical side to Valera, who after all was writing his *Doctrinal* after many years of active experience in politics. Although he always begins with a general principle, based on the traditional Christian virtues which a prince was to hold, in his narration of examples he frequently takes contingency into account, showing much more than the general principles they ostensibly demonstrate. One interesting example of justice is Sancho IV, son of Alfonso X. When he found out that certain nobles wanted to kill him,

> él se ovo así discretamente con ellos, disimulando que dello no sabía, que los allegava mucho más que ante que fuese certificado de la traición en que andavan. E toda cosa que qualquiera dellos le demandava, ge la dava con muy alegre cara, fasta tanto que ellos creyeron que el rey ninguna cosa del fecho sabía.[68]

When they felt secure, he invited them to a castle, trapped them and killed them.[69] In this passage, for practical reasons, Valera seems to imply that the ends jus-

64 Penna, *Prosistas castellanos*, 174.
65 Ibid.
66 Ibid.
67 Ibid., 175.
68 Ibid., 176.
69 Ibid., 176–77.

tify the means. His consideration of this one example leads him to undermine the idea that a monarch must always be good according to traditional Christian virtues; instead, he must adapt his behavior to contingent circumstances in order to bring justice to his subjects.[70]

The *Doctrinal de príncipes* represents the culmination of Valera's views on monarchical politics. Throughout his writing career, he had been developing his contingent sense of politics through his use of the words *fortuna* and *prudencia*. The contingency of political affairs is a principal theme in his *Exortación de la pas*. Although this text opens as a plea for peace, it quickly becomes a short treatise on kingship. In the administration of justice, the king must take into consideration contingency, that is, the particular situation of each case: "quién es el que fabla, y en qué tienpo e lugar, e si el tal está sañudo o sosegado, e si es amigo o enemigo de quien fabla, e si es honesto o infame, e si es tenprado o salido."[71] Liberality, for example, should be controlled by taking into account "la calidad del dador e los méritos del recibiente e la oportunidad de los tienpos e lugar, que mucho añade al precio de la cossa la forma del dar y el lugar e tienpo e oportunidad."[72]

In this same treatise, Valera provides a traditional definition of prudence, but then hints at an innovative one which he will develop later. Citing Cicero, Gregory the Great and Saint Augustine, Valera summarizes as follows: "Segunt las quales definiciones, a la prudencia conviene saber las cosas que el ánima deve fazer, amando aquellas en que en Dios se puede ayudar e aborresciendo las contrarias. A la qual virtud pertenesce bien e derechamente elegir, bien e como deve executar lo elegido."[73] This is followed by an interesting quote from Seneca, who adds the dimension of time to the faculty of prudence: "presencia ordina, futura provide, preterita recordare."[74] Although Valera's comments do not reflect this dimension here, he refers to the same quote in one of the notes in his *Tratado de providencia contra fortuna*.

This last treatise is a landmark in the history of contingent political thought in Spain, because in it Valera does not follow the medieval tradition, derived from Boethius, of considering fortune as our imperfect perception of providence. Instead, he discusses ways in which humans can deal with and prepare for that which is unknown in the political affairs of this life. Valera begins by establishing fortune's fickle nature, citing several authorities including Cato, the Psalms and Boethius. Just after this, however, Valera says that there is no need to appeal to authority, because history may be interpreted as a reflection of the present and a presentiment of the future:

70 See Penna's discussion in ibid., cxxx–cxxxiii.
71 Ibid., 82.
72 Ibid., 80.
73 Ibid., 84.
74 Ibid.

> Pues, con esvelado estudio acatad las cosas pasadas por ordenança de las presentes e providencia de las venideras; que quien las cosas pasadas no mira, la vida pierde, y el que en las venideras no provee entra en todas como no sabio. Ca el que próvido es, no dize: "No pensé que esto se fisiera," que no dubda, mas espera, no sospecha, mas guárdase; e los daños antevistos menos suelen enpescer. E bien aventurado es aquel a quien los agenos peligros fasen sabio.[75]

Far from a recommendation to have faith in God's divine providence, here Valera discusses the possibility for humans to learn from experience and foresee the future. In opposition to fortune, Valera recommends his readers to be *próvidos*, to be able to foresee the adversity which she inevitably will bring.

In a note, Valera explains his use of the word *próvido* by dividing the word from which it derives, *providencia*, into two definitions, divine and secular:

> Este vocablo es derivado de providencia, onde conviene saber que ay providencia divina e providencia humana. Providencia divina, segunt Boecio es esa mesma divina razón que todas las cosas dispone. Providencia humana es virtud por la qual el próvido acata e mira las cosas venideras e provee en ellas quanto la humana razón alcança. Y es parte de la prudencia como segunt Séneca a ella convenga recordar las cosas pasadas e ordenar las presentes e preveer las venideras.[76]

Following medieval authority, Valera explains that divine providence is the result of God's divine will as He establishes "todas las cosas." This divine kind of providence is atemporal, because God's vision encompasses all time. In contrast, Valera alludes to a human providence, which he defines as the ability to foresee future events as far as human reason allows. Because our perspective is limited as compared to God's all-encompassing point of view, human providence takes the perspective from one point in time. As a result, this ability is part of the virtue prudence, which is responsible, according to Seneca, for systematically organizing, as far as the human intellect allows, past, present and future. As we have seen, Valera directly quotes this passage from Seneca in the original Latin in his *Exortación a la pas*. Here, Valera develops the idea that human providence and prudence exist not in the realm of certainty but in the limited human perspective of probability.

75 Ibid., 141.
76 Ibid., 145.

Machiavelli's Rereading of the European Tradition of Political Thought

If Charles VIII's descent into Italy produced an intellectual crisis in Naples, the consequences felt in Florence were revolutionary.[77] Throughout the Quattrocento, the Medici held power while simultaneously maintaining the façade of republican institutions by sharing their rule with the other wealthy aristocrats of the city, placing the most important functions of government within small bodies of seventy and one hundred whose members were exclusively aristocrats friendly to them. After the collapse of the Medici in 1494 the government, following the suggestion of Girolamo Savonarola and the example of Venice, grouped everything together in the Great Council. Thus the aristocrats found themselves having to deal for the first time with middle-class members of government. Throughout this period, these two classes struggled within the Great Council, because their interests differed greatly: the wealthy aristocrats were concerned with international trade, while the middle-class businessmen and artisans paid attention only to the local market. It is easy to understand why control of the port of Pisa was so important to the former and not at all to the latter. This situation explains why the aristocrats, who were always in charge of diplomatic affairs, never wanted war, which would mean a collapse in economic relations. As a result, they always delayed making decisions and sought the middle road, the *via del mezzo*. The aristocracy made repeated demands for constitutional reform, but the Great Council would hear nothing of it. Finally a compromise was reached when they extended the term of *gonfaloniere* to life; however, the aristocrats were disappointed when the appointee, Piero Soderini, took no further steps toward more reform. When in 1512 the Spaniards were at the gates of Florence and Soderini fled in exile, the aristocracy thought that they finally had their chance by welcoming the return of the Medici; however, the Medici ignored any proposals and established a fairly autocratic rule, under the guidance of Cardinal Giovanni, later Pope Leo X, always maintaining the appearance of republican government.

As Felix Gilbert shows by looking at the protocols of the *pratiche* which took place during the popular government, by this time the aristocrats were all well educated according to the humanist tradition, and they used humanist vocabulary and historical methods in their speeches.[78] They constantly referred to examples from both classical literature and experiences from recent history which could be applied to contemporary situations. They alluded frequently to the contrast between fortune and virtue and spoke of the common good.

[77] For what follows I have relied on the account of Florentine popular rule from 1494 to 1512 found in Gilbert, *Machiavelli and Guicciardini*, 3–152.

[78] Gilbert, *Machiavelli and Guicciardini*, 28–45.

One such Florentine aristocrat, Bernardo Rucellai, an intellectual in the circle centered around Lorenzo the Magnificent and Marsilio Ficino, was instrumental in the development of the vocabulary of contingency prior to Machiavelli. Rucellai traveled to Naples twice as ambassador and participated in conversations in Pontano's circle. He also most likely was familiar with a copy of Pontano's *De prudentia* edited by Giovanni Corsi, a member of Rucellai's "Orti Oricellari" circle. In his *De bello italico* he employs Pontano's definition of prudence, with its many parts, in his account of Charles VIII's 1494 military campaign into Italy. Following Pontano's precept, Rucellai aimed for his history to be both moral and political, that is, for it to provide examples, both positive and negative, which readers could apply to contemporary politics. His portraits of the political leaders involved in this episode, which included Piero de' Medici, Alfonso of Aragon, Ludovico Maria Sforza and Charles VIII himself, pivot around the opposition between prudence and fortune: those who are prudent use reason to control their actions as much as fortune allows, while those who are not prudent let fortune control them completely.[79]

Machiavelli's ethics are intimately related to his conception of human nature as constant throughout history, on the one hand, and of the world of politics as inherently unstable, on the other. Santoro traces Machiavelli's use of the word *fortuna* throughout his writing career. In his early political writings, and those which were most likely speeches prepared for Soderini, Machiavelli follows the humanist tradition of stressing man's power to use reason in order to overcome fickle fortune.[80] However, in a letter to Soderini dated probably from 1513, Machiavelli attributed much more power to fortune than he had previously. Two men acting the same way reach two different outcomes, one happy, the other miserable. Therefore, success results from the encounter, the *riscontro*, between a man's actions and the circumstances, the situation in which he finds himself. The problem Machiavelli poses in this letter, however, is that men act according to their natures, their *ingegno* or *fantasia*, an idea that he could have borrowed from Pontano, such that they find success when their natures agree with the circumstances. Because circumstances change, and men do not change their behavior but follow their natures, if they live long enough, their fortune will inevitably change.

Less than a year later, after intense reflection, Machiavelli returned to his treatment of man's nature in the *Prince*. But now, based on his reading of ancient history and his memory of recent experiences in the political life of Italy and Europe, he proposed to re-examine traditional notions of behavior. In doing so,

79 Santoro, *Fortuna, ragione e prudenza*, 135–78.

80 This gendered discourse is intentional: we must remember that the humanists recovered the contrast between a feminine Fortuna and a masculine virtue. See Hanna Fenichel Pitkin, *Fortune Is a Woman* (Berkeley and Los Angeles: University of California Press, 1984).

he claims to be breaking from past thinkers, especially the humanists.[81] As Santoro notes, Machiavelli simultaneously restores the most important methods of humanism, especially that of imitation, by applying them to real-life contemporary politics, while he also denounces the humanists for limiting their own methods to the fields of rhetoric, art and speculation. Pontano certainly went through a similar crisis; however, he never lost hope in reason. In his works he tries to portray to his readers an entirely virtuous man, who uses prudence to adapt his behavior to the whims of fortune. Now, while this might mean some flexibility with respect to traditional values when necessity demands it, as we have seen, the virtuous man never sacrifices his own integrity, his own internal sense of right and wrong based on reason. In his treatment of prudence, Pontano did concede times when necessity forces man to be somewhat morally flexible; Machiavelli emphasizes and gives much more power to necessity, in such a way that prudence must show men to be much more ethically flexible. Machiavelli observes in the *Prince* 15 how, while ideally it would be best if a man could be virtuous in every way, in reality the conditions of human political life do not permit him to achieve this state of being. Therefore a prince must develop his prudence in order to learn how to control his actions according to the effectual results that they will produce. This implies, in contrast to what he had said in his letter to Soderini, that it is possible to control one's nature to some extent.[82]

Throughout his political works, Machiavelli recovers the ancient opposition between male virtue and the feminine goddess Fortune as a way of conceptualizing the uncertain, contingent nature of political life in general. This gendered opposition is behind Machiavelli's infamous suggestion in the *Prince* 25 that Fortune favors the impetuous over the careful: "perché la fortuna è donna ed è necessario, volendola tenere sotto, batterla e urtarla."[83] At the same time, empire, or the dominion of one prince or republic over another, in particular is understood especially as being associated with fortune. In a well-known passage found in *Discourses* 1.6, Machiavelli argues that necessity forces governments to organize their states in such a way that they are prepared to carry out imperial expansion:

> Ma sendo tutte le cose degli uomini in moto, e non potendo stare salde, conviene che le salghino o che le scendino, e a molte cose che la ragione non t'induce, t'induce la necessità; talmente che, avendo ordinata una republica atta a mantenersi non ampliando, e la necessità la conducesse ad ampliare, si verrebbe a tôr via i fondamenti suoi, e a farla rovinar piú tosto.[84]

81 See also Allen H. Gilbert, *Machiavelli's Prince and Its Forerunners:* The Prince *as a Typical Book* De Regimine Principum (New York: Barnes & Noble, 1968).

82 Santoro, *Fortuna, ragione e prudenza*, 179–231.

83 Niccolò Machiavelli, *Il Principe*, ed. Giorgio Inglese (Torino: Einaudi, 1995), 167.

84 Niccolò Machiavelli, *Discorsi sopra la prima deca di Tito Livio*, ed. Francesco Bausi (Roma: Salerno Editrice, 2001), 48.

Here, as in all of his political writings, Machiavelli assumes that human politics is not ruled by reason, but is instead at least somewhat chaotic. If it were possible for a state to remain independent within its own borders, then it could hope for a long life of peace and stability, free of the turbulence which elsewhere he allegorically associates with the fickle goddess Fortune. However, in the unstable reality of European politics, necessity dictates that states prepare to defend themselves through conquest; if they do not, they will fall prey to their neighbors.

Mikael Hörnqvist has traced a history of Florentines who, following Sallust's depiction of the Roman republic, linked Florentine republican love of liberty with imperial expansion. Salutati, Rinuccini, Bruni, Gregorio Dati, Palmieri and Savonarola all believed that because Florence defended liberty, it therefore had the right and the obligation to take foreign cities under its dominion in order to protect them from tyranny, whether it came from within or without. Machiavelli turns this relationship from a right into a logical conclusion: when people enjoy freedom at home, they then turn to expansion abroad, because human nature is acquisitive.[85] With reference to *Discourses* 1.2, 1.5-6 and 1.9, Hörnqvist goes on to argue that Machiavelli offers up the example of Rome's and France's mixed regime, which contains some institution or institutions which protect the many from the few, thus isolating the prince from the few and freeing him to direct his tyrannical tendencies outside the state to the realm of foreign affairs and imperial expansion. In short, Machiavelli argues that imperial expansion, correctly institutionalized, will help the prince or governing body provide for the common good, avoiding civil strife by keeping both themselves and the people occupied, directing their acquisitive natures outside of the state.[86]

In both medieval monarchical manuals as well as the Renaissance republican tradition, the common good of the political community is the goal of good political regimes. Throughout his works, Machiavelli places this same goal above traditional morals as a higher priority for princes and republican leaders alike. In a world of constant flux, dominated by the goddess Fortune, this secular notion of the common good becomes for Machiavelli a universal principle that may guide men in an effort to bring peace and stability to political life. He realized that at times the personal good of the ruler, including his desire to save his soul, did not necessarily coincide with the secular common good of the political community. Therefore, in order to carry out this goal, Machiavelli reorganizes the traditional Aristotelian division between king and tyrant, virtue and vice.

In the medieval tradition, virtues and vices are defined relative to each other: following Aristotle, the virtues are found in moderation, halfway between two

85 Mikael Hörnqvist, *Machiavelli and Empire* (Cambridge: Cambridge University Press, 2004), 73–74.

86 Ibid., 221–27.

vices. Let us look closely at one virtue, liberality, as an example, in order to comprehend how Machiavelli carries out this reorganization. In chapter 1.2.17 of his *De regimine principum*, entitled "Qué cosa es liberalidad," Giles of Rome locates liberality between prodigality and avarice: "Según que dice el Filósofo en el IV.º de las Eticas, esta virtud es medianera entre el gastar e el retener, templando los gastamientos e reprimiendo las avaricias, ca en estas dos maneras fallesce el omme, gastando lo suyo más que deve, o reprimiendo do lo deve dar."[87] Essentially, the king finds liberality by avoiding spending too much, on the one hand, or too little, on the other. Nevertheless, the king should prefer to spend too much rather than too little: "Los reyes más deven ser gastadores que avarientos, ca más sería de denostar por ser avarientos que por ser gastadores."[88] This is so because liberality resembles prodigality more than avarice: "El gastamiento es más cercano a la virtud de la liberalidad que la avaricia."[89] In addition, spending will benefit the many, so that it may contribute to the king's goal of providing for the common good: "El rey es puesto en el reyno para salud del reyno e aprovecha a todos. E cierto es que la avaricia no aprovecha a ninguno, mas el gastamiento aprovecha a muchos, ca el gastador a sí solo es malo e a todos los otros es bueno."[90]

Drawing from this tradition, Diego de Valera also declares that a king must be liberal; however, much more so than Giles, he recognizes the contingency of any given situation: "Conviene, con todo eso, tener modo a la larguesa, acatando la qualidad del dador y los méritos del rescibiente e la oportunidat de los tienpos … Porque, pensando ser liberales, no seamos pródigos e pensando ser templados, no seamos avaros."[91] This kind of advice derives from the moderation that medieval manuals recommend. Nevertheless, rather than a search for an ideal middle ground between avarice and prodigality, he points out that the best action in any given particular situation requires a specific approach that general rules cannot adequately express. In addition, Valera recognizes the imperfection of human perception: at times, we think we are being virtuous, but the result is negative.

Machiavelli takes this kind of focus on the contingent nature of human perception to a logical extreme. Machiavelli's keen sensitivity to the importance of reputation, the public perception of political leaders, is well known. He points out in the *Discourses* that often virtuous leaders are under-appreciated, while the development of tyranny goes unnoticed until it is too late to remedy the loss of a community's liberty.[92] Faced with this problem, Machiavelli's solution is a strict adherence to the principle of the common good in this life, regardless of

87 García de Castrojeriz, *Glosa castellana*, 153.
88 Ibid., 159.
89 Ibid., 160.
90 Ibid.
91 Penna, *Prosistas castellanos*, 179.
92 See, for example, *Discourses* 3.16 and 3.28.

the traditional division between virtues and vices. In fact, Machiavelli shows that instead of an ideal middle ground between two vices, the right way is a mean between virtue and vice. Prudence and strength of will are used to adapt oneself to the changing circumstances, and therefore they are the only true general virtues. Machiavelli uses virtue in a new sense, different from moral virtue or goodness.[93] To return to our example of the virtue of liberality, in polemical contrast to the medieval tradition, Machiavelli points out in the *Prince* 16 that being liberal during peacetime often results in the need to levy excessive taxes during wartime. While Giles recommended excessive spending rather than stinginess, because it resembles liberality in abstract, theoretical terms, Machiavelli points out that in reality being stingy helps the prince be prepared for any contingency. In addition, Machiavelli refutes the claim that excessive spending benefits the common good, as the medieval manuals had claimed, pointing out that in reality it usually only benefits a small number of powerful noblemen who are close to the king. Instead, he recommends the prince to be stingy to the few, so that he will not have to burden the many.

Now, Machiavelli must have seen the traditional characterization of kings and tyrants as an obstacle to this goal of the secular common good. A prince might believe that he should be liberal, for example, if he believes that in failing to do so he will be labeled a tyrant. He therefore confounds the two, teaching his prince that he should use kingly methods as long as he can, but must be willing and able to perform tyrannical actions when they are necessary for the common good. In this way, by realistically presenting one authority figure who simultaneously carries out virtuous actions associated with the prince and wicked ones associated with the tyrant, Machiavelli combines what the Aristotelian tradition had separated.[94]

As we have seen, medieval manuals drew from Aristotle their definitions of king and tyrant, based primarily on whether or not they look after the common good. Following this same model, they maintain a strict division between the king and the tyrant. In chapters 3.2.9–11 of his *De regimine principum*, Giles lists the actions of the king and the tyrant in such a way that they are presented as exact opposites by definition:

> Diez cosas deve facer el verdadero rey. La primera es que deve procurar el bien común e acrescentar las rentas del reyno con derecho e extenderlas en bien del reyno e no darlas a malas mugeres, ni a lisonjeros, ni a personas sin pro, como facen los tiranos, según que dice Aristóteles. Lo segundo, deven guardar los bienes comunes e los derechos del reyno, la cual cosa infringe el tirano de lo facer e no lo face…[95]

93 Strauss, *Thoughts on Machiavelli*, 237–42.

94 Hörnqvist, *Machiavelli and Empire*, 205–8.

95 García de Castrojeriz, *Glosa castellana*, 793.

One by one, each rule that the king must follow is subsequently broken by the tyrant. This rhetorical strategy, employed again later on in the Counter-Reformation by the anti-Machiavellians, effectively simplifies politics for the readers, enabling them to distinguish easily between acceptable and unacceptable actions: the king's actions are praised and the tyrant's actions are condemned.

As part of this rhetorical division, medieval manuals employ a rhetoric of fear, suggesting to readers that subjects will constantly attempt to overthrow the tyrant. In *De regimine principum* 3.2.13, Giles lists six reasons why. First, their subjects fear the tyrant: "La primera es por el gran temor que han, creyendo que no podrán escapar de sus manos."[96] Second, they hate him: "La segunda es porque le han muy gran sanna por los tuertos e por las injurias que rescibieron dél."[97] Third, his subjects have contempt for him: "La tercera razón es porque los tiranos facen tales cosas porque son mucho de menospreciar, ca no han cuidado de cosa del mundo sino de haver delectaciones carnales. E por la mayor parte son destemplados en comer e en beber e en fecho de mugeres e por esto a las veces los súbditos, despresciándolos, acométenlos e mátanlos."[98] Fourth, they fear for their honor and their possessions. Fifth, they desire to demonstrate their bravery by committing a wondrous act. Sixth, they desire to free themselves from slavery.[99]

While tyranny is a frequent subject of the *Discourses*, it is never once mentioned in the *Prince*. Nevertheless, Machiavelli undoubtedly had the Aristotelian contrast between king and tyrant in mind when he wrote his revolutionary contribution to the *De regimine principum* tradition. In fact, one early group of his readers considered the *Prince* to be an exposé of tyranny that revealed the *arcana imperii*, the secret methods of political leaders, to the uninitiated.[100] Another strain of the early reception of Machiavelli confronts his writings with those of Aristotle along similar lines, as we have seen.

In the infamous chapters 15–19 of the *Prince*, Machiavelli plays with the Aristotelian rhetoric of fear. Medieval writers such as Giles of Rome suggest that tyrants live in fear because their subjects desire to overthrow them, out of either hate or contempt. Machiavelli teaches his prince that in order to bring about the common good, at times he will be forced to deviate from the traditional virtues. Nevertheless, he should not worry about gaining the reputation for a necessary vice, just so long as he avoids the hatred and contempt of his subjects. This line of reasoning culminates in the *Prince* 19, where Machiavelli combines an explicit rhetoric of hope, telling his princely reader that he need not worry about conspiracies, with a subtextual rhetoric of despair, which

96 Ibid., 814.
97 Ibid.
98 Ibid.
99 Ibid., 815.
100 Donaldson, *Machiavelli and Mystery of State*, 111–21.

suggests to this same reader the need to worry.[101] Like the tyrant, the prince should always be wary of rebellion. Similarly, to maintain peace among his subjects, he should rely more on fear than on love, because friendship or loyalty based on love is inconstant, whereas fear is a better, more reliable motivator. Like the medieval manuals before him, Machiavelli states that the prince should strive to be both loved and feared whenever possible; unlike them, he adds that in the likely event that this noble goal is not possible, he should aim, more reasonably, to be feared and not hated.

In his writings, Machiavelli offers an alternative theoretical framework and vocabulary for political leaders to help them deliberate upon and deal with the contingent nature of political action and public perception. His discourses give them the flexibility to deviate from traditional morals whenever they deem it necessary for the common good of the body politic. In the chapters that follow, we shall see that throughout the early modern period, Spaniards appropriated Machiavelli's reorganization of the traditional princely virtues as well as his discourses of prudence, fortune and the avoidance of hatred and adapted them to their own Catholic worldview.

101 Hörnqvist, *Machiavelli and Empire*, 211–21.

2

Machiavelli and Spanish Imperialist Discourse in the Sixteenth Century

When Isabel and Ferdinand finally defeated their opposition and gained control of Castile, they effectively ended the internal political crisis which had been raging ever since the ascension of the house of Trastámara to the crown of Castile. They now turned their attention to a program of territorial expansion which eventually would become an empire so expansive that it would include colonies located all over the world. After conquering Granada, Ferdinand continued the kingdom of Aragon's long tradition of economic and political interests in the Mediterranean; Isabel made the Indies her own personal imperial project. When Charles succeeded the Catholic Monarchs, therefore, he inherited a collection of kingdoms and colonies in both Europe and America. This situation, combined with his election as Holy Roman Emperor, resulted logically in a preoccupation with the idea of empire on the part of the political thinkers of his court. Since the revival of the Roman legal tradition in the twelfth century, the Hohenstaufen emperors, utilizing the Roman concept of *dominus mundi*, thought of themselves as lords of the whole world, in an attempt to assert independence from the papacy, which continued to consider the emperor as the pope's secular agent. When Charles was elected emperor, he seemed to be on the verge of turning this idea from *de iure* to *de facto*, creating the first worldwide empire, including the Indies.[1]

According to José Antonio Maravall, Charles, who at first conceived of his empire as universal, over the course of his rule developed more and more a perspective of "particularismo político,"[2] through which he considered the particular situations of each individual kingdom in Christendom, rather than one universal empire, and how this community was inherently unstable. While at the beginning of his reign he and his courtiers thought of his role as emperor as being the head of a peaceful Christian community, as he faced more and more obstacles to this ideal, such as antagonism from successive popes and from

1 James Muldoon, *Empire and Order: The Concept of Empire, 800–1800* (London: Macmillan, 1999), 87–88.

2 José Antonio Maravall, *Carlos V y el pensamiento político del Renacimiento* (Madrid: Instituto de Estudios Políticos, 1960), 72.

Francis I of France, and finally the division of Germany brought on by Luther's revolution, he eventually came to rely on force in order to impose and secure his rule. In the end, Charles's vision of his European empire, far from some ideal notion of a Christian community, was eventually reduced to a union of his possessions based on the Spanish crowns combined with the Low Countries and Milan. This Spanish, Flemish and Italian complex of power, separate from the German Holy Roman Empire, but which nevertheless constituted an empire *de facto*, would finally be passed on dynastically to his son, Felipe II.[3]

In sum, as time passed, Charles, Felipe and their courtiers comprehended more and more that his universal, Christian conception of empire would have to give way to a more practical understanding of political power that took into account the contingent demands of each particular kingdom. At the same time, idealistic conceptions of empire, based on a Christian notion of justice, would slowly give way to practical, militaristic considerations of political expansion. The purpose of this chapter is to demonstrate that the writings of Machiavelli played a fundamental role in this transition. Essentially, Spaniards in the second half of the sixteenth century answered Machiavelli's call for a more militaristic and imperialist interpretation of Christianity.

Ideal Empire in the First Half of the Sixteenth Century

In the first decades of Charles's reign, his Castilian courtiers remained idealistic about their king's role as emperor of the Christian community. Antonio de Guevara is perhaps the best example of this early strain of Spanish idealism in the political thought of the first half of the sixteenth century. Throughout his writing he consistently separates the ideal from the real in his consideration of politics. He recognizes that political life is unstable, dominated by fortune, and his solution is to urge the monarch and his courtiers to pursue political actions which conform with moral and religious ideals. His division between the real and the ideal is noticeable in the dichotomy he sets up in *Menosprecio de corte y alabanza de aldea*. Guevara's ideal would be for Charles's empire to embrace the virtues of the *aldea*, rejecting the artificiality and inconsistency of the *corte*.[4] Guevara expresses this inconsistency by referring to the traditional notion of fortune: "En la corte, como la fortuna es inconstante en lo que da y muy incierta en lo que promete, de una hora a otra cae uno y sube otro…"[5] The reason fortune has so much power in the court is because people follow opinion rather than reason and because hardly anyone there tells the truth.[6] This is the way

3 Ibid., 61–161.

4 Ibid., 184.

5 Antonio de Guevara, *Menosprecio de corte y alabanza de aldea. Arte de marear*, ed. Asunción Rallo Gruss (Madrid: Cátedra, 1987), 183.

6 Ibid., 183, 192–93.

fortune works: "La vara con que mide la fortuna los méritos y deméritos de los cortesanos es, no la razón, sino la opinión."[7] While Guevara evokes the ancients, he does not do so in any historical sense, like the Florentine civil humanists, but in an idealistic way: they represent a kind of Golden Age of morality, before the ethics of the *aldea* had been corrupted by the *corte*.[8]

This separation between the real and the ideal is also present in Guevara's *Marco Aurelio con el Relox de príncipes*, which follows the medieval tradition of advice books to princes in terms of ideology, but whose innovative form, a fictionalized biography of a Roman emperor, made this work one of the most popular throughout sixteenth-century Europe. Guevara makes his idealistic goal clear in his General Prologue: "no es mi fin de dezir en este libro a los príncipes y grandes señores qué tales son, sino amonestarles qué tales deven ser; no dezirles lo que hazen, sino avisarlos de lo que deven hazer."[9] Guevara's principal piece of advice to his monarch is that he be virtuous according to the traditional, Christian notion of virtue, putting his faith in the divine providence of God: "Y no se tenga en poco ser el príncipe buen christiano, porque no ay más bienaventurada república que la que es regida por príncipe de buena conciencia."[10] One of Guevara's examples of a pious ruler is interesting precisely because he was not manly. In fact, Narsetes was a Greek eunuch, whom his empress, Sophia, humiliated and treated like a woman.[11] Nevertheless, Guevara praises Narsetes: "era tan buen christiano y tan devoto, que todos pensavan que le dava el Señor las victorias más por las oraciones que hazía que no por las armas con que peleava, porque jamás le vieron derramar sangre de sus enemigos en la batalla, que primero no uviesse derramado lágrimas de sus ojos en alguna yglesia."[12] In other words Guevara is not interested in returning to the ancient opposition between manly virtue and the feminine goddess Fortuna; instead a ruler owes his success entirely to God. True to his Franciscan education, Guevara asserts that a prince is good only if he is a devout Christian.

Guevara's portrait of an emperor, which was meant to serve as an example for Charles, coincides essentially with the ideal, Christian ruler found in Erasmus's *Institutio principis christiani* (1516).[13] Thus, in Marcus Aurelius's speech to his son, he claims that "el amor del pueblo y la libertad de su offiçio no la han de ganar o sustentar con armas derramadas por la tierra, sino con muchas virtudes iunctas en su persona."[14] At the end of his speech, the emperor speaks

7 Ibid., 234.

8 Maravall, *Carlos V*, 185–86.

9 Antonio de Guevara, *Relox de príncipes*, ed. Emilio Blanco (Madrid: ABL Editor, 1994), 14.

10 Ibid., 151.

11 Ibid., 168.

12 Ibid., 163.

13 Kathleen Bollard de Broce, "The Rhetoric of Exemplarity in Two Spanish Sixteenth-Century *Specula Principis*," *Symposium* 53, no. 2 (1999): 86–88.

14 Antonio de Guevara, *Obras completas* (Madrid: Turner, 1994), 2:190.

of an Egyptian tablet that he had found, which contained twelve statements on governance, all of which agree with Erasmus. One in particular reveals a familiarity with the traditional rhetoric of love and hate: "Siempre trabajé ser amado de buenos, y nunca tuve pena por ser aborrecido de malos."[15] In other words, Guevara's portrait of Marcus Aurelius modifies slightly the traditional Aristotelian division between the good king and the tyrant: like the good, Christian king, he chooses to be loved by his good citizens; unlike the tyrant, he does not worry about whether or not he is hated by the evil ones.

Guevara's idealistic conception of politics determines his consideration of empire. The episode of the "Villano del Danubio" constitutes a critique of the conquest of America as it was being carried out by Charles's subjects.[16] The implicit analogy between the relationships Romans-to-Germans and Spanish-to-Amerindians must have been readily recognized by Charles and his courtiers. Guevara expresses in the words of the *villano* the idea that might does not make right: "el hombre que toma por fuerça a lo ajeno pierde el derecho que tiene a lo suyo proprio."[17] The *villano*'s society before the arrival of the Romans was one characterized by a Golden Age of innocence before the Fall of mankind: they had no king because they had no need for one. The *villano* challenges one by one any reason that the Romans might have given to justify their conquest. The last one especially must have reminded the Spaniards of one of their own principal justifications for the violent conquest of the Indies: "Si dezís que nos embiastes a conquistar a fin que no fuéssemos bárbaros ni viviéssemos con tyranos, sino que nos queríades hazer vivir debaxo de buenas leyes y fueros … ¿cómo es possible que vosotros deys orden de vivir a los estrangeros, pues quebrantáys las leyes de vuestros antepassados?"[18] According to Guevara's ideal conception of empire, Charles should make every effort to create peace within the Christian community, rather than unlawfully conquer any other.

Alfonso de Valdés's conception of empire is similarly traditional and idealistic in character. As Kathleen Bollard de Broce has shown, his writings find a unique middle ground between his position of authority as a close advisor and defender of Charles and his Erasmian pacifist vision of what kind of emperor his lord should be. The emperor is the monarch of the whole world; and, following the teachings of Erasmus, it is his job to bring about a reform of Christianity in his community. In this way the emperor is supposed to carry out God's providence. The role of the emperor is to defend the Christian community and maintain justice in this world; the role of the pope is to attract this same community to the teachings and life of Christ through example. If the

15 Ibid., 2:942–43.

16 Guevara, *Relox de príncipes*, 698–713.

17 Ibid., 701.

18 Ibid., 706.

pope fails in this role, as he has, the emperor is obligated to bring about reform. In his *Diálogo de las cosas acaecidas en Roma*, Alfonso de Valdés simultaneously exculpates Charles for the sack of Rome and condemns the military expansion of empire. Appropriating Erasmus's pacifism, Valdés attempts to advise Charles to change his policy of imperial expansion, which led to the sack in the first place. Valdés adopts Erasmus's ideal of the *pax christiana* to Charles's goal of becoming the head of a universal Christian monarchy, even though Erasmus never would have supported such a goal. Nevertheless, in this dialogue and even more so in his *Diálogo de Mercurio y Carón*, Valdés discourages Charles from continuing his policy of imperial expansion.[19] Instead, he wanted Charles to take advantage of the situation to convoke a Council, a desire which never became reality.[20]

In his *Diálogo de Mercurio y Carón*, Valdés continues to conceive of monarchical government in traditional, universal terms. The political portraits of the souls which pass Mercurio and Carón on their way to the afterlife are presented in traditional terms. Carón explains to the bad king that he is going to Hell based on the medieval distinction between king and tyrant which we have already seen:

> CARÓN: Veamos, ¿tú pensabas que eras rey para provecho de la república o para el tuyo?
> ÁNIMA: ¿Quién es rey sino para su provecho?
> CARÓN: A la fe, hermano, el que piensa ser rey para su provecho y tiene más cuidado de lo que cumple a sí mesmo que a la república, aquel tal no es rey, sino tirano…[21]

Following the medieval tradition, Valdés distinguishes between king and tyrant based on whether or not he works for the common good of his kingdom. Much like Guevara's, Valdés's good king, Polidoro, is modeled after Erasmus's *Institutio principis christiani*. He goes to heaven because he realizes that he has not been a good pastor for the sheep that God has charged him with. He had neglected his own flock in search of others, not to help them but to take advantage of them. In other words, similar to Guevara, Valdés also considers imperial conquest unjust, especially if the good of the conquered is not considered. Although Valdés does not deny the validity of war against the infidel, the ideal is pacifist conversion. Ultimately, the good king should be a reflection of God.[22]

19 Kathleen Bollard de Broce, "Authorizing Literary Propaganda: Alfonso de Valdés' *Diálogo de las cosas acaecidas en Roma*," *Hispanic Review* 68, no. 2 (2000): 131–45.

20 Marcel Bataillon, *Erasmo y España: Estudios sobre la historia espiritual del siglo XVI*, 2nd ed. (México: Fondo de Cultura Económica, 1966), 367–85.

21 Alfonso de Valdés, *Diálogo de Mercurio y Carón*, ed. Rosa Navarro Durán (Madrid: Cátedra, 1999), 150.

22 Bataillon, *Erasmo y España*, 400–2.

In this way Valdés's general conception of monarchy is traditional in nature. Mercurio's characterization of the king of France and the emperor Charles is meant to contrast these two figures along the same lines. They both wait for the right *oportunidad* or *ocasión* to carry out their military campaigns; however, the king of France does this out of malice; Charles, "para provecho del pueblo."[23] The king of France attacked the Spaniards, taking the opportunity while Charles was in Germany. When Leon X declared himself enemy of the king of France, Charles took the opportunity to recover Milan from the king of France, who had held it in tyranny. However, afterwards he decided it would be better for the Milanese if he gave its administration to Francisco Maria Sforza.[24]

Machiavelli and the Development of a Militant, Imperial Christianity

Throughout his political works, but most especially in the *Discourses*, Machiavelli consistently holds up the ancient Roman republic as an example for modern political leaders to follow. Specifically, a subtle allusion to the Roman triumph appears in his discussion of the differences between the ancient Roman religion and modern Christianity in *Discourses* 2.2.[25] Here, Machiavelli praises the way the Roman religion encouraged civic-minded ambition and a search for worldly glory in its citizens:

> Perché, avendoci la nostra religione mostro la verità e la vera via, ci fa stimare meno l'onore del mondo; onde i gentili, stimandolo assai e avendo posto in quello il sommo bene, erano nelle azioni loro piú feroci. Il che si può considerare da molte loro constituzioni, cominciandosi dalla magnificenza de' sacrificii loro alla umiltà nostri, dove è qualche pompa piú delicata che magnifica, ma nessuna azione feroce o gagliarda. Qui non mancava la

23 Valdés, *Mercurio y Carón*, 94.

24 Ibid., 93–95.

25 For Machiavelli's treatment of religion, see Alberto Tenenti, "La religione di Machiavelli," *Studi storici* 10 (1969): 709–48; J. Samuel Preus, "Machiavelli's Functional Analysis of Religion: Context and Object," *Journal of the History of Ideas* 40 (1979): 171–90; Vickie B. Sullivan, *Machiavelli's Three Romes: Religion, Human Liberty, and Politics Reformed* (DeKalb: Northern Illinois University Press, 1996); Emanuele Cutinelli-Rèndina, *Chiesa e religione in Machiavelli* (Pisa: Istituti editoriali e poligrafici internazionali, 1998); John H. Geerken, "Machiavelli's Moses and Renaissance Politics," *Journal of the History of Ideas* 60, no. 4 (1999): 579–95; Marcia L. Colish, "Republicanism, Religion, and Machiavelli's Savonarolan Moment," *Journal of the History of Ideas* 60, no. 4 (1999): 597–616; Cary J. Nederman, "Amazing Grace: Fortune, God, and Free Will in Machiavelli's Thought," *Journal of the History of Ideas* 60, no. 4 (1999): 617–38; Benedetto Fontana, "Love of Country and Love of God: The Political Uses of Religion in Machiavelli," *Journal of the History of Ideas* 60, no. 4 (1999): 639–58; John M. Najemy, "Papirius and the Chickens, or Machiavelli on the Necessity of Interpreting Religion," *Journal of the History of Ideas* 60, no. 4 (1999): 659–81; Maurizio Viroli, *Machiavelli's God* (Princeton, NJ: Princeton University Press, 2010).

> pompa né la magnificenza delle cerimonie, ma vi si aggiugneva l'azione del sacrificio pieno di sangue e di ferocità, ammazzandovisi moltitudine d'animali; il quale aspetto, sendo terribile, rendeva gli uomini simili a lui.[26]

Christian ceremonies may be magnificent, but they lack the ferocity that the Roman triumph, with its bloody sacrifice of the white oxen, inspired in its citizens. Machiavelli goes on to contrast the Roman triumph, which raised the value of worldly glory to the level of godliness, to the way Christians now glorify humility and contemplation in this world, with the hope of finding the ultimate good in the next life:

> La religione antica, oltre di questo, non beatificava se non uomini pieni di mondana gloria, come erano capitani di eserciti e principi di republiche. La nostra religione ha glorificato piú gli uomini umili e contemplativi che gli attivi. Ha dipoi posto il sommo bene nella umiltà, abiezione, e nel dispregio delle cose umane; quell'altra lo poneva nella grandezza dello animo, nella fortezza del corpo e in tutte le altre cose atte a fare gli uomini fortissimi. E se la religione nostra richiede che tu abbi in te fortezza, vuole che tu sia atto a patire piú che a fare una cosa forte.[27]

As a result of this Christian education, according to Machiavelli, men are more apt to accept their suffering at the hands of evil men who know that their victims will not seek vengeance. This critique of Christianity later became, in fact, a common point of contention for the early, sixteenth-century detractors of Machiavelli, such as Girolamo Osorio, Reginald Pole and Juan Ginés de Sepúlveda, as well as the seventeenth-century anti-Machiavellians of the reason-of-state tradition, as we shall see. Nevertheless, Machiavelli does not attack the Christian doctrine, per se, but corrupt members of the Church as well as those who, according to Machiavelli, have interpreted Christ's teachings erroneously:

> E benché paia che si sia effeminato il mondo e disarmato il cielo, nasce piú, sanza dubbio, dalla viltà degli uomini, che hanno interpetrato la nostra religione secondo l'ozio, e non secondo la virtú. Perché, se considerassono come la ci promette l'esaltazione e la difesa della patria, vedrebbono come la vuole che noi l'amiamo e onoriamo, e prepariamoci a essere tali che noi la possiamo difendere.[28]

Drawing from a long tradition of a social and political application of Christian *caritas* that flourished during the civic humanism of the Florentine Quattrocento, Machiavelli offers a more militaristic interpretation of the Gospels, one which

26 Machiavelli, *Discorsi*, 317–18.
27 Ibid., 318.
28 Ibid., 318–19.

calls for the armed defense of one's *patria* as well as civilized Christendom as a whole. In other words, in his writings, Machiavelli does not simply call into question the legitimacy of the institution of the Catholic Church, as historians have often noted; in addition, he implies that political leaders, following the example of the Romans, may use the Christian religion, interpreted correctly, for political ends, to encourage a devotion to the common good as well as to motivate their citizens and give confidence to their soldiers.[29]

Machiavelli's inclusion on the Roman Index of 1559 was anticipated by a series of authors who found his works offensive to the Church. Machiavelli's first attackers did not form a concerted effort, but were instead isolated from each other. In his *Democrates primus*, published by Blado in 1535, Juan Ginés de Sepúlveda criticizes those who think the Christian religion makes men weak, without giving any names. However, Alejandro Coroleu discovered that in a manuscript of this work conserved in the Biblioteca Vaticana, Sepúlveda refers explicitly to Machiavelli in this passage.[30] Jeronimo Osorio da Fonseca, in his *De nobilitate christiana*, written in the 1530s, makes a similar criticism of Machiavelli, without naming the "impurus quidam scriptor ac nefarius."[31] In 1539, Reginald Pole condemns Machiavelli in his *Apologia ad Carolum Quintum*.[32] These three authors were not aware of each other at the time they composed their works. However, from the early 1550s there begins to emerge a movement which would eventually lead to the prohibition of Machiavelli's entire *corpus*. In 1550, Girolamo Muzio da Capodistria wrote a letter to the Roman Inquisitors in which he groups Machiavelli among the "infedeli" in opposition to the "heretici," because "nelle sue scritture fa apertamente di questi officii, che quegli altri fanno sotto la maschera del Christo. Che egli senza respetto alcuno insegna a non servar fede, né charità, né religione & dice che di queste cose gli huomini se ne debbono servire per parer buoni, & per le grandezze temporali, alle quali quando non servono non se ne dee fare stima."[33] In 1552, the Florentine publication of Osorio's work coincided with the release in Rome of Ambrogio Catarino Politi's *Enarrationes*, which contains a criticism of Machiavelli, calling him an atheist.[34] These early anti-Machiavellians cite passages from the *Prince* 18 and *Discourses* 2.2 in order to demonstrate his opposition to Church doctrine. Nevertheless, I argue that these early readers of Machiavelli simultaneously reject Machiavelli's characterization of the Christian religion as effeminate and answer his call for a more militant Christianity capable of supporting an aggressive imperial enterprise.

29 Hörnqvist, *Machiavelli and Empire*, 81–86; Viroli, *Machiavelli's God*.

30 Procacci, *Machiavelli*, 85–86.

31 Ibid., 87.

32 Ibid., 87.

33 Ibid., 95–96.

34 Ibid., 89–91.

Jeronimo Osorio da Fonseca wrote his *De nobilitate civile et christiana* in the 1530s, but it was not published until 1542 in Lisbon and 1552 in Florence.[35] It contains two books on civil nobility and three on Christian nobility. His lengthy discussion of fortitude and magnanimity in book 5 consists of a response to Machiavelli's critique of these Christian virtues found in *Discourses* 2.2. He argues that martial zeal is perfectly compatible with Christianity, as the examples of Moses and David prove. The love of Christ and the promise of immortality give courage to soldiers. On the other hand, unchristian courage, fury and cruelty are bestial and barbarous. The bloody sacrifices that Machiavelli praises in truth only induce fear in the public. He asserts that when Machiavelli blames the interpreters of Christianity, rather than Christianity itself, he is merely trying to exculpate himself. Nevertheless, in the remainder of his treatise, where he leaves Machiavelli aside and attacks pacifism, Osorio essentially agrees with Machiavelli, offering precisely the alternative interpretation of Christianity that Machiavelli calls for. In what Anglo calls "a positively Machiavellian outburst,"[36] Osorio rejects the pacifist claim that war is contrary to Christian charity on the grounds that there is a difference between private and public morality: it is true that one should suffer private injuries; on the other hand, one must defend country and religion.[37]

Later on, Osorio incorporates Machiavelli's views without acknowledgment into his *De regis institutione*, dedicated to King Sebastian of Portugal in 1571. One of the interlocutors, Menesius, puts forth the idea that princes cannot always keep their word when the common good demands that they break it, citing the example of Lysander, who in turn cites Hercules, who covered himself with the skins of both the lion and the fox. Osorio repeats his refutation of the idea that the Christian prince cannot be martial, urging the central idea that good arms are essential. He repeats Machiavelli's argument that "virtus" and not money is the "nerve of war."[38] Treaties alone are not sufficient, because enemies break them at the first sign of weakness or opportunity. Otiosity brings corruption and weakness, so it is necessary for the prince to always keep his subjects exercised and prepared for war. In fact, war is preferable to peace if this otiosity is allowed.[39]

Perhaps inspired by Machiavelli's negative characterization of the Catholic Church in *Discourses* 2.2, in his *Apologia ad Carolum Quintum* (1539) Reginald Pole reveals how Thomas Cromwell, corrupted by demons, used Machiavelli's *Prince*, penned by the devil himself, to induce Henry VIII into splitting with the Catholic Church, declaring himself the head of a new church, in order to

35 Ibid., 87.
36 Anglo, *Machiavelli—The First Century*, 154.
37 Ibid., 145–55.
38 Ibid., 161.
39 Ibid., 156–62.

satisfy his own personal lustful desires. In this way Henry VIII anticipated the arrival of the Antichrist, if indeed he did not already embody him himself. Pole focusses on the *Prince* 18, in which he found the idea that the prince should only worry about the appearance of religion. Pole finds a contradiction between this notion and Machiavelli's insistence that the prince avoid hatred, citing 2 Thessalonians 2, which tells us that all deception, the *mysterium iniquitatis*, will eventually come to light through God's will. It is impossible to dissimulate this vice, as proved by the case of Henry VIII himself, as well as the absence of any case in history to support Machiavelli's view.[40] As Donaldson has argued, Pole understood Machiavellism as a doctrine of concealment in opposition to God's divine Revelation. As such he portrays himself as a profit of the Last Days and of the Second Coming. This self-characterization was dependent on his characterization of Machiavelli's text as the instrument of the Antichrist. In other words, Osorio, in fact, invented a characterization of Machiavelli, misrepresenting him in such a way that his own position would be considered an exact opposite.[41] As we shall see, the anti-Machiavellians of the Baroque appropriated this same method for a similar purpose.

We have seen how Juan Ginés de Sepúlveda criticizes Machiavelli for putting forth the view that the Christian religion makes men weak. Nevertheless, in his writings Sepúlveda appropriates Machiavelli's use of the Roman model for contemporary empire. In part because of this, Machiavelli's Romans would become an important element in the way Spaniards conceived of Charles V's imperial project.

Elsewhere I have placed the publication of Juan Lorenzo Ottevanti's *Discursos de Nicolao Machiaueli*, a Spanish translation of the *Discourses* published in 1552, within the context of the debate between Bartolomé de las Casas and Juan Ginés de Sepúlveda that took place just one year before.[42] In sum, both Sepúlveda and Las Casas made use of the example of the ancient Romans as part of their argument.[43] Their different treatment of the Romans is intimately related to their two distinctive notions of empire: Sepúlveda, who like Machiavelli holds the Romans up as positive examples, emphasizes the secular justifications of imperial conquest; Las Casas, who points to the paganism of the Romans, returns to a more traditionally papal conception of the emperor, stressing the obligation on the part of the Spaniards to proselytize their new subjects

40 Donaldson, *Machiavelli and Mystery of State*, 1–31; Anglo, *Machiavelli—The First Century*, 131–32.

41 Donaldson, *Machiavelli and Mystery of State*, 30.

42 Juan Lorenzo Ottevanti, *"Discursos de Nicolao Machiaueli": Juan Lorenzo Ottevanti's Spanish Translation of Machiavelli's "Discourses on Livy" (1552)*, ed. Keith David Howard (Tempe: Arizona Center for Medieval and Renaissance Studies, forthcoming).

43 See David A. Lupher, *Romans in a New World: Classical Models in Sixteenth-Century Spanish America* (Ann Arbor: University of Michigan Press, 2003), 103–49.

in the Indies. Sepúlveda's treatment of the ancient Romans, which agrees with Machiavelli's, constitutes one important instrument that he used to put forth his vision of the worldwide Spanish imperialist project.

When discussing the specific reasons by which the Spaniards were justified in depriving the Indians of their possessions in book 2 of his *Demócrates segundo*, Sepúlveda, just like Machiavelli, presents the Romans as exemplary military conquerors. In *Discourses* 2.4, Machiavelli distinguishes between three modes of expanding: first, through leagues, whereby no one republic is above another, like the ancient Tuscans; second, by getting direct subjects, like the ancient Spartans and Athenians; third, a kind of compromise between these two extremes: "farsi compagni, non tanto però che non ti rimanga il grado del comandare, la sedia dello imperio e il titolo delle imprese: il quale modo fu osservato da' Romani.'[44] The Roman method of expanding is the best, because they became "partners" with their neighbors, leaving them autonomous, but in such a way that the Romans maintained the title and seat of empire as well as the right to military command. Machiavelli goes on to explain that this method was actually a deception used by the Romans to trick these same early partners: after these partners helped Rome expand beyond Italy, conquering various peoples as direct subjects and making them provinces of Rome, before they were aware of it Rome became so powerful that these partners were unable to hold on to their autonomy. Thus it is revealed that the other two methods of expanding listed above become two successive stages in the history of Roman expansion: first Rome forms a kind of slightly advantageous league with its powerful neighbors; second, after Rome grows mighty enough, these neighbors become direct subjects.[45]

Sepúlveda's own account of Roman imperial expansion is strikingly similar, when in book 2 he sets up the Romans above all other examples of moderation after military conquest:

> pues algunas ciudades vencidas por ellos eran primeramente convertidas en estipendiarias, con ligeras desventajas y no bajo inicuas condiciones, las que después convertían en provincias; a otras las dejaban libres y las consentían utilizar su propia legislación, pero cuando lo exigían la culpa o naturaleza de los enemigos, los despojaban de sus ciudades y campos, y aun a algunas ciudades las arrasaban por completo.[46]

Here Sepúlveda refers to cities conquered by Rome but left autonomous for a while, either completely free or obliged to pay a tribute; either way, Rome's

44 Machiavelli, *Discorsi*, 330–31.

45 Hörnqvist, *Machiavelli and Empire*, 135–39.

46 Juan Ginés de Sepúlveda, *Demócrates segundo o de las justas causas de la guerra contra los indios*, ed. Ángel Losada, 2nd ed. (Madrid: Instituto Francisco de Vitoria, 1984), 95.

superiority to these cities was only slight. However, under pretense of either their guilt or their very nature, Rome's subjected cities could be reduced to complete obedience or destroyed. The progression from near equality to complete subjugation, spelled out in Machiavelli's account, is here only implied. In fact, keeping in mind the importance of the authority of Aristotle for his general argument, Sepúlveda's simultaneous reading of Machiavelli constitutes one more example of a tendency among European humanists around the middle of the sixteenth century to interpret the Florentine's writings through the lens of the works of "The Philosopher," and vice versa.[47] Fadrique Furió Ceriol subsequently continued this tendency in Spain; however, Furió Ceriol's debt to Machiavelli is much more pervasive than Sepúlveda's, because he accepted Machiavelli's reorganization of the traditional Aristotelian strict division between kingly virtues and tyrannical vices.

Fadrique Furió Ceriol

Fadrique Furió Ceriol belonged to a group of Spaniards who studied at the University of Louvain around the beginning of Philip II's reign. We know about this group from a report that Fray Baltasar Pérez submitted to the Inquisition of Seville in 1558 expressing his concern with the Spaniards' exposure to heretical ideas. Furió Ceriol in particular had come under scrutiny because he published an essay defending vernacular translations of the Bible in 1556, five years after this activity was banned in Spain.[48] He was also accused of owning prohibited books and spent time in jail in either 1556 or 1557. However, he successfully defended himself from his accusers and from around 1563 he was a member of Philip II's court.[49]

Furió Ceriol published his political treatise, *El concejo y consejeros de príncipes*, in Antwerp in 1559. It is a relatively short essay which gives the king advice regarding how his administration should be organized and how his councillors should be elected. In his preface, Furió Ceriol explains that what he is now offering to his king is really just a small fraction of a complete treatment of kingship. It is significant that Furió Ceriol decides to focus his treatise on councils and councillors: he understood that Philip depended on his courtiers, ministers and even common soldiers to maintain his extensive empire. As we shall see, Machiavelli provided him with a vocabulary which helped him express to his monarch the problems involved with maintaining an empire of such large proportions. Furió Ceriol not only appropriated Machiavelli's vocabulary in general and adapted it to Philip II's monarchical ideology but also borrowed

47 For this Aristotelian reading of Machiavelli, see Procacci, *Machiavelli*, 63–81.

48 Truman, *Spanish Treatises*, 89.

49 Fadrique Furió Ceriol, *El concejo y consejeros del príncipe*, ed. Henry Méchoulan (Madrid: Tecnos, 1993), xiii–xix.

extensively from the *Prince* in order to advise his king on the best way to deal with the rebellion in the Low Countries.

Historians have debated to what extent Furió Ceriol was influenced by Machiavelli. Maravall and Antonio Risco both point to Furió Ceriol's division between the good prince and the good man, to which we will return shortly, as evidence of Machiavelli's influence: like the Florentine, Furió Ceriol recovers the so-called "double truth," or the separation between reason and faith associated with the thirteenth-century naturalist, Averroist commentators on Aristotle.[50] Neither of these authors point out specific passages from Machiavelli's works that Furió Ceriol could have had in mind when writing his treatise.

Truman has recently highlighted the similarity between several passages of the *Concejo* and the *Prince* 22 and 23, which deal specifically with the subject of Furió Ceriol's entire treatise, the prince's councillors.[51] For example, Machiavelli mentions that princes are usually judged according to the merit of their councillors:

> E la prima coniettura, che si fa del cervello d'uno signore, è vedere li uomini che lui ha d'intorno: e quando sono sufficienti e fedeli, sempre si può reputarlo savio; perché ha saputo conoscerli sufficienti e sa mantenerli fedeli; ma quando sieno altrimenti, sempre si può fare non buono iudizio di lui: perché el primo errore che fa, lo fa in questa elezione.[52]

Furió Ceriol uses the same language to convey the same message. In fact, Furió Ceriol's passage is so similar that it appears to be at least an adaptation if not a loose translation of Machiavelli's:

> Vemos primeramente que el primer juizio que se suele hazer sobre el Príncipe i de su habilidad, es de la reputación de los de su Concejo; porque, quando son sabios i suficientes, siempre es reputado sabio el Príncipe, pues supo entender quáles eran los suficientes, i después conservárselos fieles i leales. Pero quando no son tales, no se puede esperar buena reputación en el Príncipe, pues ierra en lo principal; i el que ierra en lo que más importa, es casi necessario que en todo lo otro ierre.[53]

Similarly, when dealing with how princes should take advice from their councillors, Machiavelli writes: "E perché e' sono di tre generazione cervelli,—l'uno intende da sé, l'altro discerne quello che altri intende, el terzo no intende né sé

50 Maravall, "Maquiavelo y maquiavelismo," 58; Antonio Risco, "El empirismo político de Fadrique Furió Ceriol," *Cahiers du Monde Hispanique et Luso-Bresilien* 29 (1977): 128–34, 149-50.

51 Truman, *Spanish Treatises*, 104–8.

52 Machiavelli, *Principe*, 153–54.

53 Furió Ceriol, *Concejo y consejeros*, 67–68.

né altri: quel primo è eccellentissimo, el secondo eccellente, el terzo inutile."[54] Furió Ceriol's own remark on the same subject is strikingly similar:

> Porque vemos que hai tres maneras de entendimientos: uno entiende, comprehende, i sabe por sí solo; otro siendo amonestado, o enseñado, otro ni con lo uno, ni con lo otro. Este postrero es inútil, i nasció esclavo en perpetua servidumbre. El segundo es bueno, pero el primero es divino, i nasció derechamente para mandar i governar.[55]

As Truman points out, these passages clearly demonstrate that Furió Ceriol was at least familiar with the *Prince*.[56] Nevertheless, Truman concludes that Furió Ceriol differs from Machiavelli because "his view of government leaves room for an ideal of public service and personal integrity in the service of the public good and of the prince himself."[57] Similarly, Henry Méchoulan admits that Furió Ceriol agreed with Machiavelli's pessimistic view of human nature, but asserts that they are fundamentally different for two reasons: first, Furió Ceriol does not applaud duplicity, recommending it only when needed; second, Furió Ceriol's objective is the common good.[58] For his part, Fernández-Santamaría accepts that some passages in Furió Ceriol's *Concejo* resemble others in the *Prince*. However, he rejects the possibility of there being any presence of Machiavellism on the grounds that "the crucial ingredient is missing: the open acknowledgement that Christian virtue and political action are mutually exclusive."[59]

The problem with all of these objections is that these historians' conceptions of Machiavellism are in reality anachronistic for a discussion of Furió Ceriol, because they are based not on a close reading of those works by Machiavelli which were available to Furió Ceriol, but rather on the later, Counter-Reformation anti-Machiavellians' own misleading representations of the Florentine as a diabolical teacher of evil, such as those created by Pedro de Ribadeneyra and his imitators, as we shall see. We must remember that Furió Ceriol is reading and writing before this Counter-Reformation portrait of Machiavelli has been constructed. To be sure, Machiavelli does promote a moral flexibility, which includes the possibility of using mendacity; however, similar to Furió Ceriol, he writes that rulers should always be good when they can, and only enter into evil when necessity demands it.[60] In effect, an analysis of Furió Ceriol's texts reveals a significant Machiavellian influence. From his own experience Furió

54 Machiavelli, *Principe*, 154.

55 Furió Ceriol, *Concejo y consejeros*, 8.

56 Truman, *Spanish Treatises*, 106.

57 Ibid., 107.

58 Furió Ceriol, *Concejo y consejeros*, xxvi, xxxiv.

59 J. A. Fernández-Santamaría, *The State, War and Peace: Spanish Political Thought in the Renaissance, 1516–1559* (Cambridge: Cambridge University Press, 1977), 292–93.

60 See, for example, Machiavelli, *Principe*, 118.

Ceriol had come to understand well that empire was inherently unstable and uncertain; he appropriates Machiavelli's vocabulary of contingency in order to express this problem to his king, Philip II.

Furió Ceriol begins his treatise with a long dedication to Philip II in which he discusses the institution of the king generally. In this more universal discussion, Furió Ceriol adapts Machiavelli's vocabulary of contingency to a long tradition of medieval political thought marked by a monarchical ideology. He begins by dividing the king into two persons: on the one hand, there is the man who, like any other man, comes from nature; on the other, there is the institution of the king which is "merced de Fortuna, i favor del Cielo, hecha para gobierno i amparo del bien público, a cuia causa la nombramos persona pública."[61] It is important to note here the reference to the goddess Fortune with respect to the king as an institution, not as a man. This anticipates Furió Ceriol's incorporation of the Machiavellian contrast between prudence and fortune into his consideration of kingship, and more specifically of empire, as we shall see. Furió Ceriol refers here to the medieval tradition of understanding the king as having two bodies: the natural man and the body of the whole kingdom, the *corpus mysticum*, of which he is usually presented as the head, as we have seen. Furió Ceriol adapts this tradition to a secular, rational analysis of politics. Similar to Machiavelli's famous accusation in the *Prince* 15 that all previous political philosophers had limited their discussions to imaginary kingdoms, Furió Ceriol accuses all former political thinkers of unrealistically confusing these two persons of the king. For example, when they say that the king must learn precepts taken from theology, natural philosophy, law, mathematics or medicine, they are treating the king as a man and not as a king per se. In other words, according to Furió Ceriol, these writers think that in order for a man to be a good king, he must be a good man in a general sense, not realizing that a despicable man can be a good king, just like he can be a good musician or a good pilot. In this way, he agrees with Machiavelli's reorganization of the traditional dichotomy between virtue and vice, in order to allow a prince to pursue the common good more freely. Furió Ceriol encourages the king, as a man, to be flexible with respect to traditional morals so that the king, as an institution, may better serve the common good.

As an alternative, Furió Ceriol defines the good king as one who knows well, and prudently carries out, his own art: "que sepa i pueda con su prudente industria conservarse con sus vassallos de tal modo que no solamente se mantenga honradamente en su estado i lo establezca para los suios, sino que (siendo menester) lo amplifique, i gane vitoria de sus enemigos cada i quando que quisiere, o el tiempo pidiere."[62] In this general discussion, while Furió Ceriol still

61 Furió Ceriol, *Concejo y consejeros*, 5.
62 Ibid., 7.

considers it the function of the king to look after the common good, the "bien público," of the entire kingdom, he secularizes the institution of kingship: just like in Machiavelli's political works, the king is considered in practical terms of power with respect to his subjects, and independence and conquest with respect to neighboring states.[63] Internally, the goal of the king is to conserve his power over his subjects. Externally, his role is to conquer the neighboring states whenever necessary. It is significant that Furió Ceriol excludes the possibility of a king remaining confined to his own borders, defending his lands whenever his neighbors might attack; when he finds himself in conflict with an enemy, he must know how to "amplify" his territory. As we have seen, in *Discourses* 1.6 Machiavelli explains that in the political world of men, dominated by fortune, this 'via del mezzo' is not possible, because necessity will inevitably lead a state to defend itself through imperial expansion. In Machiavelli's zero-sum world, rulers must choose between conquest or subjugation.[64]

Furió Ceriol's proposed system of councils was not by itself very innovative: Philip had inherited from his father Charles a bureaucratic administration which generally resembles Furió Ceriol's proposal. His contribution is to adapt Machiavelli's vocabulary for thinking about empire to this system. According to Furió Ceriol, the prudent and effective use of his councils will allow Philip to control his own fortune. For example, the consequences of not using well his Council of War are severe:

> En el principado do no hai un tal Concejo, ierra el Príncipe en quantas cosas emprende militares, muévelas sin tiempo ni sazón, no las sabe guiar, ni menos acabar, todo cuelga de la fortuna; en el vencer es sobervio, ni sabe usar de la vitoria; si fuere vencido, deturbado i congoxoso no sabe dónde se está, como flaca i vil mugercilla se araña i messa, sino en público, a lo menos en secreto.[65]

Philip's Council of War will help him take into account the contingency of each particular situation. If he does not use his councils well, this passage suggests, he will give up the destiny of his kingdoms to the whims of Fortune. Machiavelli's recuperation of the ancient Roman opposition between the feminine goddess Fortune and masculine virtue fits particularly well in this context of military power. The contrast between the ideal brave, masculine soldier and the weak, pitiful woman is evident. In this way, Philip is presented with the image of how Fortune will emasculate him if he does not use his councils prudently.

63 Marcia L. Colish, "The Idea of Liberty in Machiavelli," *Journal of the History of Ideas* 32 (1971): 323–50.

64 Hörnqvist, *Machiavelli and Empire*, 88–89.

65 Furió Ceriol, *Concejo y consejeros*, 20.

In the same context, Furió Ceriol chastises those who look to higher powers to explain a negative outcome in war:

> Unos se quexan de la fortuna; i ellos no veen que la fortuna mui ruin lugar tiene donde está la prudencia. Otros dizen, que Dios es servido de hazerlo assí; io no entro en el poder de Dios, pero sé bien dezir, i digo con San Pablo, si son ellos secretarios de Dios, o si han recibido cartas dello firmadas de mano de la Trinidad, con que se asseguren que assí sea, como dizen. Otros dizen que nuestros pecados lo causan; i esto es mui gran verdad, porque los ierros i faltas del Príncipe, i de sus ruines Consejeros, son pecados que nos acarrean la perdición nuestra i suia.[66]

Here, Furió Ceriol continues the opposition between fortune and virtue, specifically human prudence. The close etymological relation between *prudence* and *providence* is subtly evoked here: he does not deny divine providence, but he does question the idea that we can perceive it and understand it. Instead, kings and councillors must look to their own human prudence to determine their own fortunes in war. His agreement with those who say that military misfortune is due to our sins is ironic: the sins, or rather faults, to which Furió Ceriol makes reference are purely secular and may be prevented through human prudence.

According to Machiavelli, in order to acquire and maintain a large empire, Rome was forced to give some power to the plebs.[67] This idea could have been transferred to the Spanish context in two ways: first, throughout the sixteenth century, the crown opened up its bureaucratic administration to *letrados* from a wide variety of social backgrounds; second, many non-nobles served as soldiers and colonizers, especially in the Indies. As a consequence, the Spanish crown was forced to depend on others to provide for the common good of each of its multiple possessions. Furió Ceriol evidently has this shift of responsibility in mind when presenting his characterization of the ideal councillor:

> La novena calidad que muestra la suficiencia del alma en el Consejero, es que no solamente ame el bien público, pero que en procurarlo, se olvide de su propio provecho i reputación; de tal manera que, do se pueda aprovechar al bien común, el Consejero se deve emplear en ello con todas sus fuerças i diligencia, aunque de allí se le haia de recrescer daño propio en fama, vida i bienes.[68]

By Furió Ceriol's time, the concept of the common good had become a commonplace in the Aristotelian *De regimine principum* tradition, as we have seen. Nevertheless, this reference to the common good in the context of a general

66 Ibid., 20.
67 Pocock, *Machiavellian Moment*, 198–99.
68 Furió Ceriol, *Concejo y consejeros*, 43.

anxiety, allegorized as the capricious Fortuna, about the uncertainty of imperial projects fits very well with Machiavelli's vocabulary and conceptual framework. Furió Ceriol adapts this framework to the administration of the Spanish empire: in order for the empire to maintain itself and expand, the monarch's councillors must look to the common good rather than their own particular advantage. According to Furió Ceriol, the very survival of Philip's empire depends on this quality: "i ningún imperio, hasta el día presente, alcançó grandes fuerças i se conservó en ellas sino por medio de hombres que tuviessen esta novena calidad de que trato: i por el contrario, el día que vinieron a ser governados por hombres de contraria calidad, esse día mesmo començaron a declinar hasta caer."[69] Furió Ceriol knows, like Francisco Vitoria before him, that each of Philip's possessions has different needs in order to bring about its own common good.[70]

Those subjects who are not included in their monarch's administration will begin to fear for the common good of their own particular community. As a result, they will consider themselves slaves and seek to become free of their natural lord:

> Porque los pueblos se resienten en ver que ellos son desechados de la administración i govierno principal, pues no veen en el Concejo ningún hombre de su tierra, piensan (i no sin causa) que el Príncipe los tiene en poco, o que los tiene como por esclavos, o que no se fía dellos: lo primero, engendra odio; lo segundo, busca libertad; i portanto hazen conjuraciones, i llaman príncipes estraños: lo tercero, les da osadía, i aun obstinación para armar qualquier traición contra su natural Príncipe.[71]

In this passage, Furió Ceriol brings together several statements on conspiracy that Machiavelli puts forward in both the *Prince* and the *Discourses*, and he transfers Machiavelli's language to the question of whether or not Philip should include the diversity of his subjects in his imperial administration. If he does not, his subjects will react in one of three ways, causing one of three results, all three of which have to do with their conception of his opinion of them, and increase the risk of rebellion: first, they will think that Philip thinks lowly of them, which will create hatred; second, they will think that he considers them slaves, which will lead them to seek their freedom and conspire with foreigners; third, they will think that he does not trust them, which will give them the daring to carry out treasonous plots. In the *Prince* 19, as part of his general

69 Ibid., 44.

70 In his *De potestate ciuili*, Vitoria distinguishes between Christ's kingdom, whose aim is the salvation of souls, and secular kingdoms, whose purpose is "human happiness and peace within the commonwealth." Francisco de Vitoria, *Political Writings*, ed. Anthony Pagden and Jeremy Lawrance (Cambridge and New York: Cambridge University Press, 1991), 25.

71 Furió Ceriol, *Concejo y consejeros*, 70.

thesis, spelled out in chapter 17, that princes should avoid the hatred of their subjects, Machiavelli discusses conspiracies at length, offering several examples. Chapter 20, in which he points out specific means by which princes may maintain their security, may be considered a continuation of this discussion of conspiracies. There, when he addresses the question of whether or not a prince who has acquired new subjects should arm them, his language closely resembles Furió Ceriol's: "Ma quando tu gli disarmi, tu cominci a offendergli: mostri che tu abbi in loro diffidenzia, o per viltà o per poca fede, e l'una e l'altra di queste opinioni concepe odio contro di te."[72] This statement, transferred from the question of arms to that of administration, corresponds to Furió Ceriol's first and third reactions, regarding Philip's low opinion or lack of trust for his subjects, and to his first result, fomenting hatred in his subjects. *Discourses* 3.6 constitutes a short but exhaustive treatise on conspiracies. There Machiavelli notes one cause of plots which, interestingly, he had left out of the *Prince*: "Una altra cagione ci è, e grandissima, che fa gli uomini congiurare contro al principe; la quale è il disiderio di liberare la patria, stata da quello occupata."[73] This idea of liberating the *patria* from an oppressor corresponds to Furió Ceriol's second reaction and result: if Philip's subjects think that he considers them slaves, they will seek their freedom.

Besides these specific borrowings, here Furió Ceriol shows that he is an excellent student of Machiavelli's general reconsideration of kingship. All three of these possible reactions on the part of Philip's subjects warn him of the risk of rebellion. Implicit in this argument is the idea, subtly invoked by the parenthetical phrase "i no sin causa," that in reality they would have the right to do so. In other words, Furió Ceriol is suggesting to Philip that he runs the risk of becoming a tyrant, while being careful never to declare as much openly or even use the term. In this way, Furió Ceriol adopts Machiavelli's blurring of the lines between king and tyrant: Philip should include his subjects in his administration, not to cultivate their love, but in order to avoid their hatred.

As these passages suggest, Furió Ceriol was familiar with Machiavelli's vocabulary and theoretical framework associated with political contingency, and he incorporated it into his academic *Concejo* in order to warn Philip about the inherent problems involved with empire in general. Later on, around 1573, as a member of Philip's court, Furió Ceriol put into practice this same approach to empire in his brief *Remedios*. Borrowing heavily from the *Prince*, these *Remedios* consisted of recommendations for means by which the resistance in the Netherlands could be reduced to obedience. In the early 1570s it had become clear that the Duke of Alba's violently repressive approach had not succeeded in quelling the unrest there, which while fomented by the French Huguenots,

72 Machiavelli, *Principe*, 139.
73 Machiavelli, *Discorsi*, 553.

was more immediately caused by excessive taxes such as the infamous Tenth Penny and Alba's cruelty itself: even some Spanish captains and officials joined the Netherlanders in their frequent complaints. After Charles IX of France, influenced by his mother Catherine de' Medici, renounced his ties with the Huguenots, setting off the Saint Bartholomew's Day Massacre, the threat from France was effectively neutralized. Furió Ceriol was among several intellectuals at court, such as the humanist Benito Arias Montano, who answered Philip's general call for new ideas with the suggestion that Philip begin to employ a strategy of moderation and clemency in the Low Countries. In this context, Machiavelli's lessons on the avoidance of hatred were particularly relevant, because at this point Philip was forced to deal with a situation in which Alba and his officials had used fear immoderately, to the point that the local populace of that region hated the Spaniards. As we shall see, Furió Ceriol recommends that Philip attempt to change this opinion, cultivating love when he can, but above all reducing this hatred at all costs.

He introduces his *Remedios* by repeating, perhaps from memory, what Machiavelli says at one point in the *Prince* 18, mistakenly replacing *centauro* with *minotauro*: "que la efigie minotauro de medio arriba hombre, que es el buen govierno, que a de ser superior y primero, y de medio avajo vestia, que es la potencia con las armas, que ha de ser la ymferior y postrera."[74] Philip had already tried to suppress the rebellion with force and fear; now, he should turn to good government, using his "prudencia, liberalidad y misericordia."[75] Nevertheless, if we return Machiavelli's passage to its original context, we realize that he alluded to the centaur in order to demonstrate that both the beast and the man are used in politics, and that of the beast the prince should use both the lion, representing force, and the fox, or cunning. As we shall see, while Furió Ceriol does reject the continuation of the lion as a solution to the situation that Alba had created up to this point, his advice still contains elements of the fox. Perhaps Furió Ceriol's reference to the minotaur, body of a man and head of a bull, is not a mistake after all, but a subtle suggestion that Philip continue to use the beast, but that he shift his emphasis from force to cunning.

Just as he advises in his *Concejo*, Furió Ceriol's remedies 7 through 10 involve giving the Netherlanders important positions in Philip's councils, because "eso aprovecha mucho para romper la ymbidia de las naciones subjetas y para conservarlas en amor y berdadera obediencia."[76] This focus on the means with which Philip may make his subjects love him is meant to counteract the hatred that Alba had produced. Furió Ceriol is concerned with public opinion, noting that Philip's subjects may perceive that they are free, even though they are in fact

74 Furió Ceriol, *Concejo y consejeros*, 113–14.
75 Ibid., 113.
76 Ibid., 118.

"naciones subjetas." He even goes so far as to say that Philip should promise offices and privileges to those under suspicion of being malcontent and having the intention to create disturbances, even if he does not mean to keep his word.[77] In this example, Furió Ceriol encourages Philip to put into practice the idea that necessity demands moral flexibility from the traditional perspective: in order to end the resistance and bring order and peace to one of his possessions, it is legitimate to lie.

Several of the remedies that Furió Ceriol offers could have been taken directly from the first chapters of the *Prince*, which consider ways in which a prince may maintain dominion over another state, "come membro,"[78] a situation comparable to Philip's with respect to the Netherlands. When the subject state is used to living with its own laws and privileges, Machiavelli recommends three modes: "il primo, ruinarle; l'altro, andarvi ad abitare personalmente; il terzo, lasciàgli vivere con le sua legge, traendone una pensione e creandovi dentro uno stato di pochi, che te lo conservino amico."[79] One of Furió Ceriol's remedies resembles this third mode:

> confirmarles de nuevo todas sus leyes, fueros, previlegios, ynmunidades, usos y lohables costumbres que usaban antes de los alborotos: porque ellos nezesariamente han de tener que Vuestra Magestad no se los derrroge y quite a causa de las pasadas y presentes alteraciones, y conzediéndoselas de nuebo, adorarán en Vuestra Magestad.[80]

Furió Ceriol's reference to the "fueros, previlegios, ynmunidades" clearly implies that he is referring to a privileged few, "uno stato di pochi," whom Philip must make indebted to their Spanish monarch.

With respect to subject states whose language and customs are different from the prince's, Machiavelli makes specific recommendations with respect to that subject state's neighbors:

> farsi capo e defensore de' vicini minori potenti, e ingegnarsi di indebolire e' potenti de quella, e guardarsi che per accidente alcuno non vi entri uno forestiere potente quanto lui: e sempre interverrà ch'e' vi sarà messo da coloro che saranno in quella malcontenti o per troppa ambizione o per paura.[81]

Two of Furió Ceriol's remedies, as a pair, apply this advice to the situation under consideration:

77 Ibid.
78 Machiavelli, *Principe*, 10.
79 Ibid., 29.
80 Furió Ceriol, *Concejo y consejeros*, 119.
81 Machiavelli, *Principe*, 16.

> El décimo tercio remedio es que Vuestra Magestad, por vía de enbaxadores, o de visitas, o de otros medios, entretenga con su buena gracia a los príncipes vecinos de aquellos estados. El décimo quarto rremedio es que Vuestra Magestad no rrompa por agora guerra públicamente en Yngalatera, sino que entretenga debaxo de especie de amistad en público, y de favor y ayuda en secreto de gente dinero y consejo y a la contravanda que tiene en aquel rreyno y principalmente a los mal contentos y a los que están llebantados.[82]

In the thirteenth remedy, Furió Ceriol advises Philip to keep close relations with the neighboring princes, presumably to keep them under control. In the next remedy, Philip should not declare open war with England, while at the same time he should secretly help the malcontent in that kingdom. Although Furió Ceriol gives no further explanation for these remedies, these stratagems agree with the passage from the *Prince* cited above. First, Philip should make himself the friend and leader of the surrounding minor neighbors. Next, he should secretly attempt to weaken England, a very strong neighbor, and above all make sure that England does not invade the Low Countries in an open act of war, because, following Machiavelli's explanation, those Dutch who are unhappy there will see this opportunity as a means to free themselves from Spain's dominion. Protestant England under Queen Elizabeth sympathized with and had been aiding William of Orange and the Dutch rebels. Furthermore, we know that at the time Philip had expressed interest in creating an international Catholic alliance against England. Nevertheless, the advice of Furió Ceriol and others seems to have had its intended effect, and in May of 1573 the two countries agreed to renew trade and an uneasy peace lasted until Furió Ceriol's fears finally came true and England invaded the Netherlands in 1585.[83]

Finally, Furió Ceriol's last remedy coincides with the one Machiavelli considers the most important for subject states whose language and customs are different from the prince's: "uno de' maggiori remedi e piú vivi sarebbe che la persona di chi acquista vi andassi ad abitare."[84] Furió Ceriol similarly recommends that Philip go to the Netherlands to carry out these remedies personally:

> El dézimo quinto rremedio es que para usar de tan altos grados y actos de prudencia, liberalidad y de misericordia, como son los sobre dichos, no ay persona que lo pueda hazer, ni aunque lo deva hazer, porque los prudentes príncipes cometen a sus ministros la justicia, y reservan para sí la gracia, sino es Vuestra Magestad o no puede o no deve de pasar a aquellos estados por justas causas.[85]

82 Furió Ceriol, *Concejo y consejeros*, 119–20.

83 Henry Kamen, *Philip of Spain* (New Haven, CT: Yale University Press, 1997), 142.

84 Machiavelli, *Principe*, 13.

85 Furió Ceriol, *Concejo y consejeros*, 120.

In order to understand this passage, it is necessary to point out that Furió Ceriol recommends Philip to carry out his justice personally, following Machiavelli's recommendation, even though by doing so he might go against another, more general *ordine*, also found in the *Prince*, for avoiding hatred: "che e' principi le cose di carico debbono fare sumministrare ad altri, quelle di grazia loro medesimi."[86] While it is true that the prince should reserve for himself the "gracia," as Machiavelli recommends, Philip should see to these remedies himself, even though he risks exposing himself to the hatred that the Netherlanders had accumulated toward the Spaniards over the years, especially toward the Duke of Alba and his Tribunal de los Tumultos, which, according to Furió Ceriol, "engendra odio en el ánimo de aquellos vasallos."[87] Nevertheless, if Philip personally carries out these changes in policy, the Dutch will begin to differentiate between Alba, whom they hated, and Philip, whom they could at least not hate, if not love. In these passages we see that Furió Ceriol applies to a specific case the general rule, learned in Machiavelli's political treatises, that the best way for a prince to maintain his political position of power is to combine policies which bring about the common good for his subjects with a strict avoidance of hatred directed at his person.

Furió Ceriol adapted Machiavelli's vocabulary of contingency to the Spanish monarchical context in both theory and practice. In his own political treatises, Furió Ceriol used Machiavelli's vocabulary as a rhetorical discourse aimed at making Philip II aware of the problems involved in empire in general as well as persuading him to take a specific set of actions in order to maintain his imperial dominion over the Low Countries.

Balthazar de Ayala

Roughly a decade after Furió Ceriol wrote his *Remedios*, and just one year before Machiavelli's works were included in Quiroga's index of prohibited books, Balthazar de Ayala, Jurisconsult and Judge Advocate General of the Royal Army in the Low Countries, continued this line of reasoning, adapting Machiavellian rhetoric to a Catholic worldview and specifically to Philip's imperial project. In his *De iure et officiis bellicis et disciplina militari* (Douai, 1582), Ayala draws heavily, without acknowledgement, from the *Discourses*, and to a lesser extent from the *Prince*, not only Machiavelli's ideas but also the same examples taken from Roman history, to which he adds additional authority from biblical and historical sources. Clearly he checked Machiavelli's references against the original source material, mostly in Livy, adding or correcting names here and there; nevertheless, for the most part Ayala agrees with Ma-

86 Machiavelli, *Principe*, 126.

87 Furió Ceriol, *Concejo y consejeros*, 116.

chiavelli's analysis of the historical examples, as we shall see, and the sheer abundance of coincidences between Ayala and Machiavelli suggest that he used Machiavelli's text as a guide while he wrote his own text.

To begin, he adapts Machiavelli's preface to the *Discourses* to his own dedication to Alessandro Farnese, Lieutenant Governor and Captain General of Philip II in the Low Countries: his purpose is to highlight the military glory of the ancient Romans in order to demonstrate how their military discipline may be imitated in modern times. In book 1, on the laws of war, we find isolated borrowings from the *Prince*. For example, in chapter 1.2, on just war and just causes of war, Ayala uses the same example of Quintius's speech to the Acheans, found in the *Prince* 21, arguing against remaining neutral when Antiochus and the Aetolians were at war with the Romans.[88] Just like Osorio before him, in chapter 1.8, on trickeries and deceit in war, Ayala repeats the idea found in the *Prince* 18, which originally derived from Plutarch, attributed to Lysander, to the effect that it is necessary to cover oneself with the skins of both the lion and the fox.[89] In the same chapter, he also retells the two main episodes from *Discourses* 3.20, on how an act of decency can be more powerful than arms: how Camillus won over the Falisci by handing over to them the treacherous schoolmaster; and how Fabricius told Pyrrhus of a plot to poison him.[90]

However, it is throughout book 2, on the duties connected with war, that we find the bulk of Ayala's borrowings from the *Discourses*.[91] In general, he answers Machiavelli's call for a more militaristic interpretation of the Gospels. Much like what we have seen in Machiavelli's *Discourses* 2.2, Ayala argues in the opening chapter 2.1 that the defense of one's fatherland is compatible with Christianity.[92] Citing Saint Augustine, he writes that it is not a mortal sin to expose oneself to death in defense of one's country and the Catholic Church.[93] With respect to how religion should be used during war, Ayala repeats what Machiavelli says in *Discourses* 1.14 on how the Roman generals would interpret the auspices and oracles according to their needs.[94] In this way, Ayala not only justifies and bolsters Philip II's imperial project, especially in the Netherlands, where Ayala grew up and lived most his life: in addition, he teaches Spanish military leaders to exploit their soldiers' desire to be good Christians, suggesting to them that it is their duty to defend their monarch's dominion in the region, even if that defense leads to their own death.

88 Balthazar de Ayala, *De jure et officiis bellicis et disciplina militari libri III*, ed. John Westlake, trans. John Pawley Bate (Washington, D. C.: Carnegie Institution of Washington, 1912), 2:14.

89 Ibid., 2:84.

90 Ibid., 2:86.

91 See Anglo, *Machiavelli—The First Century*, 551–52.

92 Ayala, *De jure et officiis bellicis*, 2:102–3.

93 Ibid., 2:103.

94 Ibid., 2:116.

Throughout the rest of book 2, Ayala draws many specific ideas and examples from the *Discourses* regarding how war should be waged. Chapters 2.2 and 2.3 focus on the commander or general of an army. In chapter 2.2, Ayala draws the examples of Coriolanus and Alexander from *Discourses* 3.13 in order to argue that it is better to have a good general than good soldiers.[95] He also takes the example of Fabius from *Discourses* 3.33 to demonstrate that it is essential that the general inspires his troops with confidence.[96] Ayala draws from *Discourses* 3.18 the two examples that highlight the importance of knowing and understanding the enemy's plans and actions: first, Cassius and Brutus; second, a battle between the Romans and the Volscians, correcting Machiavelli's reference to the Aequians.[97] Ayala agrees with Machiavelli, who in *Discourses* 2.31 wrote that it is dangerous to believe refugees or exiles, although he uses different examples.[98] Ayala gives the same reasoning and the same example of Fabius as is found in *Discourses* 2.33 to demonstrate the importance of giving discretionary authority to generals.[99] Likewise, Ayala gives the same reasoning and the same examples of Sergius and Virginius and that of Varro found in *Discourses* 1.31 to demonstrate the importance of not punishing generals for making mistakes.[100] In chapter 2.3, which offers more specific advice for commanders, Ayala uses the same examples of the three Roman tribunes who were defeated by the Veians and of how Agrippa handed over his authority to Quintius, as found in *Discourses* 3.15, to illustrate the importance of there being only one head of an army.[101] Finally, Ayala uses the same example found in *Discourses* 3.17 to demonstrate the danger of giving command to someone who has been criticized or disgraced, referring to the correct name, Marcus Livius, as opposed to Claudius Nero, whom Machiavelli erroneously cites.[102]

In chapters 2.4 through 2.9, Ayala carries out an extended Machiavellian analysis of the contingency of war. His debt to Machiavelli for both ideas and examples is clear and extensive. Ayala draws from *Discourses* 3.19, 3.21 and 3.22 the contrasting examples of Hannibal and Scipio, those of Manlius and Valerius, and those of Appius and Quintius, in order to discuss the merits of both cruelty and humaneness. Like Machiavelli, Ayala warns that too much kindness can bring contempt and, on the other hand, that too much cruelty can attract hatred. Ayala repeats Machiavelli's statement, found in *Discourses* 3.22, about previous writers who incline toward Valerius rather than Manlius, and he

95 Ibid., 2:109–10.
96 Ibid., 2:116.
97 Ibid., 2:118.
98 Ibid.
99 Ibid., 2:121–22.
100 Ibid., 2:122–23.
101 Ibid., 2:125–26.
102 Ibid., 2:127–28.

even repeats a citation of Xenophon, who attributed much kindness to Cyrus. Machiavelli makes the distinction between republics, whose generals should not become loved for danger of them becoming tyrants, and monarchies, where the prince should cultivate the love of his subjects. Ayala, who is only concerned with monarchies, concludes by leaning more in favor of kindness and humanity, because love and fear cannot coexist.[103]

In chapter 2.5, Ayala uses different ancient Roman examples to put forth the same idea as Machiavelli in *Discourses* 3.41: citing Cicero as his authority, Ayala argues that all actions that bring about the well-being of the state are just and lawful. In the same chapter, Ayala repeats Machiavelli's analysis of the nature of Fabius Maximus found in *Discourses* 3.9, demonstrating that a man's nature sometimes conforms with the circumstances that fortune dictates, while sometimes it does not. Surprisingly, he even goes so far as to repeat Machiavelli's conclusion that free republics are preferred to monarchies, because they have a greater variety of character.[104] In chapter 2.6, Ayala uses the same examples of Annius's speech to the Latins, Apollonides's speech to the Syracusans, and the Lavinians failure to help the Latins, found in *Discourses* 2.15, in order to demonstrate the harm caused by slow and contentious deliberations in times of war.[105] In chapter 2.7, Ayala takes from *Discourses* 2.14 the example of the war between the Romans and the Latins in order to demonstrate the error of supposing that pride can be overcome by moderation and patience.[106]

In chapter 2.8, Ayala cites all of the same examples of Cyrus and Tomyris, the Athenians, Antaeus, king of Libya, Carthage, Agathocles, Scipio and Hannibal found in *Discourses* 2.12, in order to present the debate about whether it is better to wait for one's enemies within one's own borders or go to attack them in their territory. After citing a few more examples, Ayala reaches the same conclusion as Machiavelli: if you are dealing with an enemy that is armed and warlike, then it is better to draw them to you away from their home; if you are dealing with an enemy that is unarmed and unwarlike, then it is better to take the fight to their home.[107] In chapter 2.9, Ayala repeats the example of the Roman consuls, Decius and Fabius, in order to demonstrate that it is better to hold off the first attack of an enemy and then counterattack, than to charge impetuously from the beginning.[108]

Chapters 2.10 and 2.11 deal with the motivation of a people and especially soldiers. Among others, Ayala cites the same example in chapter 2.10 as Machiavelli in *Discourses* 2.25 in order to demonstrate that it is bad policy to rely

103 Ibid., 2:129–31.
104 Ibid., 2:135–36.
105 Ibid., 2:137–38.
106 Ibid., 2:140–42.
107 Ibid., 2:144–49.
108 Ibid., 2:150–51.

on the civil unrest of the enemy, because external threats will unite a people, as the Veientes discovered when they tried to attack Rome when Gaius Manlius and Marcus Fabius were consuls.[109] In chapter 2.11, Ayala repeats Machiavelli's assertion in *Discourses* 3.12 that a general should make it necessary for his own soldiers to fight, but on the other hand he should contrive to eliminate that necessity for the enemy. Ayala repeats Machiavelli's examples as well. Manlius was killed by the Veientes because he hemmed them in, preventing them from retreating, and so they fought madly. Both cite Livy's rendering of a speech by Vettius Messius, the Volscian general, who pointed out to his troops that while in all other things they were equal to the Romans, they were superior in necessity, because they were hemmed in by the Romans. They both also cite the example of Camillus, who during the siege of Veii had proclaimed that the unarmed would be spared.[110]

Chapters 2.12 and 2.13 deal with the best ways to handle victory and the end of war. First, in chapter 2.12 Ayala draws from *Discourses* 2.27 the same idea that one should be content with peace after victory, supported by the same example of Hanno: when news of Hannibal's victory at Cannae reached Carthage, Hanno advised that they sue for peace while they still held the advantage.[111] In chapter 2.13, Ayala draws from *Discourses* 2.23 the idea that a subject people should either be crushed or be treated generously. He repeats the negative example of the Samnites when they had caught the Romans in the Caudine Forks. He then repeats Camillus's speech regarding how the Latins should be treated and the example of how the Roman Senate treated the Privernians.[112]

***

If we take Furió Ceriol and Balthazar de Ayala as examples, we may understand to what extent it was possible for Spaniards to profit from a careful reading of Machiavelli. After Machiavelli was prohibited in Rome in 1559, but before that same prohibition was decreed in Spain, Spaniards living and writing about the Low Countries cautiously applied his ideas and examples, without acknowledgment, to Philip II's imperial project. On the other hand, after Machiavelli was prohibited in Spain in 1583, while this silent use continued, writers were obliged to express ostensibly an attitude of open hostility toward Machiavelli, whose name became associated with the new, frowned-upon kind of politics known as "reason of state."

109 Ibid., 2:154.
110 Ibid., 2:156–60.
111 Ibid., 2:161–62.
112 Ibid., 2:163–67.

3

Machiavelli and the Foundations of the Spanish Reason-of-State Tradition: Giovanni Botero and Pedro de Ribadeneyra

The "French Face" of Machiavelli

In an episode in the history of Machiavellian reception that would have a profound impact on European culture, whose effects are felt even today, the figure of Machiavelli simultaneously became immensely popular and greatly distorted. During the French Wars of Religion, anti-Machiavellism became a polemical weapon, used by both Catholics and Huguenots to slander their opponents. As Edmond M. Beame has put it, French pamphleteers who used Machiavelli's name indiscriminately, rather than serious scholars, were responsible for the "French face" of Machiavelli.[1]

For three decades after his appearance in 1544 in French translation, Machiavelli remained tolerated in France, perhaps because this period coincided with the rise of a group of French scholars, such as Louise Le Roy, who began to consider questions of state as autonomous, even overriding those of religion. During this period reference to Machiavelli's name was infrequent. In his *Methodus* of 1566, Jean Bodin praises Machiavelli's republican thought; however, ten years later in his *République* he condemns Machiavelli and goes to great length to dissociate himself from the Florentine, despite the fact that his treatise agrees with him on many points.[2] After the Saint Bartholomew's Day Massacre of 1571, Machiavelli gained popularity among pamphleteers, who assigned him the status of spokesperson for whichever opponent they wished to attack: the crown, the Catholic League and most frequently the *politiques*.[3]

As Donald R. Kelley has shown, during the 1560s *politique* was used as a derogatory term, sometimes associated with Machiavelli, to label those who

1 Edmond M. Beame, "The Use and Abuse of Machiavelli: The Sixteenth-Century French Adaptation," *Journal of the History of Ideas* 43, no. 1 (1982): 35.

2 G. Cardascia, "Machiavel et Jean Bodin," *Bibliothèque d'Humanisme et Renaissance* 3 (1943): 129–67.

3 Beame, "Use and Abuse," 36–41.

thought public utility was more important than religious principle. Eventually the word lost its negative associations when some began to believe that a good *politique* and a good Christian were not incompatible. Kelley attributes this change primarily to the Saint Bartholomew's Day Massacre, when the Huguenot victims began to use the term to designate themselves. These "bons politiques" turned Machiavelli into the embodiment of tyranny.[4] Stories began to emerge of how Catherine de' Medici, mother of Charles XI and Henry III, applied what she had learned from Machiavelli, whose *Prince* was dedicated to her father Lorenzo, to instigate the Massacre and encourage her children to pursue repressive, anti-reformist governmental policies.[5]

At first, Machiavelli's name was used almost exclusively by the Protestants. After the Peace of Bergerac in 1577, reference to Machiavelli died down. But in the mid-1580s, during the final series of the Wars of Religion, the Florentine was used by both Catholics and Protestants to attack their opposing parties. Eventually, however, Machiavelli came to be associated less with tyranny and more often with the *politiques* themselves, "those who prefer the peace of the kingdom … to the salvation of their souls," in the words of Gaspard de Saulx-Tavannes.[6] The defenders of the Catholic League now began to label the Huguenot *politiques* as Machiavellians. The figure most frequently attacked in this sense was Henry III. At first, his advisors were blamed; after the assassination of the Duke of Guise, however, he was considered Machiavellian himself. From then on, his expressions of Catholic faith were construed as Machiavellian "pageantry and fiction."[7] Eventually, as League apologists increasingly feared that religious toleration was becoming a means to undermine Catholicism, *politique* became practically synonymous with Machiavellian.[8]

The first polemical anti-Machiavellian was Innocent Gentillet, whose *Discours sur les moyens de bien gouverner et maintenir en bonne paix un royaume ou autre principauté. . . contre Nicolas Machiavel Florentine* was first published in Geneva in 1576. Gentillet built on the Huguenots' previous minor anti-Machiavellian expressions, especially the association they had been developing between the Florentine and the royalty's repressive policies. His political treatise uses Machiavelli's name to attack tyranny, focusing his attention on the Massacre.[9] Gentillet attacks Machiavelli's method, which according to him contains two fundamental flaws: his experience and his knowledge of history were both extremely limited. According to Gentillet, Machiavelli's aim was to establish

4 Donald R. Kelley, "Murd'rous Machiavel in France: A Post Mortem," *Political Science Quarterly* 85, no. 4 (1970): 552.

5 Ibid., 551–53.

6 Beame, "Use and Abuse," 46.

7 Ibid., 49.

8 Ibid., 45–50.

9 Kelley, "Murd'rous Machiavel," 553.

tyrannical governments. France's court and government has become full of Italians and Italianized who are Machiavellians. This is the cause of all of France's corruption and civil strife.[10]

Gentillet's method was to misrepresent Machiavelli's own thought by taking single sentences out of their context in the *Prince* and the *Discourses* and turning them into maxims, which he would then proceed to refute through logic and historical examples. Gentillet divided his Machiavellian maxims into three books, based on three principal themes. First, Machiavelli's absolute power should be replaced by a monarchy controlled by laws and a system of estates. Second, he attacked what he called Machiavelli's atheism and insisted that government should be founded on the Christian religion. Third, he claimed that Machiavelli's recommendation for cunning and hypocrisy was worse than any disease. It is interesting to note that Gentillet attacked Machiavelli in order to argue in favor of religious tolerance, while later Catholic anti-Machiavellians would attack him in order to argue the opposite. In short, the Huguenots blamed Machiavelli himself and "Machiavellism" for France's plight in general and the Massacre in particular.[11]

Anglo has demonstrated Gentillet's importance for the subsequent development of the anti-Machiavellian tradition. Antonio Possevino's *Judicium* (Rome, 1592) is a collection of attacks on dangerous authors, including François de la Noue, Jean Bodin, Philippe Du Plessis Mornay and Machiavelli. It also contains an extract from Osorio's *De nobilitate christiana*. As Anglo has demonstrated, Possevino never read any of Machiavelli's works, using Gentillet to summarize and condemn him instead. Possevino's summary is based on twenty-two chapter headings taken in the same order from Lambert Daneau's anonymous Latin translation of Gentillet's *Contre-Machiavel*. He not only carelessly thought that all of these maxims were taken only from the *Prince*, but he even refers to books 1, 2 and 3 of the *Prince*, because that is how Gentillet divided his maxims.[12] This summary of Machiavelli's thought would be appropriated subsequently by Ribadeneyra and his imitators as well, as we shall see.

Giovanni Botero

It is well known that with his *Della ragion di stato* of 1589, Giovanni Botero initiated the Counter-Reformation reason-of-state tradition. In Spain, Antonio de Herrera's Spanish translation of Botero's treatise, published just three years later, should be considered the first Spanish contribution to this tradition, because he adapted Botero's text to the Spanish audience three years before Pedro de Ribadeneyra published his *Tratado de la Religion y Virtudes que deue tener el*

10 Anglo, *Machiavelli—The First Century*, 285–88.

11 Kelley, "Murd'rous Machiavel," 553–55; Beame, "Use and Abuse," 41–43.

12 Anglo, *Machiavelli—The First Century*, 386–88.

Principe Christiano. In his own preface to his *Diez libros de la razon de estado*, Antonio de Herrera paraphrases the original preface, beginning with the following phrase: "El intento que ha tenido Iuan Botero en esta obra de la razon de Estado, ha sido…"[13] Through Herrera's paraphrase, Botero portrays Machiavelli and Tacitus as "en todo contrarios a la ley de Dios" because they claim that "vnas cosas son licitas por razon de Estado, y otras por conciencia, siendo esto la cosa mas bestial, que puede auer."[14] Ribadeneyra will later rework this dichotomy between reason of state and conscience into one between bad and good reason of state. Following the model of the earliest anti-Machiavellians, Botero also initiates in the reason-of-state tradition the characterization of Machiavelli as an atheist: "porque el que aparta de la conciencia la juridicion vniuersal que tiene de todo lo que sucede entre los hombres, assi en cosas publicas, como en particulares, claramente muestra que ni tiene alma, ni Dios."[15]

Despite this negative characterization of Machiavelli, a close reading reveals that Botero is in reality an excellent student of Machiavelli, adapting key Machiavellian concepts to his own Catholic and monarchical ideology. This two-facedness with respect to Machiavelli, the rhetorical pretense of anti-Machiavellism combined with the acceptance of important aspects of Machiavelli's thought, would go on to become the hallmark of the entire reason-of-state tradition of the Hispanic Counter-Reformation.

At this point, while Botero's preface concludes, Herrera goes on to address Philip II directly, speaking to the utility of his translation for his son, the future Philip III:

> Y como V. Magestad me ha mandado que ponga esta obra en vulgar Castellano, ha mostrado V. Magestad en ello, como en todo lo demas su prudentissimo juyzio, pues que para el Principe nuestro señor serà este libro de mucho fruto: porque la cosa con que mas le ha ilustrado el autor es, con auer muy bien considerado las heroycas costumbres y acciones de V.M. y las formas tan catolicas y prudentes con que ha gouernado sus Reynos y Estados, en paz, y en guerra, y espejandose en esto, como se conoce en el discurso del tratado, ha criado su Principe a imagen y semejança de V. M. con que marauillosamente consigue su intento.[16]

This portrayal of Philip II as the perfect model for subsequent Spanish monarchs is a trope that will reappear throughout the reason-of-state tradition. Here, Her-

[13] Giovanni Botero, *Diez libros de la razon de estado. Con tres libros de las causas de la grandeza, y magnificencia de las ciudades de Iuan Botero. Tradvzido de Italiano en Castellano, por mandado del Rey nuestro señor, Por Antonio de Herrera su criado* (Madrid: Luys Sanchez, 1592), n.p.

[14] Ibid.

[15] Ibid.

[16] Ibid.

rera's translation is presented as a traditional "mirror of princes" for Prince Philip in which his father is presented as the ideal example to imitate, for the benefit of their Spanish vassals:

> Y pues el mayor bien que podran tener los vassallos de V. M. ha de ser que el Principe nuestro señor sea su verdadero imitador, y el retrato de sus virtudes, con ninguna dotrina (creo yo) que se puede alcançar tan gran bien, mas que con esta, sin cansar a su Alteza con demasiados exemplos de diuersos autores, ni letura de muchos libros.[17]

Prince Philip need not read anything else besides this translation, nor turn to any other example besides that of his father, because in this book he will find the best "doctrine" to follow in his future political life.

Botero dedicates book 1 of the treatise proper to the definition of reason of state: "Razon de Estado, es vna noticia de los medios conuenientes para fundar, conseruar, y engrandecer vn señorio."[18] While Botero does include founding and amplifying in this definition, throughout the remainder of his treatise he presupposes the existence of the state and therefore focusses almost exclusively on its conservation, as he is careful to declare: "la causa desto es, que la razon de Estado prosupone que ay señorio, y Principe que le possee, y no prosupone la fundacion del estado."[19] In the rest of his treatise, Botero adopts Machiavelli's vocabulary and theoretical framework to his discourses on the conservation of the Catholic, monarchical state, both internally and externally.

In his discussion of internal threats, Botero employs Machiavelli's rhetoric on the avoidance of hatred in the *Prince* 17 and 19. He writes that princes lose their states not so much by being cruel as by sinning with the flesh: "porque la crueldad engendra aborrecimiento, y miedo con aquel que la vsa: la deshonestidad y vicio de la carne engendra aborrecimiento y menosprecio."[20] Both behaviors bring hatred upon the prince, but while cruelty brings also fear, sins of the flesh bring contempt or scorn. In the first phrase, Botero follows the Aristotelian mirror-of-princes tradition by grouping together cruelty and fear, both of which were considered typical tools of the tyrant. Nevertheless, in the second phrase, Botero adds a distinction between hatred and contempt drawn from Machiavelli's advice in the *Prince* 19, at the conclusion of his restructuring of the Aristotelian tradition, that the prince should avoid behavior that makes him "odioso o contennendo … Odioso soprattutto lo fa, come io dissi, essere rapace e usurpatore della roba e delle donne de' sudditi … Conten-

17 Ibid.
18 Ibid., 1.
19 Ibid.
20 Ibid., 3.

nendo lo fa essere tenuto vario, leggieri, effeminato, pusillanime, irresoluto."[21] Herrera's translation of Botero's "libidine"[22] as "deshonestidad y vicio de la carne" is only one cause of contempt, while Machiavelli lists several. Nevertheless, it corresponds very well with Machiavelli's characterization of a prince who is "effeminato, pusillanime." This distinction leads Botero to differentiate the results of one and the other: "assi que la crueldad tiene por contrario al odio, pero el miedo la sustenta, aunque flacamente porque dura poco tiempo; pero la deshonestidad no tiene ningun arrimo, porque el odio y el menosprecio son sus contrarios.[23] In other words, in contrast to contempt, fear is characterized as an effective tool of conservation, albeit not one that should be considered permanent.

While Botero does not reach the same conclusion as Machiavelli, he reveals himself to be well informed by the Florentine's revolutionary advice on cruelty in the *Prince* 17: the prince should choose to be feared rather than loved, if he must make that choice, so long as he avoids hatred. While Botero insists on the avoidance of contempt, rather than hatred, his characterization of fear is similar to Machiavelli's. Botero concludes this consideration with a typically Machiavellian comment: "y de mas desto, la crueldad priua de la vida, o delas fuerças a los que ha ofendido, lo qual no haze el vicio de la carne."[24] A similar statement may be found in Machiavelli's discussion, in the *Prince* 3, of the violent use of colonies in newly acquired provinces: "quegli che gli offende, rimanendo dispersi e poveri, non gli possono mai nuocere; e tutti li altri rimangono da uno canto inoffesi … da l'altro paurosi di non errare, per timore che non intervenissi a loro come a quelli che sono stati spogliati."[25] Botero and Machiavelli agree that cruelty not only renders impossible any retaliation by those it offends, but also keeps everyone under control through fear.

Botero continues this Machiavellian re-evaluation of traditional values when he considers the foundation of kingdoms at the dawn of civilization. He asks his readers to consider, when the original kings were elected, which was more important, love or reputation gained through their valor? "Sin duda fue la reputación, porque los pueblos no se mouieron a ello, por fauorecer y complacer a nadie, sino por el bien publico, y por esto no eligieron a los mas graciosos y blandos, sino a los mas valerosos."[26] The king who more likely will bring about the common good is not necessarily one who earns the love of his subjects, but the one who will use his valor to defend his own position of power from internal threats as well as his entire country from external ones. Similar to Machia-

21 Machiavelli, *Principe*, 120.

22 Giovanni Botero, *Della ragion di stato*, ed. Chiara Continisio (Roma: Donzelli, 2009), 9.

23 Botero, *Razon de estado*, 3.

24 Botero, *Razon de estado*, 3.

25 Machiavelli, *Principe*, 15.

26 Botero, *Razon de estado*, 11.

velli, Botero portrays a king who relies on love as effeminate, "gracious and soft," in contrast to the masculine, valorous king.

For Botero, two qualities bring kings reputation: prudence and valor. To begin his consideration of prudence, he continues his Machiavellian reconsideration of love and friendship. In order to support his revolutionary view that the prince, if forced to choose, should aim to be feared rather than loved, Machiavelli undermines a charitable view of friendship in the *Prince* 17:

> Perché le amicizie si acquistono col prezzo, e non con grandezza e nobilità di animo, si meritano, ma elle non si hanno, e alli tempi non si possono spendere; e li uomini hanno meno rispetto a offendere uno che si facci amare, che uno che si facci temere: perché lo amore è tenuto da uno vinculo di obligo, il quale, per essere gl'uomini tristi, da ogni occasione di propria utilità è rotto, ma il timore è tenuto da una paura di pena che non ti abbandona mai.[27]

Following Machiavelli's logic, Botero insists that kings should not rely on love and friendship, but rather assume that their vassals support them out of interest:

> Tenga por cosa muy cierta y aueriguada, que en las determinaciones de los Reyes, es el interesse el que todo lo atrauiessa: y por tanto no se deue de fiar de amistad, ni de parentesco, de liga, ni de otro vinculo, en el qual el que con el trata, no tenga fundamento de interes.[28]

In book 7 Botero further demonstrates his agreement with the Machiavellian reorganization of the traditional virtues in his discussion on liberality. In the *Prince* 16, Machiavelli reconsiders the value of liberality: in order to cultivate a reputation for being liberal the prince must spend all his wealth:

> e serà necessitato alla fine, se si vorrà mantenere il nome del liberale, gravare e' populi estraordinariamente ed essere fiscale e fare tutte quelle cose che si possono fare per avere danari; il che comincerà a farlo odioso a' sudditi, o poco stimare da ciascuno divenendo povero. In modo che, con questa sua liberalità avendo offeso gli assai e premiato e' pochi, sente ogni primo disagio e periclita in qualunque primo periculo.[29]

Machiavelli's conclusion is that the prince should not worry about being called miserly:

> perché col tempo sarà tenuto sempre piú liberale veggendo che, con la sua parsimonia, le sua entrate gli bastano, può difendersi da chi gli fa guerra, può

27 Machiavelli, *Principe*, 110–11.
28 Botero, *Razon de estado*, 40.
29 Machiavelli, *Principe*, 105.

> fare imprese sanza gravare e' populi. Talmente che viene a usare liberalità a tutti quelli a chi e' non toglie, che sono infiniti, e miseria a tutti coloro a chi e' non dà, che sono pochi.[30]

Botero not only expresses the same idea, but he uses the same vocabulary as Machiavelli as well. For him, the worst thing a prince can do is "hazer profession de acumular dinero, sin justa causa," because, "por fuerça ha de trabajar a sus vassallos extraordinariamente, y mas de lo que es razon, y no pudiendo ellos sufrirlo, dessean mudança de Estado, y de gouierno, y al cabo daran en algun escandalo."[31] Botero's original phrase here is "aggravare i sudditi più dell'ordinario,"[32] a close rendering of Machiavelli's "gravare e' populi estraordinariamente." The prince must have a certain amount of money readily available in case of war. Botero's solution is that "se han de juntar dineros, sin hazer profession dello: lo qual se harà en dos maneras, con tener en pie, y libres todas las rentas de vuestro estado, y con guardarse de no gastar demasiadamente, y de hazer mercedes impertinentes."[33] Herrera's "rentas" is a translation of Botero's "entrate,"[34] the same word used by Machiavelli. Similarly, Herrera translates as "hazer mercedes impertinentes" Botero's "dare impertinentemente,"[35] which is the same verb *dare* as is found in Machiavelli. Herrera's use of the term *mercedes* captures very well Machiavelli's focus on the negative consequences of being excessively liberal to an elite few.

Despite this general acceptance of the Machiavellian rhetoric of the avoidance of hatred, Botero sets up a dichotomy between reason of state and God's divine law:

> Porque causa el Principe Christiano ha de cerrar la puerta de su consejo secreto, al Euangelio, y a Christo? Y leuantar vna razon de estado contraria a la ley de Dios, como altar, contra altar? Y como puede esperar, que las cosas le sucedan dichosamente, si las ha consultado sin respeto del autor de la buena dicha?[36]

Ribadeneyra and his imitators will adopt this same kind of rhetorical division when they differentiate between good, Catholic reason of state and bad, godless reason of state. Nevertheless, this rhetoric does not prevent Botero from imitating Machiavelli's use of the Roman example for demonstrating the utility of religion.

30 Ibid., 106.
31 Botero, *Razon de estado*, 118.
32 Botero, *Ragion di stato*, 112.
33 Botero, *Razon de estado*, 121.
34 Botero, *Ragion di stato*, 114.
35 Ibid.
36 Botero, *Razon de estado*, 60.

To this end, Botero draws from *Discourses* 1.14, where Machiavelli discusses at length how the Romans prudently used their pagan religion in order to motivate their soldiers: "mai sarebbono iti ad una espedizione, che non avessono persuaso ai soldati che gli dei promettevano loro la vittoria."[37] As Botero declares: "No ay cosa que mas aumente el animo de los soldados, ni que mas despierte la esperança, que acudir a la diuina Magestad."[38] Among his numerous examples are the Romans, who "no hazian ninguna empressa, antes de hazer sus sacrificios." It is interesting to note that Herrera's "sacrificios" is an inaccurate translation of Botero's "auspici,"[39] one of the terms employed by Machiavelli, along with *augurii*.[40] Elsewhere, Botero repeats the same idea: "Los Romanos no tratauan de empressa, ni de ningun negocio publico, si primero no deliberauan la procuracion de los prodigios, y sobre el aplacar la ira de los dioses, o de ganar su gracia y amor, y dalles gracias por los bienes recebidos. Tenian finalmente la religion por principal articulo de su gouierno, y no sufrian que fuesse mudada, ni violada."[41]

Botero differs from Machiavelli when he goes on to say that religion is only useful if the king is truly Catholic:

> pero es dificultosa cosa, que el que no es verdadero religioso sea tenido por tal: porque no ay cosa que menos dure que la disimulacion. Deue pues el Principe de todo coraçon humillarse delante de la diuina Magestad, y reconocer della el Reyno, y la obediencia de los vassallos, y quanto el es colocado en mas alto estado sobre los otros, tanto mas se deue prostar delante de la preferencia de Dios: no tratar negocio, no intentar empressa, ni otra cosa, de la qual no sea cierto y seguro que va conforme a la ley de Dios: porque el mesmo Dios manda al Rey, que tenga mucha cuenta con su santa ley, y que con mucho cuydado la guarde.[42]

Dissimulation, permitted in other matters, is forbidden when it comes to religion.

Despite this warning, Botero emphasizes the utility of the Christian religion especially:

> y entre todas las leyes no ay ninguna que sea mas en fauor de los Principes que la Christiana, porque esta no solamente los somete los cuerpos, y haziendas de los vassallos, para lo que conuiene, pero tambien los animos y las conciencias, y liga las manos, los efetos y pensamientos dellos: y quiere que se obedezca, no solo a los Principes sabios, pero aun a los muy

37 Machiavelli, *Discorsi*, 94.
38 Botero, *Razon de estado*, 157.
39 Botero, *Ragion di stato*, 150.
40 Machiavelli, *Discorsi*, 93–94.
41 Botero, *Razon de estado*, 59.
42 Ibid., 59–60.

> desconcertados, y que se sufra qualquiera cosa por no perturuar la paz, y no ay cosa ninguna, por la qual el subdito se pueda desobligar de la obediencia que deue a su señor, sino la ley de naturaleza, y de Dios, y aun en estos casos quiere que se piense, y mire mucho antes que venir a manifiesto rompimiento.[43]

This description agrees in part with Machiavelli's critique of Christianity found in *Discourses* 2.2, as we have seen: Christian fortitude encourages vassals to put up with evil princes as well as good ones. From a prince's point of view, Christianity may be used as an instrument of state, because it helps him maintain his power, even if he does not behave perfectly. Recent history supports Botero's claim:

> Y en nuestros tiempos emos visto, que en todas partes han sido oprimidos los Catolicos en Escocia, Inglaterra, Francia, y Flandes, y en muchas partes de Alemania, lo qual es indicio de la verdad de la Fè Catolica, que haze los vassallos obedientes a su Principe, y los liga su conciencia, y los haze desseosos de paz y enemigos de escandalos, y rumores: pero Lutero, y Caluino, y los otros hereges, apartandose de la verdad Euangelica en todas partes siembran zizañas, y reboluciones de Estados, y destruyciones de Reynos.[44]

Catholicism is true because it encourages obedience; Reformation denominations are false, because they cause rebellion. Underneath this dichotomy between truth and falsehood is the subtle suggestion that Catholicism is more useful than Reform, because the prince may use it as an instrument to keep his subjects obedient and thus to conserve his state.

In his discussion of external politics, Botero uses Machiavelli's rhetoric of fortune. For example, he describes the precarious state of a prince who has conquered a new province:

> Deue primeramente el Rey, procurar con todo cuydado de interessar los vassallos conquistados en su dominio y gouierno, y hazellos casi naturales, porque no teniendo la inclinacion de los pueblos, su Reyno será como vna planta sin rayzes: porque como cada pequeño viento derriua el arbol que no està bien arraygado, cada ligera ocasion aparta de su señor los vassallos, poco o nada aficionados a su seruicio, con la fortuna se mudan ligeramente, y siguen la bandera del vencedor, de lo qual nacen las mudanças y rebueltas de los estados.[45]

43 Ibid., 62.
44 Ibid., 63.
45 Ibid., 88.

Fortune is powerful in this situation, because these subjects feel no natural love toward their new lord. One method that Botero recommends is the following:

> fauorecer la religion, las letras, y la virtud: porque los religiosos, los letrados, y los virtuosos, casi son cabeças de los otros, y ganando a estos, se ganarà los demas: porque los religiosos tienen en su mano las conciencias de los pueblos, los hombres de letras, los ingenios y juyzios destos, y de los otros, y son de gran autoridad a cerca de todos, por la santidad, por la dotrina, por la reuerencia, y por la reputacion: y assi todo lo que estos hazen y dizen, es tenido por bien dicho, y por bien hecho.[46]

Here we see again the utility of religion as an instrument for the conservation of the prince's state: in this case, religion is used to cultivate a good reputation among new subjects, thereby gaining their love. Religion is an instrument of the state used to counteract the power of fickle fortune in a new dominion.

We have seen how Machiavelli consistently encourages the imitation of the Roman model for imperial expansion. In his own discussion of empire, Botero adopts several key precepts that he had found in Machiavelli's *Discourses*. First, at the end of book 7, Botero elaborates on the need for an abundance of people for the creation of an expansive empire: "Primeramente es necessario tener mucha gente, porque (como dezia Seruio Tulio) de ninguna cosa tiene mas necessidad vna ciudad, que aspira a grandes empressas, que de muchos ciudadanos, de los quales pueda confiar, y seruirse en las cosas de la guerra."[47] In his own discussion in *Discourses* 1.6, Machiavelli had referred to the Romans as the best example of a regime that by giving pre-eminence and political power to the plebs, through the institution of the tribunes, had allowed themselves to expand imperially. As counter-examples, Machiavelli offers the Spartans and the Venetians, who both attempted to expand but failed because their regimes excluded the plebs. Then again, in *Discourses* 2.3, Machiavelli repeats the same negative example of Sparta, which lost its entire empire when the Thebans rebelled. Botero repeats this same example, even referencing the cause of the Spartans' downfall as the Theban rebellion.

For his discussion of external threats, Botero follows Machiavelli's analysis of Sparta and Venice found in *Discourses* 1.5–6. In Machiavelli, these city-states were examples of the general rule that oligarchies, as long as they limit themselves to their own borders, conserve their states; however, as soon as they attempt to expand, they ruin themselves. Rome is an example of a mixed regime, which gives power to the plebs and therefore is more apt to expand. Botero ignores the difference, found in Machiavelli, between oligarchies and mixed regimes. Nevertheless, he uses the same examples to conclude that middle-sized

46 Ibid., 89.
47 Ibid., 126.

states are best, because unlike small states they protect themselves from their neighbors, and unlike large states they do not become full of vice.[48] Also like Machiavelli, he goes beyond this conclusion to state that the reality is that these middle-sized states do not last long: "Y aunque la mediania es mas aparejada para la conseruasion de vn dominio, que sus excesos con todo esto los estados medianos duran poco, porque no se contentan los Principes, desseando hazerlos grandes, y por esto saliendo de los limites de la mediania, salen de los de la seguridad: como acontecio a los Venecianos."[49] Their reasoning is slightly different, because while Machiavelli considers both principalities and republics, Botero only considers the former: Machiavelli refers to fortune and general rules of movement and necessity in politics; Botero alludes to the psychology of princes, who always desire to expand. Nevertheless, Botero follows Machiavelli's example of reaching a temporary conclusion based on reason alone, only to reject that conclusion after taking into account a particularly pessimistic vision of reality, whether that pessimism comes from a cosmological or psychological perspective.

At the beginning of book 8, Botero declares that there are two ways of augmenting the amount of people, and therefore military forces, available to a regime: first, by propagating one's own; second, by attracting and admitting outsiders. For this second method, Botero's source is Machiavelli's *Discourses* 2.3–4. There Machiavelli explains, always offering the excellent example of the Romans, that there are two modes of increasing a city's population, which is the necessary condition for imperial expansion: "per amore e per forza. Per amore, tenendo le vie aperte e sicure a' forestieri che disegnassono venire ad abitare in quella, acciò che ciascuno vi abiti volentieri; per forza, disfaccendo le città vicine, e mandando gli abitatori di quelle ad abitare nella tua città."[50] Botero simply repeats this explanation, offering the Romans as an example worthy of imitation for his readers:

> Acrecentaron lo [*sic*] Romanos lo propio con lo ageno, agregando y ayuntando assi a los enemigos que vencieron, que fueron los Albanos, Sabinos, y otros, destruyendo las ciudades vezinas, poniendo con esto a los moradores dellas en necessidad de recogerse a Roma. Hazian ciudadanos Romanos a muchos, y en particular a infinitas personas de valor, y de buenas calidades, y a las ciudades enteras.[51]

Likewise, Botero's source for his discussion of leagues is Machiavelli's *Discourses* 2.4. There, as we have seen, Machiavelli observes that there are

48 Ibid., 5–7.
49 Ibid., 7.
50 Machiavelli, *Discorsi*, 324.
51 Botero, *Razon de estado*, 137.

three modes of expanding: first, through leagues between equals; second, through leagues between unequals, what he calls "compagni";[52] finally, by making other states completely subject to oneself. According to Machiavelli, the best mode, the mode followed by Rome, is the second one. As Machiavelli explains, Rome basically tricked its powerful neighbors into subjugating themselves over time. When quoted in full, it is clear that Botero draws heavily from this explanation:

> E perché la [Roma] è stata sola a vivere cosí, è stata ancora sola a diventare tanto potente; perché, avendosi lei fatti dimolti compagni per tutta Italia, i quali in dimolte cose con equale legge vivevano seco, e dall'altro canto (come di sopra è detto) sendosi riserbata sempre la sedia dello imperio e il titolo del comandare, questi suoi compagni venivano, che non se ne avvedevano, con le fatiche e con el sangue loro a soggiogare se stessi. Perché, come ei cominciarono ad uscire con gli eserciti d'Italia, e ridurre i regni in provincie, e farsi suggetti di coloro che, per essere consueti a vivere sotto i re, non si curavano di essere suggetti e, avendo governatori romani e essendo stati vinti da eserciti con il titolo romano, non riconoscevano per superiore altro che Roma, di modo che quegli compagni di Roma che erano in Italia si trovarono in un tratto cinti da sudditi romani e oppressi da una grossissima città come era Roma. E quando ei s'avviddono dello inganno sotto il quale erano vissuti, non furono a tempo a rimediarvi, tanta autorità aveva presa Roma con le provincie esterne, e tanta forza si trovava in seno, avendo la sua città grossissima e armatissima. E benché quelli suoi compagni, per vendicarsi delle ingiurie, le congiurassero contro, furano in poco tempo perditori della guerra, peggiorando le loro condizioni, perché di compagni diventarono, ancora loro, sudditi.[53]

Botero repeats Machiavelli's example of the Roman method for imperial expansion:

> Marauillosa y excelente manera fue de ganar los animos de los vassallos conquistados, la que vsò Tarquinio Priscio: porque auiendo vencido a los Latinos gente muy poderosa, no los hizo tributarios, ni vassallos, sino juntolos consigo, como compañeros, lo qual fue vno de los principales fundamentos de la grandeza Romana: porque los Latinos combatieron como los Romanos valerosamente en todas partes.[54]

Botero makes the same distinction between leagues among equals and alliances in which one state has superiority over the other. To explain this second kind of league, Botero summarizes Machiavelli's observations:

52 Machiavelli, *Discorsi*, 330.
53 Ibid., 332–33.
54 Botero, *Razon de estado*, 90.

> Superioridad tenian los Romanos en sus ligas con los Latinos, porque determinauan las empressas, nombrauan el general, y todos los ministros de importancia, y tenian el gouierno de las empressas, y el fruto de las vitorias, y assi no eran mas los Latinos, que ministros de los Romanos. Y si todavia eran compañeros, era en los trabajos y peligros de la guerra, sin participar de la honra, del prouecho, del Imperio, ni de nada, en lo qual mostraron los Romanos grandissima prudencia: por que debaxo de nombre de liga, y de compañia, ganaron para si solos con las fuerças comunes, el Imperio del mundo: y queriendo los Latinos remediallo tuuieron contrarias las fuerças Romanas, y de los pueblos sus sujetos; y de los Principes sus amigos, y confederados.[55]

We have seen how, in order to reach the goal of internal peace and stability, Machiavelli recommends in *Discourses* 1.2, 1.5–6 and 1.9 that regimes institutionalize imperial expansion, so that the people's acquisitive nature is directed outside of the state. In his discussion on how to entertain the people, who are naturally desirous of novelties, Botero repeats Machiavelli's advice, found in the *Prince* 21, that the prince cultivate an image of magnificence in public opinion through military conquests. As the example of Ferdinand of Aragon's conquest of Granada makes clear, imperial expansion keeps the great occupied: "tenne occupato in quella gli animi di quelli baroni di Castiglia, e' quali, pensando a quella guerra, non pensavano a innovazioni: e lui acquistava in quel mezzo reputazione e imperio sopra di loro, che non se ne accorgevano."[56] For very similar reasons, Botero also recommends a policy of military imperialism:

> Mucho mayor entretenimiento dan las empressas militares, porque no ay cosa que mas suspensos tenga los animos de los hombres que las guerras, que se emprendan para asegurar los confines, y ampliar y acrecentar el Imperio, para justamente ganar riquezas y gloria, defender los adherentes, fauorecer los amigos, o para conseruar la Religion, y el culto diuino, porque suelen yr a semejantes empressas todos aquellos que valen algo en obras, y en consejo, y alli contra los enemigos comunes, purgan y desechan los humores.[57]

Those people who are worth anything direct their restlessness outside the confines of the kingdom, purging their unquiet humors. Machiavelli concludes his consideration of the example of Ferdinand by suggesting that it shows that continual war keeps one's subjects occupied: "E cosí sempre ha fatte e ordite cose grandi, le quali hanno sempre tenuti sospesi e ammirati gli animi de' sud-

55 Ibid., 141.

56 Machiavelli, *Principe*, 147.

57 Botero, *Razon de estado*, 72.

diti, e occupati nello evento di esse."[58] For his part, Botero uses the same language to suggest that this same policy is today the cause of Spain's greatness and internal peace, while on the other hand France's ills are understandable, because it did not implement a similar policy:

> Y si consideramos bien de donde proceda, que en nuestros tiempos España se halla con gran sossiego, y Francia con grandes y perpetuas guerras ciuiles, hallaremos, que por auerse España empleado en guerras forasteras, y empressas remotas, en las Indias, en Flandes contra Hereticos, contra Turco, y Moros: y hallandose ocupadas las manos y pensamientos de los españoles, su tierra ha estado en paz, y diuertido en otra parte todo humor pecante: y por el contrario Francia estando en paz con los estrangeros, se han rebuelto contra si misma: y no teniendo para ello pretesto alguno, ha tomado el de la heregia de Caluino, y de vn nueuo euangelio, que adonde quiera que llega, no da alegria, sino lloro; no paz, sino guerra espantosa, y no pone en los animos buena voluntad, sino furia, y rabia.[59]

In sum, following Machiavelli's analysis, Botero suggests that the Catholic king should conserve his position of power by establishing a policy of imperial expansion that keeps both the nobles and the many of his kingdom "occupied" in a constant succession of military campaigns.

Almost as a side note, Botero concludes this line of thought by disagreeing with Machiavelli's advice that the prince go in person to a newly conquered state to reside there.[60] By overtly criticizing one small point, Botero diverts attention from the fact that he covertly agrees with Machiavelli's general approach to imperialist politics. By silently adapting Machiavellian discourse in his own treatise, Botero renders it acceptable for his readers' Catholic worldview and monarchical ideology. Through Herrera's Spanish translation, Botero's method would serve as a model for all of the subsequent writers in the Spanish reason-of-state tradition, beginning with its founder, Pedro de Ribadeneyra.

Pedro de Ribadeneyra

Pedro de Ribadeneyra went to Rome at the age of 13 and soon came into contact there with Ignatius Loyola, who received him into the new Society of Jesus. After a brief time studying, along with several other young Jesuits, in Paris and Louvain, he returned to Rome in 1543, where he stayed, holding a series of administrative posts in the Society, until 1574. Back in Spain, he was free to devote himself to writing. Both his *Life* of Ignatius Loyola, first published in

58 Machiavelli, *Principe*, 148.
59 Botero, *Razon de estado*, 73.
60 Ibid., 76.

1572, and his treatise on the *Christian Prince*, which came out in 1595, went through multiple editions in Spanish, Latin, Italian and French throughout the seventeenth century. The title of the latter political treatise expresses clearly Ribadeneyra's aim: *Tratado de la religión y virtudes que debe tener el príncipe cristiano para gobernar y conservar sus estados, contra lo que Nicolás Maquiavelo y los políticos deste tiempo enseñan*. It is divided into two books: Ribadeneyra dedicates book 1 to teaching the king how he should behave with respect to religion; in book 2 he discusses all the other virtues a king needs in order to rule justly.

In his prologue, "Al cristiano y piadoso lector," he declares that he is writing against those who would subordinate religion to matters of state. Following Possevino, he groups Machiavelli with the French *politiques*, naming the Huguenots François de la Noue and Philippe Du Plessis Mornay along with Jean Bodin. For his brief portrait of Machiavelli, he summarizes Possevino's selection of Gentillet's chapter headings.[61]

> Enseña que el príncipe debe creer más a sí que a ningun sabio consejo, y que no hay otra causa justa para hacer guerra sino la que parece al príncipe que le es conveniente o necesaria; y que para cortar toda esperanza de paz, debe hacer notables injurias y agravios a sus enemigos; y que para destruir alguna ciudad o provincia sin guerra, no hay tal como sembrarla de pecados y vicios; y que se debe persuadir que las injurias pasadas jamas se olvidan, por muchos beneficios que se hagan al que las recibió. Que se debe imitar algun tirano valeroso en el gobierno, y desear ser más temido que amado, porque no hay que fiar en amistad; y otras cosas semejantes a estas...[62]

Gentillet's and Possevino's exaggerated misrepresentation of Machiavelli is an easy tool that Ribadeneyra appropriates in order to be able to condemn his works in their entirety, agreeing in this way with Quiroga's prohibition of 1583. Nevertheless, perhaps surprisingly, Ribadeneyra was a very good reader of Machiavelli in the original Italian, rendering into Spanish quotations from both the *Prince* and the *Discourses* and adapting Machiavellian discourse to his own advice to the Christian king.[63]

At the very beginning of his prologue, he creates a portrait of Machiavelli which is only partly true: "Nicolas Maquiavelo fué hombre que se dió mucho al estudio de la policía y gobierno de la república y de aquella que comunmente

61 Anglo, *Machiavelli—The First Century*, 389–90.

62 Pedro de Ribadeneyra, *Obras escogidas*, Biblioteca de Autores Españoles 60, ed. D. Vicente de la Fuente (Madrid: Imprenta de Hernando y Compañía, 1899), 455.

63 Anglo, *Machiavelli—The First Century*, 391, would disagree: "There is little acuity of thought, no originality, and a real but severely limited knowledge of Machiavelli in Ribadeneira's work. Nevertheless, the Spanish Jesuit was a historian of European reputation."

llaman razon de estado. Escribió algunos libros, en que enseña esta razon de estado, y forma un príncipe valeroso y magnánimo, y le da los preceptos y avisos que debe guardar para conservar y amplificar sus estados."[64] Here Ribadeneyra follows Botero, attributing to Machiavelli the origins of reason of state. In this portrait, Ribadeneyra focusses on the Florentine's consideration of secular power, both internal and external: that is, in terms of the relationships between the prince and his subjects, on the one hand, and between the prince and neighboring states, on the other. He completely leaves out of this picture Machiavelli's republican ideology or concern for the common good. In Ribadeneyra's day, Spanish Catholics, and especially the Jesuits, had observed how the Wars of Religion had torn France apart, and they concluded that religious tolerance, "la libertad de conciencia" in Ribadeneyra's own words,[65] an idea promoted by a "secta que Satanás ha inventado,"[66] whose principal proponent was Machiavelli, was counterproductive to a unified Church, which they considered a necessary condition for the conservation of the secular state.[67]

Imitating the early anti-Machiavellians, especially Osorio, when creating this misleading portrait of Machiavelli, part of Ribadeneyra's intention is to characterize him as an enemy of Christianity. Toward the end of his treatise, when he turns to a discussion of fortitude, he translates the same passage from *Discourses* 2.2 that we have already seen in order to refute it:

> Pensando dónde pueda nacer que en aquellos tiempos antiguos los pueblos fuesen más amigos de la libertad que en éstos, creo que nazca de la misma causa que ahora hace á los hombres ménos fuertes, la cual pienso yo que sea la diversidad de nuestra educacion y de los antiguos, fundada en la diversidad de la religion nuestra y suya; porque, habiéndonos nuestra religion enseñado la verdad y el verdadero camino (estas y otras semejantes palabras suelen decir los políticos para mejor engañar), hace que estimemos ménos la honra del mundo; y como los gentiles la estimasen tanto y la tuviesen por su sumo bien, eran sus acciones más feroces.[68]

Ribadeneyra dedicates several chapters to refuting this part of Machiavelli's "doctrina," calling it not only "impía," "falsa" and "peligrosa," but also "necia y desatinada."[69] To do so, he has recourse to the medieval, Christian definition of fortitude as consisting primarily of patience: without Christian virtue, fortitude

64 Ribadeneyra, *Obras escogidas*, 455.

65 Ibid., 482.

66 Ibid., 452.

67 José María Iñurritegui Rodríguez, *La gracia y la república: El lenguaje político de la teología católica y "El príncipe cristiano" de Pedro de Ribadeneyra* (Madrid: Universidad Nacional de Educación a Distancia, 1998), 325–29.

68 Ribadeneyra, *Obras escogidas*, 567.

69 Ibid., 567.

is equivalent to bestial ferocity. By calling Machiavelli's thought a "doctrine," he implies that Machiavelli is attempting to replace the Christian doctrine with his own. What Ribadeneyra conveniently leaves out is that at the end of this same paragraph of the *Discourses*, Machiavelli makes a distinction between Christ's own doctrine and its subsequent interpreters:

> E benché paia che si sia effeminato il mondo e disarmato il cielo, nasce piú, sanza dubbio, dalla viltà degli uomini, che hanno interpetrato la nostra religione secondo l'ozio, e non secondo la virtú. Perché, se considerassono como la ci promette l'esaltazione e la difesa della patria, vedrebbono come la vuole che noi l'amiamo e onoriamo, e prepariamoci a essere tali che noi la possiamo difendere.[70]

Machiavelli is making an attempt to portray Christ's original doctrine as compatible with the kind of fortitude he admires in the ancient Romans, one which will help citizens actively defend their state's liberty. In the passage that Ribadeneyra translates, Machiavelli refers to the "truth" and to the "true way" taught to us by Christ; however, Ribadeneyra adds his own phrase in parenthesis to suggest that Machiavelli does not believe in Christianity at all. This misleading portrait of Machiavelli would become the standard characterization for Spaniards throughout the seventeenth century and beyond.

Nevertheless, much like the early anti-Machiavellians before him, Ribadeneyra answers Machiavelli's call for a militant, imperialist understanding of Christianity. He provides a long list of ancient and modern examples of Christian soldiers and captains who demonstrated true fortitude during their military campaigns whose aim was to expand the influence of Christ's teachings. In one interesting example, Ribadeneyra reminds his readers of the exploits of Hernán Cortés: "¿a quién no pone admiracion el ánimo con que Fernan Cortés acometió con tan pocos españoles el reino de Méjico, y el valor con que le sojuzgó, y destruyó la monarquía de Motezuma, y la fortaleza con que le defendió de inumerables indios, y la felicidad con que ganó y sujetó tantas y tan ricas provincias, y se hizo señor de tantos y tan grandes tesoros, que han enriquecido el mundo?"[71] Readers apparently are to assume that Cortés was a Christian, and that therefore his fortitude was the true Christian kind; nevertheless, Ribadeneyra focusses on the earthly gains he made through conquest, the territorial expansion and monetary profit, making no mention whatsoever of the salvation of the pagan souls that Cortés's actions were supposed to bring about through evangelization.

As he repeats throughout his treatise, Ribadeneyra's principal objection to Machiavelli is precisely how he does not take into consideration God's divine

70 Machiavelli, *Discorsi*, 318–19.

71 Ribadeneyra, *Obras escogidas*, 574.

providence, replacing it with the pagan goddess Fortuna. At the head of his complaints against Machiavelli is that he attributes "la felicidad del hombre al caso y á la fortuna, y no á la religion y á la virtud."[72] Later, he repeats this same idea in another way: that Machiavelli and the *políticos* teach kings how to rule "como si el Señor no tuviese providencia dellos, y el mundo se gobernase acaso ó con sola la malicia y astucia humana."[73] We may recall how Furió Ceriol was critical of those who attributed worldly misfortune to higher powers and advised rulers to do exactly what is criticized here. Ribadeneyra, on the other hand, a prominent member of the Company of Jesus, is working from a different set of assumptions: he cannot accept a secular vision of politics that goes without a providential view of history.[74] Much of book 1 is dedicated to demonstrating, mostly through examples taken from the Bible and early Church histories such as Eusebius, that the only way for a king to be good is to place all of his faith and hope in God's grace.

The problem for Ribadeneyra was that from the end of the Middle Ages European political thinkers had been steadily shifting their attention from the afterlife to this life. Therefore, in order to make an effective argument, he had to convince kings that putting their faith in God not only would benefit them in their effort to save their own souls but also help them achieve the same political ends in this world that Machiavelli and the French *politiques* strived for as well. Ribadeneyra points out how even Machiavelli and the *políticos* teach that religion is necessary to conserve the state; the difference is that they teach that any religion will do and that only appearances matter. As evidence, he translates a passage from *Discourses* 1.12:

> Los príncipes de una república ó de un reino deben conservar los fundamentos de la religion que tienen, y con esto fácilmente conservarán su república religiosa, y por consiguiente buena y unida. Y deben favorecer todas las cosas que son en favor de su religion (aunque las tengan por falsas), y acrecentarlas; y tanto más lo deben hacer, cuanto fueren más prudentes y más sabios de las cosas naturales.[75]

In contrast, following the model established by Botero, Ribadeneyra teaches that only the true Catholic religion works, and then only when the prince truly

72 Ibid., 455.

73 Ibid., 470.

74 Iñurritegui Rodríguez, *La gracia y la república*, 316–21.

75 Ribadeneyra, *Obras escogidas*, 459. A comparison between this passage and Ottevanti's 1552 translation reveals that Ribadeneyra's is more accurate, because he understood better Machiavelli's use of the subjunctive: "come che le giudicassono false" (*Discorsi* 84), which Ottevanti renders as "como si las juzgasen por falsas" (*Discursos* 41) and Ribadeneyra as "aunque las tengan por falsas." From this comparison, we may conclude that Ribadeneyra's reading does not depend on Ottevanti's translation.

believes and loves religion. While the *políticos* only aim for the conservation of their states and peace in this world, Ribadeneyra says that God established government for happiness in this life and the next.[76]

Ribadeneyra is caught in a double bind.[77] On the one hand, he wants to convince rulers that the only way to conserve their states is by being truly virtuous according to God's law. However, in order to do so, the king must not subordinate religion to the state. Therefore, his aim must not be the conservation of the state, a temporal good, but eternal happiness in the next life. He must somehow convince rulers that the only way to conserve their states is to not worry about conserving their states, but put their faith only in God: "el primero y más principal cuidado de los reyes y príncipes debe ser el acudir á Dios y guardar su santa ley, y procurar que todos sus súbditos la guarden; y cuando lo hacen así, Dios les da prosperidad y conserva los reinos, y hace que sean felices y bienaventurados acá temporalmente, y en el cielo sin fin."[78]

This double bind explains some of Ribadeneyra's phrases, which otherwise would be difficult to interpret. For example, he introduces chapter 9, "Cuál sea la verdadera felicidad de los reyes, y premio de sus trabajos," with a rhetorical question asking if the king's rewards are found in this world:

> ¿Son por ventura grandes tesoros, ricos estados, reinos poderosos, copia de mantenimientos, salud, fuerzas, vida larga, vitoria de sus enemigos, paz, honra y gloria, y aquello que el mundo llama felicidad, y los políticos tienen por sumo bien y por el blanco y fin de todo su gobierno? Todos estos bienes suele nuestro Señor dar con abundancia á los reyes y principes cristianos que fielmente le sirven, cuando les conviene; pero si en ellos se rematase su galardon, no serian bienes tan grandes como son, sino muy cortos, bajos y de poco valor. Y muchas veces no habría diferencia del católico al hereje, del buen Rey al malo, del cristiano al pagano, si por solos ellos se hubiese de medir su felicidad; pues el Señor los reparte á los unos y los otros, para declarar la poca estima que dellos debemos hacer.[79]

Rulers who read this rhetorical question will see enumerated everything they might desire for their political life in this world. Why should they not desire these things? Ribadeneyra's answer is puzzling. At first he seems to imply that the king should not worry, because God provides all of these worldly desires to those kings which faithfully serve him. However, it turns out that this rule is not always true: he rewards his followers only "cuando les conviene," a condition that remains unexplained. The next sentence is difficult to interpret, revealing

76 Ribadeneyra, *Obras escogidas*, 458–59.

77 I employ the term borrowed from the field of psychopathology by Alison Weber, *Teresa of Avila and the Rhetoric of Femininity* (Princeton, NJ: Princeton University Press, 1990), 45–46.

78 Ribadeneyra, *Obras escogidas*, 467.

79 Ibid., 471.

the tensions created by Ribadeneyra's double bind. It appears to say that in the cases when the king does not receive these worldly rewards, he should conclude that they are not as great as normally he might think, but lowly, short-lived and of little worth. In context, this interpretation agrees with Ribadeneyra's arguments throughout his treatise and with his conclusion in this passage: that God hands out these worldly rewards rather arbitrarily, to both good and bad kings, so that we understand how little we should value them. However, Ribadeneyra's use of tense and mood is curious: the imperfect subjunctive (*se rematase*) indicates the possibility that the good king might not be rewarded; however, his use of the conditional (*no serian*) and the present indicative (*son*) implies that these worldly rewards are in fact great, but that they would not be so only in the case that the king did not receive them. In other words, this passage seems to imply that the king should desire these worldly goods only if God does indeed reward him; if he does not, then the king should not desire them at all. This particular inconsistency is the result of Ribadeneyra's need to convince his readers that good kings will be rewarded not only in the next life but in this world as well, only if they follow God's laws.

Ribadeneyra's solution to this double bind is to divide reason of state into two kinds, true and false: "una falsa y aparente, otra sólida y verdadera; una engañosa y diabólica, otra cierta y divina; una que del estado hace religion, otra que de la religion hace estado; una enseñada de los políticos y fundada en vana prudencia y en humanos y ruines medios, otra enseñada de Dios..."[80] As this passage reveals, Ribadeneyra's method for establishing this division is to create a rhetorical opposition between the two, polarizing them by setting up one semantic opposition after another: false, true; apparent, solid; deceptive, certain; diabolical, divine. He further highlights this opposition through a chiasmus that changes the meaning of the verb *hacer*: "one makes a religion of the State, the other makes a state out of religion."[81] In essence, Ribadeneyra returns to the medieval, rhetorical dichotomy between king and tyrant and adapts it to the new, popularized political vocabulary of reason of state of his own times.

Throughout his treatise, Ribadeneyra makes every effort to remind his readers of the medieval conception of kingship by invoking its traditional theological imagery: the king's origins are divine; like God, he looks after his flock like a shepherd; he is the head of the *corpus mysticum*, etc.[82] The basic distinction between true and false reason of state is based on the medieval distinction between the good king and the tyrant, as Ribadeneyra makes explicit:

> Y porque esto mejor se entienda de una vez, quiero declarar aquí la diferencia que hay entre el rey cristiano y justo, de quien nosotros hablamos, y el tirano,

80 Ibid., 456.

81 Truman, *Spanish Treatises*, 279.

82 Ribadeneyra, *Obras escogidas*, 532–33.

> de quien hablan los políticos. El verdadero rey está sujeto a las leyes de Dios y de la naturaleza; el tirano no tiene otra ley sino su voluntad. El Rey hace profesion de guardar la piedad, la justicia, la fe; el tirano no tiene cuenta con Dios ni con fe ni con justicia. El uno está atado al bien público y a la defension de su pueblo; el otro no hace cosa sino por su interese...[83]

Following the Aristotelian tradition, Ribadeneyra declares that the good, Christian king looks out for the common good of his subjects, while the tyrant only worries about his own interests. He simply brings the medieval tradition up-to-date by incorporating into it the new language of reason of state: while the good, Christian king uses the true, Christian reason of state, the tyrant operates with the false, Machiavellian reason of state.

In the rest of the treatise, Ribadeneyra applies this opposition between true and false reason of state, regardless of whether or not Machiavelli's advice actually corresponds to the latter. In many examples, Ribadeneyra's false reason of state turns out to be any course of action that results in the ruler's downfall. To give an example, he writes that, "por falsa razón de estado," Ludovico Sforza invited Charles VIII into Italy to conquer Naples in 1494. This of course resulted in Ludovico's own downfall, which Ribadeneyra portrays, curiously, using the imagery of the goddess Fortuna, something he had criticized in Machiavelli and the *políticos*: "Pues él, que estaba tan ufano y pagado con su grandeza y prosperidad, que se llamaba hijo de la fortuna, cuando ella le volvió las espaldas y le derribó de lo alto de su rueda inconstante y presurosa, conoció que no tiene firmeza y que cuanto más se nos ríe, más nos engaña."[84] However, it is not clear how this should be an example, as Ribadeneyra claims, "para escarmiento de todos los príncipes que en sus consejos no miran a Dios."[85] Machiavelli's own famously negative judgment of Ludovico's action, as expressed toward the end of his *Florentine Histories*, was that it was the cause of the ruin of Italy. On a conceptual level, Machiavelli would have agreed that Ludovico's action was misguided, not because it somehow went against God's laws, but because he invited a stronger ruler to come into his own lands to fight his battles for him. We might compare this example to Machiavelli's criticism of the Venetians when they invited Louis XII into Lombardy in the *Prince* 3. This juxtaposition of a Machiavellian discourse of Fortuna alongside a providential analysis of Ludovico's actions not only suggests that Ribadeneyra's critique of Machiavelli is purely rhetorical; in effect it renders Machiavelli's generally secular approach to historical analysis acceptable to a Catholic readership.

Ribadeneyra was, in fact, very familiar with the *Prince* in addition to the *Discourses*. He quotes a long passage from chapter 18 in order to demonstrate,

83 Ibid., 532.
84 Ibid., 478.
85 Ibid.

in his own words, that Machiavelli teaches that "para engañar mejor y conservar su estado, debe fingir el príncipe que es temeroso de Dios aunque no lo sea, y templado aunque sea disoluto, y clemente siendo cruel, y tomar la máscara de las otras virtudes cuando le viene á cuento, para disimular sus vicios y ser tenido por lo que no es."[86] The passage that Ribadeneyra quotes is in fact one of the most important paragraphs in the *Prince*, because it summarizes Machiavelli's reorganization of the traditional dichotomy between virtues and vices, and because it expresses well the idea that necessity justifies moral flexibility. Ribadeneyra's translation is accurate, with one small exception, as well as elegant:

> No es necesario que un príncipe tenga todas las calidades que habemos dicho, más bien es necesario que parezca que las tiene; ántes oso decir que teniéndolas y guardándolas siempre son dañosas, y pareciendo que las tiene son provechosas; como parecer piadoso, fiel, humano, religioso, entero, y serlo; mas de tal manera, que cuando fuere menester, el príncipe pueda y sepa mudarse y hacer lo contrario. Y hase de entender que un príncipe, especialmente nuevo, no puede guardar todas las cosas por las cuales los hombres son tenidos por buenos, porque muchas veces, para conservar su estado, están obligados á hacer contra la fe, contra la caridad, contra la humanidad y contra la religion; pero[87] es menester que de tal manera disponga su ánimo, que esté aparejado á mudar las velas segun los vientos y la variedad de la fortuna, y como dije arriba, no partirse del bien pudiendo; mas saber entrar en el mal cuando lo pidiere la necesidad. Por tanto el príncipe con gran cuidado debe procurar que no le salga jamas de la boca cosa que no sea llena destas cinco virtudes, y que el que le viere y oyere, juzgue que todo es piedad, todo fe, todo entereza, todo humanidad, todo religion, y no hay cosa más necesaria que parecer que el príncipe tiene esta postrera, que es la religion; porque los hombres, comunmente hablando, más juzgan con los ojos que con las manos, porque el ver es de todos, y el palpar y tocar con las manos es de pocos.[88]

It is important to note here that Ribadeneyra's translation accurately transmits Machiavelli's message to rulers that they should be good when they can; however, they must also know when necessity demands that they be bad. At the end of the quotation, Ribadeneyra attributes a diabolical motive to its author: "Todas éstas son palabras de Maquiavelo, salidas del infierno para destruir la religion y arrancar del pecho del príncipe cristiano de un golpe todas las verdaderas virtudes."[89]

Nevertheless, throughout book 2 of his treatise, which treats all of the other virtues besides religion which are necessary for the Christian prince, Ribad-

86 Ibid., 520.

87 This "pero" is an inaccurate translation of the Italian "però" (Machiavelli, *Principe*, 118), which in Machiavelli's time meant "per ciò."

88 Ribadeneyra, *Obras escogidas*, 520.

89 Ibid.

eneyra reveals his understanding of Machiavelli's reorganization of the traditional virtues, as he justifies a similar moral flexibility for the same reasons: when necessity demands it. The rhetorically constructed opposition between true and false reason of state allows Ribadeneyra to incorporate much of Machiavelli's advice into his own treatise, without giving him credit. At one point he blames "las artes de Maquiavelo" for the fact that rulers are surrounded by enemies who will try to deceive them.[90] This volatile state of affairs is in fact the reality of European and specifically Italian politics that Machiavelli describes in his essays. By blaming Machiavelli himself for this situation, Ribadeneyra diverts the attention of his readers away from the fact that in reality he follows Machiavelli's example and advises rulers to prepare themselves in the same way. For both Machiavelli and Ribadeneyra, the reality of politics creates a necessity for rulers to be morally flexible in order to conserve their states and bring about the common good.

Ribadeneyra dedicates two chapters to demonstrate "Cómo el príncipe debe cumplir su fe y palabra" and one to offer as example "Algunos castigos que ha dado el Señor á los príncipes que han quebrantado su juramento y palabra."[91] Elsewhere he writes that the king must never lie: "porque la palabra del príncipe debe ser como una palabra de Dios."[92] However, he follows this statement with a list of actions and utterances which do not fall under the category of lying. It is not lying, for example, to be secretive. "Tampoco es mentira, sino prudencia, el disimular muchas cosas y pasar el príncipe por ellas y hacer que no las ve, puesto caso que esta disimulacion engendre en los ánimos de los otros alguna falsedad y engaño."[93] It is not lying to be careful about who one believes, although the prince should act as if he believes everyone. "Asimesmo no es mentira (cuando la necesidad ó utilidad grande lo pide) decir algunas palabras verdaderas en un sentido, aunque crea el que las dice que el que las oye, por ser equívocas, las podrá tomar en diferente sentido. Y lo que digo de las palabras se puede tambien decir de las obras."[94] This is especially true during war, "porque esto no es mentir, sino hacer las cosas con prudencia para bien de la república."[95]

At this point Ribadeneyra invokes the authority of Martín de Azpilcueta:

> como dice el doctor Navarro, hay dos artes de simular y disimular: la una, de los que sin causa ni provecho mienten y fingen que hay lo que no hay, ó que no hay lo que hay; la otra, de los que sin mal engaño y sin

90 Ibid., 524.
91 Ibid., 542–46.
92 Ibid., 525.
93 Ibid.
94 Ibid.
95 Ibid.

mentira dan á entender una cosa por otra con prudencia, cuando lo pide la necesidad ó utilidad.[96]

Ribadeneyra does not go into any of the details of Azpilcueta's complex *Commentary on the Chapter "Humanae Aures", XXII. qu. V*, where the idea of "mental reservation" justifies simulation and dissimulation, as long as it is done prudently and for just cause.[97] It is enough for Ribadeneyra to maintain his rhetorical separation between true and false reason of state: all of these exceptions are justified as long as the king does not offend God, "para que, siendo príncipes cristianos y discípulos de Cristo, no se hagan discípulos de Maquiavelo."[98] In this way, Ribadeneyra effectively makes Machiavellian prudence acceptable for the Christian king: as long as the king knows that he is lying for a good, just reason, or out of necessity (which in reality is the same justification Machiavelli's texts offer for being morally flexible), he may rest assured that he is not following the advice of the "impious" Machiavelli, that is, the mischaracterization of Machiavelli that Ribadeneyra drew from Possevino.

Ribadeneyra's objection to Machiavelli's moral flexibility is based on his different point of view regarding who is the most important judge of a prince's actions, men or God. Machiavelli's secular consideration of politics leads him to consider the prince's internal power in terms of peace and stability. In order to conserve his state, the prince must be conscious of his subjects' opinion of him. This idea is behind the famous reorganization of the traditional princely virtues that we have seen in chapters 15–19 of the *Prince*, including the above-cited passage that Ribadeneyra translates, where Machiavelli considers the situations in which princes should not worry about their reputation: as long as they look after the common good, maintain internal stability and avoid the hatred of their subjects, sometimes necessity dictates that they accept being called cruel, stingy, etc. Ribadeneyra cannot accept this secular point of view, because it does not take into consideration God's divine providence: "Pero no depende la conservacion del Estado principalmente de la buena ó mala opinion de los hombres, aunque la buena se debe procurar y granjear con las verdaderas virtudes, y no con las aparentes, sino de la voluntad del Señor, que es el que da los estados y los conserva, y lo quita y traspasa á su voluntad."[99]

Nevertheless, throughout his discussion of the virtues in book 2 of his treatise, Ribadeneyra incorporates exactly Machiavelli's rhetoric of the avoidance of hatred in his own advice to the Christian prince, focusing not on "la voluntad

96 Ibid.

97 Perez Zagorin, *Ways of Lying: Dissimulation, Persecution, and Conformity in Early Modern Europe* (Cambridge, MA: Harvard University Press, 1990), 168–75; Truman, *Spanish Treatises*, 297–98.

98 Ribadeneyra, *Obras escogidas*, 524.

99 Ibid., 521.

del Señor," but precisely on the "opinion de los hombres." For example, he advises the Christian king to give his subjects the impression that they are paying only the necessary taxes, nothing more:

> para que sus vasallos lleven con mayor paciencia su trabajo, y den sus haciendas con ménos repugnancia y disgusto, procure que entiendan que el cargarlos no es voluntario, sino pura necesidad ... porque si ven que el Rey está rico, ó que, no lo estando, hace gastos excesivos y superfluos ... afligense terriblemente, y cobran ódio y aborrecimiento al príncipe.[100]

Although this passage does not exclude the possibility that the king in truth does only collect taxes when he needs them, as Ribadeneyra says the Christian prince should do, the emphasis here is not on truth but on public opinion: he must not overburden his subjects in order to avoid their hatred.

Similarly, Ribadeneyra incorporates the Machiavellian discourse of the avoidance of hatred into his discussion of clemency: "cualquiera castigo que hiciere, hacerle de manera que se entienda que es celo de justicia, y no saña y venganza; porque la ira arrebatada y la cólera en el príncipe es muy fea y dañosa."[101] Just as in the passage cited above, Ribadeneyra's use of the verb *entender* in the subjunctive expresses how the prince should make an attempt to create an image of himself in the public eye in order to avoid the people's hatred. As these examples demonstrate, in his discussion of the various virtues that the Christian prince must have, Ribadeneyra implicitly accepts Machiavelli's lesson that necessity often obliges the prince to avoid his subjects' hatred rather than attract their love. In these passages, he forgoes his insistence on the importance of God's divine providence in favor of a secular, Machiavellian analysis of political power.

Finally, in a series of chapters on prudence, Ribadeneyra gives advice of a purely practical, secular nature. Prudence teaches kings to take into account the contingency of each particular situation: "mirar mucho la circunstancia del tiempo, sin la cual se hace muy difícil y áun imposible lo que con ella es fácil y llano. Y es cosa increible cuán presto vuela y huye la ocasion, y las mudanzas que hay en todas las cosas humanas."[102] Ribadeneyra speaks of foresight using the same medical metaphor as Machiavelli in the *Prince* 3: "Regla de prudencia es prevenir los males y sangrarse ántes que venga la enfermedad, que es más excelente género de medicina que el curarla despues de venida."[103] For both Machiavelli and Ribadeneyra, this metaphor conveys the idea that small problems, if left alone, can become irremediable big problems. Like

100 Ibid., 535.
101 Ibid., 546.
102 Ibid., 563.
103 Ibid.

Machiavelli says in the *Prince* 14, Ribadeneyra advises princes always to be prepared for war in times of peace, and that prudence teaches princes to measure their enemies' forces accurately.[104] Just like Machiavelli says in the *Prince* 21, Ribadeneyra advises princes not to be neutral if either of the warring parties is more powerful than him, because then whoever wins will be his enemy, and it is better to join forces with one of them, and "correre la fortuna sua";[105] "correr la fortuna con él."[106] Thus, despite his characterization of Machiavelli as a denier of the Christian religion and of God's divine providence, Ribadeneyra does not hesitate to use Machiavelli's secular language to teach his Christian prince human prudence.

In sum, regardless of his rhetorical opposition to the straw figure of "Maquiavelo" that he inherited from a tradition deriving ultimately from Gentillet, Ribadeneyra very effectively adapts Machiavelli's reorganization of the traditional political virtues to the Catholic worldview of his readers at the end of the sixteenth century. This double-sided technique, found in both Botero and Ribadeneyra, would appear repeatedly throughout the Counter-Reformation in the Spanish anti-Machiavellian reason-of-state tradition that they founded.

104 Ibid.

105 Machiavelli, *Principe*, 149.

106 Ribadeneyra, *Obras escogidas*, 564.

4

Machiavellian Discourse in the Hispanic Baroque Reason-of-State Tradition

At the turn of the seventeenth century, Spain was entering into a social, economic and political crisis, the consequences of which would last well beyond the end of the early modern period. The death of Philip II and the coronation of his son, Philip III, in 1598 inaugurated the practice of the *valido* or favorite, whereby the king's political power was wielded in practice by a grandee friend. While Philip II administered his kingdoms personally, Philip III handed over the responsibility of governing to his friend and mentor, Francisco Gómez de Sandoval y Rojas, Marquis of Denia and soon to be Duke of Lerma, who was less interested in governing than he was in accumulating land, wealth and titles for himself and his friends and family. When Philip III died prematurely in 1621, his 16-year-old son, crowned Philip IV, was already dominated by Gaspar de Guzmán, Count of Olivares. The new favorite continued the practice of patronage established by his predecessor; yet he was much more interested in politics, and made it his life's goal to defend the Spanish empire, if not expand it, against encroachments by the English, French and Dutch, even while he never developed an adequate financial policy to fund this project.[1]

Throughout this period, political writers addressed their advice on reason of state not only to the king, but also to the courtiers who were involved in policymaking, whether the king's favorite himself or members of the various councils that would submit advisory *juntas* to the king and his favorite. These writers make up a reason-of-state tradition, in the sense that we may assume that each writer who produced a new contribution to the tradition was familiar with the previous instances of the same tradition. Beginning with Maravall, historians have tended to divide these writers into three groups or "schools" based on their relationship to Machiavelli's works. While each historian adjusts the precise definition of these groups, in general they may be described as follows: first, those who rejected the Florentine's ideas altogether; second, those who

[1] For general studies, see J. H. Elliot, *The Count-Duke of Olivares: The Statesman in an Age of Decline* (New Haven, CT: Yale University Press, 1986); John Lynch, *The Hispanic World in Crisis and Change* (Oxford: Blackwell, 1992); and Antonio Feros, *Kingship and Favoritism in the Spain of Philip III, 1598–1621* (Cambridge: Cambridge University Press, 2000).

accepted these ideas more or less completely, even while they protected themselves either by citing Tacitus or by superficially attacking the figure of Machiavelli or both; third, those who attempted to reconcile Machiavelli's ideas with traditional Christian values. These categories in turn have been accepted for the most part by scholars interested in examining the political implications of literary works produced in this period.[2]

I argue that we should move beyond these categories, because they are based on an inaccurate and incomplete understanding, first, of Machiavelli's writings themselves and, second, of these Spanish writers' reading of Machiavelli. All of these writers follow the model established by Botero and Ribadeneyra of attacking a straw figure of Machiavelli while they simultaneously adapt specific Machiavellian ideas to their Catholic readership. In other words, the first two categories mentioned above are oversimplifications: there were very few if any Spaniards who either rejected or accepted Machiavelli's ideas completely. Maravall himself admits that his tripartite division is mostly artificial.[3] He cites Gentillet and Trajano Boccalini, and only two Spaniards, Claudio Clemente and Juan de Torres (even though the latter does not mention Machiavelli directly), as those who reject Machiavelli completely, and he adds that he has not found any Spanish author who accepted Machiavelli completely, although Tacitists such as Baltasar Álamos de Barrientos and Juan Alfonso de Lancina come the closest. All other Spaniards, according to Maravall, attempt to make Machiavelli's "realidad política natural" and his analysis of the "Estado moderno" agree with divine revelation.[4]

Thus, with few exceptions, these writers fall into the third category mentioned above: they attempted, in varying degrees, to reconcile Machiavelli's ideas with their readers' Catholic worldview. Now, in order to answer the questions of how they went about doing this and to what extent they were directly familiar with Machiavelli's works, it is necessary to examine each individual writer. In the selection of writers that follows, we shall see that while in many cases writers

2 Maravall, *Teoría española*, 365–78. See José Ignacio Barrio Olano, *La novela picaresca y el método maquiavélico* (Madrid: Editorial Pliegos, 1998), 36–40; Enrique Tierno Galván, *Escritos (1950–1960)* (Madrid: Editorial Tecnos, 1971), 32–39; Monroe Z. Hafter, *Gracián and Perfection: Spanish Moralists of the Seventeenth Century* (Cambridge, MA: Harvard University Press, 1966), 7–8. A notable exception is Fernández-Santamaría, *Razón de estado*, 14–18, who eliminates the category of those who accept Machiavelli completely. In his study of Calderón de la Barca's political ideology, *Allegories of Kingship: Calderón and the Anti-Machiavellian Tradition* (University Park: Pennsylvania State University Press, 1996), 23–26, Stephen Rupp follows Fernández-Santamaría's categorization. Gonzalo Fernández de la Mora, "Maquiavelo, visto por los tratadistas políticos españoles de la Contrarreforma," *Arbor: Revista General de Investigación y Cultura* 13, no. 43–44 (1949): 417–49, asserts that Spanish prose writers of the Counter-Reformation were unanimous in their condemnation of Machiavelli.

3 Maravall, *Teoría española*, 368–78.

4 Ibid., 377–78.

exhibit at least some direct and unique borrowing from Machiavelli, in others ideas that had appeared previously in the same reason-of-state tradition are simply repeated. Nevertheless, even those writers who do not reveal any direct familiarity with Machiavelli do in fact perpetuate the same Machiavellian discourse found in earlier examples of the tradition. In this way, this reason-of-state tradition constitutes a good example of what Harald E. Braun has called the "discursive hybridity" typical of the political language of the Spanish Baroque, which aims to provide "practical solutions to early modern challenges of uncertainty … by deliberately transgressing philosophical, moral and ideological boundaries."[5] By incorporating Machiavellian discourse into their political advice to their Catholic monarch, these ostensibly anti-Machiavellian writers successfully propose practical solutions to real political problems.

Jerónimo Gracián de la Madre de Dios

While he does not provide practical political advice to his readers, Jerónimo Gracián de la Madre de Dios is an example of a writer who appropriates and popularizes the anti-Machiavellian mischaracterization of Machiavelli, while the Spanish reason-of-state tradition is still relatively new, and his methods will be repeated throughout the tradition, as we shall see. Toward the end of his life, Jerónimo Gracián, friend and confessor of Teresa of Ávila, moved to Brussels at the behest of his friend the Marquis of Guadaleste, whom Philip III had recently appointed ambassador to Flanders. Among other works, Gracián published there his *Diez lamentaciones del miserable estado de los Atheistas de nuestros tiempos* (1611). At the beginning of his treatise, Gracián declares that there are seven kinds of atheist, one of them being: "Atheistas Politicos, discipulos de Machiauello, que anteponen a la Diuina ley su razon de estado, y aquella tienen por buena fee, que es de mayor prouecho para su augmento y conseruacion."[6] When he reaches the corresponding lamentation, he names their masters: "discipulos de Tiberio Cesar, Cornelio Tacito, Mons de la Noue, Plessis, Morneo, Bodino, y Machiauelo."[7] Gracián gives pride of place to Machiavelli among these teachers: "Pero quien mas de proposito, y con mayor daño de la Christiandad ha escrito desta maldita doctrina, fue vn Secretario del Duque de Florencia, llamado Nicolao Machiauelo, en tres libros que haze de la *Institucion del Principe*. Por la qual causa, muchos llaman Machiauelistas a estos Atheistas politicos."[8]

5 Harald E. Braun, "Baroque Constitution and Hybrid Political Language: The Case of Juan de Mariana (1535–1624) and Juan Márquez (1565–1621)," *Revista Canadiense de Estudios Hispánicos* 33, no. 1 (2008): 80.

6 Jerónimo Gracián de la Madre de Dios, *Diez lamentaciones del miserable estado de los Atheistas de nuestros tiempos* (Brussels: Roger Velpio & Huberto Antonio, 1611), 13.

7 Ibid., 183.

8 Ibid., 189.

Was Gracián familiar with all of these writers? Three pieces of evidence suggest that he was not. First, he divides Du Plessis Mornay into two individuals, "Plessis" and "Morneo." Second, he refers anachronistically to Machiavelli as the Secretary of the Duke of Florence, a post he could not have held, because Florence was not made a duchy until 1533, six years after Machiavelli's death. Finally, he erroneously divides the *Prince* into three books. How can we explain these mistakes? It turns out that Gracián is simply repeating the mischaracterization of Machiavelli created by Innocent Gentillet, Antonio Possevino and Pedro de Ribadeneyra, all of whose works he cites precisely as authorities, even against his own trepidation in the case of Gentillet:

> Vn Caluinista escriuio vn libro intitulado *Antimachiauelo*, que (aunque esta inficionado con los errores de Caluino) descubre muy al viuo los de Machiauelo. El Doctissimo y religiosissimo Padre Antonio Posseuino de la Compañia de Jesvs, escriuio admirable contra Bodino y Morneo, y en su libro primero *Bibliotecae selectae* en el capitulo veyntiseys ... y el Padre Pedro de Ribadeneyra, tambien de la Compañia de Iesus compuso en Español vn admirable libro, llamado, *De la Religion y virtudes que deue tener el Principe Christiano, para gouernar y conseruar sus Estados, contra lo que Nicolas Machiauelo, y los Politicos deste tiempo enseñan.*[9]

The exactness with which Gracián cites his authorities leads us to conclude that, unlike Machiavelli's works themselves, he probably consulted them firsthand. Gracián draws from Possevino when he repeats his erroneous citation of the "tres libros" of Machiavelli's "*Institucion del Principe.*" Moreover, the list of Atheistas Politicos derives from Possevino's list of condemned authors, which Ribadeneyra repeats.

As Gracián makes apparent at the beginning of this lamentation, his targets are the bad princes who put their own political ends above religion, and even use religion as a political instrument:

> Principes Atheistas y sin Dios. Y estos se llaman los que son tan malos, que tienen a Dios en menos estima que a su estado: y hazen a sus Republicas vltimo fin, y a Dios y a las cosas diuinas medio para alcançar el fin de su felicidad, hazienda, reputacion, conseruacion o augmento de su Republica, y para conseguir este fin, cierran los ojos a todas las razones diuinas, y solamente se gouiernan por razon de estado, profesando la abominable doctrina de algunos que escriuen, que todo lo bueno se ha de postponer por alcançar sus pretensiones temporales; y esta razon de estado tienen por ley, y por fee.[10]

9 Ibid., 190–91.
10 Ibid., 187–88.

For Gracián, the challenge that Machiavelli and the other masters of reason of state present is that they cover up their evil doctrine with beautiful rhetoric: "es dificultoso descubrir las serpientes, escondidas debaxo de las yeruas y flores destos hereges, que van con tanta Rhetorica y artificio solapando su abominable doctrina debaxo de razones dulces y aparentes."[11] Here Gracián employs the trope of the snake hidden in the grass, which was very common in sixteenth-century Spanish lyrical poetry, in order to warn his readers, not of the dangers of earthly love, but of the diabolical designs of Machiavelli and his disciples.

In order to expose the poison of these snakes, Gracián discusses twelve virtues that good princes must have: "Para que mejor se entiendan, me parecio seria bien nombrar doze fuentes de donde mana el agua de la doctrina de vn buen Principe, que estos inficionan, y entosigan con su ponçoña. Estas se pueden llamar Razon, Fee, Consejo, Obseruancia, Rectitud, Culto diuino, Recato, Beneficiencia, Verdad, Religion, Zelo, y Paz."[12] Gracián illustrates each virtue with one example and one counter-example. Jesus Christ typifies reason, and the Antichrist, its opposite; Abraham is exemplary of faith, and the princes of Sodom, the lack thereof, etc. Thus, each chapter of this lamentation is organized around a dichotomy between one virtue and one vice, which is demonstrated by the contrary examples of one good prince and one bad one. Finally, each chapter contains the corresponding bad doctrine, always introduced by the phrase "Dize Machiauelo," also highlighted by marginal notes enumerating Machiavelli's "errores." The core of these phrases all derive from Possevino's and Ribadeneyra's summary of Gentillet's maxims. Nevertheless, Gracián adds his own additional glosses and examples which help him demonstrate his characterization of Machiavelli, but which in reality further distort Machiavelli's ideas.

In one example, Gracián's attribution to Machiavelli constitutes a gross anachronism that is not present in his authorities. It appears in his account of what Machiavelli "says" in opposition to his second virtue, faith:

> El mal Principe, o es infiel en su persona, o se descuyda en conseruar la verdadera fee en su Republica; Machiabelo dize, Que el Principe, no ha de professar otra fee, sino la que le estuuiere bien para gouernar su estado con prosperidad. Si entrare a gouernar Lutheranos (para ser acepto entre sus vassallos) mude la fee Romana en la heregia Lutherana, lo mismo si Caluinista &c. y lo segundo dize. Que por conseruar sus vassallos en paz, y tener prosperidad en su Reyno (aunque el viua como Christiano) permita libertad de conciencia, y dexe al que quisiere ser Lutherano, que oyga a la predica de Luthero, y al Caluinista que haga la cena de Caluino, &c. abriendo puerta en su Reyno, para qualquier secta que a el quisiere venir, sin

[11] Ibid., 191–92.

[12] Ibid., 192.

> castigar ni estoruar ningun herege (si con esta libertad augmenta su Repub. y hazienda) viuiendo cada qual como aquellos Principes de Sodoma, que ellos y sus moradores con libertad seguian la abominacion que les daua gusto.[13]

In contrast to the good prince, who only allows Catholicism in his kingdom, Gracián attributes to Machiavelli two "errors," diligently annotated in the margins as "2 Error de Machiauelo" and "3. Error."[14] First, Machiavelli says that the prince should profess whatever faith happens to be convenient for him to govern with prosperity; second, he should allow his subjects to profess whatever faith they wish, so long as they remain peaceful. These ideas derive from Gentillet's maxim 2.2, "Le prince doit soustenir ce qui est faux en la religion, pourveu que cela tourne en faveur d'icelle,"[15] where he criticizes Machiavelli's discussion in *Discourses* 1.12–14 of how the Romans used religion, focussing in particular on the false auguries used to motivate their soldiers before battle. In his introductory characterization of Machiavelli, Ribadeneyra shifts the emphasis from "that which is false in religion" to "abraçar qualquiera Religion por desatinada que sea."[16] Gracián takes the concept of "libertad de conciencia" from Ribadeneyra as well, who uses the same term in his discussion of how false reason of state (not necessarily Machiavelli himself) teaches the prince to allow "que cada uno siga la religion que quisiere."[17] Gracián applies these two ideas to the explicit example of how a prince should be able to convert from Catholicism to Lutheranism or Calvinism and to permit his subjects to do the same. Unlike his authorities, he is clearly either unaware or unconcerned with the fact that, chronologically speaking, it would have been impossible for Machiavelli to name these two institutions in the second decade of the sixteenth century, when he was writing the *Prince*.

Juan de Santa María

Juan de Santa María, the Franciscan royal chaplain to Philip III, confessor of the Infanta Margarita, and one of the leading opponents of the Duke of Lerma, published his *Tratado de republica y policia christiana* in Madrid in 1615, as an open challenge to Philip III's *valido*.[18] In his prologue, addressed to Philip III himself, Santa María declares that his intention was to provide his prince with "dotrinas breues, ciertas, y generales, que son de mas prouecho, comprehenden mas sujetos, y se pueden aplicar a los particulares, sacadas todas de los

13 Ibid., 198–99.
14 Ibid., 198.
15 Innocent Gentillet, *Anti-Machiavel*, ed. Edward Rathé (Geneva: Droz, 1968), 24.
16 Ribadeneyra, *Obras escogidas*, 455.
17 Ibid., 482.
18 Feros, *Kingship and Favoritism*, 236–38.

Politicos, la ley Natural, y hombres de Estado, y en nada contrarias a la ley Diuina, y religion Christiana, de antiguos Filosofos, y sabios varones, de Iurisperitos, y Legisladores."[19] In stark contrast to Jerónimo Gracián, Santa María considers the doctrines that he has borrowed from the *políticos* to be in no way contrary to divine law and the Christian religion. These brief doctrines are accompanied by historical examples of kings and emperors, which will help Philip achieve the end of all kings: "mantener en paz, y justicia los reynos."[20] By employing here the term *mantener*, Santa María establishes from the beginning of his treatise that he is engaging the reason-of-state tradition, whose aim is to teach kings how to conserve or maintain their states. He goes on to emphasize the practical nature of his doctrines: "no le digan que son Metafisicas, y cosas impracticables, o casi impossibles, que antes son muy conformes a nuestra possibilidad, y praticadas entre los passados, por sabios y prudentes Reyes, y en Reynos y Republicas de grande concierto, artificio, y policia, en materia de gouierno, y razon de Estado."[21] His doctrines, in fact, were put into real practice by prudent kings who were well versed in reason of state. By imitating these examples, in time Philip should be able to put these doctrines into practice himself, "si con efeto y resolucion lo quisiere, y se siruiere de que se execute lo que le pareciere bien destos aduertimientos."[22] Santa María urges Philip to take some time to study them, because "las materias de Estado, de justicia, y gouierno, y de cosas mayores, es la ciencia que merece su cuidado, y discurso, que lo demas como quiera passa, y quien quiera lo haze," reminding him that the king is the head of the "cuerpo mystico dela Republica,"[23] following the medieval tradition.

Santa María's chapter "*Que importa mucho a los Reyes ser amados, y queridos del pueblo*" at first glance seems to follow the traditional precept that good, Christian kings should choose to maintain their position through love rather than fear. Nevertheless, his opposition to the Duke of Lerma moves him to approach this question from a decidedly more practical point of view, as the opening lines of the chapter reveal: "Y porque es impossible contentar a todos, por las inclinaciones, no solo diferentes, mas aun contrarias, que tienen, es necessario por lo menos contentar a los mas."[24] In order to elaborate on this idea, he proceeds to divide kingdoms into two kinds of people: "ciudadanos, y gente plebeya, o plebe (digamos) que lo comprehende todo, y Grandes, y titulares,

19 Juan de Santa María, *Tratado de republica y policia christiana para reyes y principes y para los que en el gobierno tienen sus veces* (Madrid: Imprenta Real, 1615), n.p.
20 Ibid.
21 Ibid.
22 Ibid.
23 Ibid.
24 Ibid., 325.

que lo son, o aspiran a serlo."[25] The answer he offers and the reasoning behind it reveal a familiarity with Machiavelli's ideas regarding the plebs and the great in both the *Prince* 9, on civil principalities, as well as *Discourses* 1.5, on where it is better to place the guard of freedom, in the people or in the great. In the *Prince* 9, Machiavelli explains that when an individual becomes a prince by the will of the citizens, he does so "o con el favore del populo o con quello de' grandi. Perché in ogni città si truovono questi dua umori diversi: e nasce, da questo, che il populo desidera non essere comandato né oppresso da' grandi ed e' grandi desiderano comandare e opprimere el populo."[26] As Machiavelli goes on to explain, the prince who comes to power with the help of the people maintains his position more easily than the one who receives help from the great, because, among other reasons, "quello del populo è piú onesto fine che quello de' grandi, volendo questi opprimere e quello non essere oppresso."[27] As Santa María similarly puts it: "Serà discrecion, y prudencia procurar contentar a la plebe (especialmente quando el Principe comiença a reynar) en lo razonable, y honesto que pide."[28] Interestingly, Santa María here incorporates Machiavelli's general focus on the new prince, even though Philip III had already been king for seventeen years at the time of publication. A plausible explanation for this approach may be found in the fact that immediately after his coronation in 1598 Philip III effectively handed over government to the Duke of Lerma. By now, however, the king was beginning to show signs of more maturity, independence of thought and disappointment in the system of personal patronage that his *valido* had by then instituted. With this context in mind, Santa María's appropriation of Machiavelli's preference for the people may be seen as a suggestion to Philip that he break free from Lerma's web of family and friends, all grandees, to become more in touch with his own subjects.

At the end of *Discourses* 1.5, Machiavelli concludes that it is better to place the guard of freedom in the people, because they are less ambitious than the great:

> si disputò assai quale sia piú ambizioso, o quel che vuole mantenere o quel che vuole acquistare, perché facilmente l'uno e l'altro appetito può essere cagione di tomulti grandissimi. Pur nondimeno, il piú delle volte sono causati da chi possiede, perché la paura del perdere genera in loro le medesime voglie che sono in quegli che desiderano acquistare; perché non pare agli uomini possedere sicuramente quello che l'uomo ha, se non si acquista di nuovo dell'altro.[29]

25 Ibid.
26 Machiavelli, *Principe*, 63
27 Ibid., 64
28 Santa María, *Tratado de republica*, 325.
29 Machiavelli, *Discorsi*, 40.

Similarly, Santa María writes that the people "no puede dessear, ni pretender lo que tienen los mayores, y grandes señores de estado, que siempre aspiran a mas, y estan hazeçando por lo que imaginan que les faltan."[30] Machiavelli adds that the great more easily carry out their desires: "E di piú vi è che, possedendo molto, possono con maggiore potenza e maggiore moto fare alterazione."[31] Santa María also adds a similar idea: "y tanto mas les crece esta codicia, quanto en mejor lugar se veen, y mas se llegan a la possibilidad de esso que dessean."[32]

In Santa María's view, the best way for kings to gain "el fauor, y amor del pueblo,"[33] "este amor popular,"[34] is to have ministers who are well-loved: "porque no ay duda, y la experiencia lo enseña, que los ministros, y criados del Principe lo hazen amable, o aborrecible, y todos sus defetos, o virtudes paran en daño, o prouecho suyo."[35] Here, while Santa María subtly displaces blame from the figure of the monarch to that of the minister, the implication is nevertheless clear: if Philip is unwilling to give up the institution of the *valido* and dismiss the Duke of Lerma, who by this time had gained a notorious reputation for venality and greed, he himself also runs the risk of becoming an object of hatred for his subjects. As part of this strategy, Santa María significantly shifts the focus from the gaining of favor or love to the Machiavellian concept of the avoidance of hatred: "Y no hagan los Reyes poco caso desto, ni se lo coloreen con razones de estado, que el que vna vez comiença a ser aborrecido con mala opinion, le cargan todo lo bien, o mal hecho."[36] Interestingly, Santa María employs the term "reasons of state" to signify the excuses or rhetorical explanations kings might offer for not following the Machiavellian advice he is giving to his king, namely to avoid hatred, or in this case to detach himself from the hatred directed at his favorite, in order to maintain more securely his position of power.

With respect to mendacity, Santa María does not display any unique reading of Machiavelli, imitating instead the rhetorical maneuvering of his authority, Ribadeneyra. Like Ribadeneyra he writes that the king must always tell the truth. Santa María quickly sets up the *políticos* as the opposition against whom he is arguing:

> contra el presupuesto de los Hereges, que esta edad llama Politicos, que para justificar su policia, y gouierno tyranico, afirman que puede el Rey

30 Santa María, *Tratado de republica*, 327.
31 Machiavelli, *Discorsi*, 40–41.
32 Santa María, *Tratado de republica*, 327.
33 Ibid.
34 Ibid., 328.
35 Ibid.
36 Ibid.

> por razon de estado, si le estuuiere bien para conseruarle, simular, engañar, quebrar la palabra, y darla sin animo de cumplirla, siendo como es la fraude, simulacion, y engaño contra la verdad, que deue el hombre a su proximo, de qualquiera condicion que sea, y contra el derecho natural, que en todo lo que se trata pide verdad, y contra el diuino, que condena al que no la dize, y anda con engaños.[37]

Santa María follows Ribadeneyra's model of presenting the thought of Machiavelli's followers as the diabolical, tyrannical, even unnatural opposite of his own position. Nevertheless, like Ribadeneyra, Santa María follows this rhetorical and ideological introduction with a statement about an exception to this rule: "Puede empero el Christiano Rey, o su ministro callar, encubrir, no darse por entendido, de las cosas, y disimular con astucia lo que entendiere dellas, todo el tiempo que le pareciere necessario el secreto para la buena expedicion de lo que trata."[38] Santa María uses Machiavelli's vocabulary of necessity to justify some moral flexibility so that the Christian king and his ministers may accomplish their goals in any particular situation. Santa María continues the practice of differentiating dissimulation and simulation and condemning the latter: "pero no podrà fingir, engañar, simular, o dar a entender con el hecho, lo que no tiene allà en su pecho."[39] On the other hand, when it comes to the confession of his Christian faith, no exceptions may be made, even when his life depends on it: "Todo lo qual no ha lugar en lo que toca a la Fè, en que por derecho diuino tenemos obligacion, no solo de creer, sino de confessar con toda verdad, y senzillez lo que creemos, sin dar a entender con la menor palabra, ni el mas ligero ademan cosa en contrario, ni por vn momento de tiempo, aunque en ello se redimiesse la vida."[40] Finally, much like Ribadeneyra before him, Santa María concludes this discussion by differentiating his view from that of the *políticos*: "Con esto quedan aduertidos los Reyes, y ministros Christianos, de como podran vsar de dissimulacion, hasta donde, y en que tiempo, sin echar por la vereda de la propria vtilidad, por donde los Politicos los pretenden guiar."[41] Thus, just as in the case of Ribadeneyra, Santa María gives permission to his Christian prince to be flexible with his morals, as long as he does not become an egotistical, opportunistic *político*, a follower of Machiavelli.

Santa María dedicates the following chapter to demonstrating that, for several reasons, kings must keep their word. Following the tradition, he writes that the true reason of state consists of following God's precepts: "Considerese primero profundamente, lo que se dize, y promete, que vaya regulado con la ley

37 Ibid., 386–87.
38 Ibid., 388.
39 Ibid.
40 Ibid.
41 Ibid.

de Dios, y preceptos de la Iglesia, y despues infaliblemente se guarde, que en esto consiste la conseruacion, y aumento de los grandes Estados, y la verdadera razon de Estado, para ser los Reyes mas poderosos, mas ricos, mas estimados, y obedecidos."[42] If the king's goal is the conservation of his state, indeed the same goal as the *políticos*, then he must follow the true, Christian reason of state. Here, following the tradition begun by Ribadeneyra, Santa María argues that the false reason of state, espoused by the *políticos*, is not only contrary to Christian authorities, but even unnatural and bestial:

> Digan los Politicos lo que quisieren, y que es buen consejo, que el Principe para conseruar su estado haga contra la Fè, y Religion, y no guarde palabra, ni juramento, que yo digo, que tal consejo es iniquo, torpe, y bestial, contra la ley diuina, natural, y escrita, y contra toda la escuela de los Doctores sagrados, que afirman, que el principe ha de guardar su palabra, aunque no la jure, y mucho mas si la jurare.[43]

Even the *políticos* would have to admit this truth:

> Y sino, quitense la mascara los mismos Politicos, y hablen claro, los que los siguen, y diganme que sienten ellos de los Principes que no hazen caso de lo que prometen, y juran quando veen que por esso se les va de las manos el lance que tienen al ojo. No dudo, sino que lo tendran por muy necia razon de Estado: porque perderan luego todo el credito, y aun para engañar no quedaran de prouecho, pues en ningun tiempo seran creydos.[44]

By setting up a false reason of state, and directing his rhetorical question to a fictional group of *políticos* who follow its precepts, Santa María masterfully characterizes the king who does not keep his faith as not only un-Christian, but as an imbecile who does not realize that he is letting himself be manipulated by his councillors into doing something that even they would admit to be illogical.

Despite all of this rhetorical presentation, within this discussion readers find yet again a subtle reference to the allowable exceptions to the strict observance of "true" reason of state. Among his authorities who condemn lying Santa María cites San Isidro, who nevertheless offers two exceptions: "quando lo que se promete no se puede cumplir sin pecado. Y quando los negocios, o personas se mudan notablemente."[45] From this, Santa María concludes: "estando las cosas en el mismo estado por conueniencias de propria vtilidad, no se puede faltar en lo prometido, y querer defender lo contrario, es armar assechanças a la verdad

42 Ibid., 402.
43 Ibid., 400–1.
44 Ibid., 401.
45 Ibid., 399.

de la Fè, y a la Religion del juramento."[46] What is left simply implied is the contrary: when the circumstances do change, and/or when motivated not by personal gain but public utility, then it is permitted to go against one's word.

Fernando Alvia de Castro

Fernando Alvia de Castro, Inspector General of the Spanish Royal Army and Naval Forces in Portugal, published his *Verdadera razon de estado* in Lisbon in 1616, which is a good example of a work that, while demonstrating no unique reading of Machiavelli, nevertheless perpetuates the rhetorical operation, typical of the reason-of-state tradition, of attacking the straw figure of Machiavelli while still including Machiavellian discourse. In his dedicatory preface to Antonio de Zúñiga, Comendador de Ribera, a member of Philip III's Council of War and Captain General of Portugal, Alvia de Castro continues the tradition of distinguishing true and false reason of state, declaring, not surprisingly, that he will be dealing with the true kind:

> Podria tener alguna estimacion por el gusto, y commodidad de hallarse recogido en este ramillete pequeño las flores (a que comparo las acciones Catholicas, las virtudes morales) no solo olorosas, vistosas, y apazibles, mas las naturales, necessarias, y prouechosas, para acertarse Christiana, justa, y prudentemente en la verdadera razon de estado: quitadas las malas, ponçoñosas y nociuas (por tales reprueuo los hechos injustos, las demostraciones hypocritas) que los politicos, o con ignorancia, o con malicia mesclan en ella.[47]

Alvia de Castro repeats Jerónimo Gracián's metaphor, distinguishing those flowers, comparable to Catholic virtues, that are not only fragrant, beautiful and pleasing but also natural, necessary and useful, from those bad, poisonous and harmful ones that the *políticos* teach. While he treats "la materia de estado, del principe Christiano, deuoto, y temeroso de Dios,"[48] its opposite will also become known and condemned: "la falsa razon de estado, Politica, y Atheysta, que tanta fuerça tiene en Europa."[49] Alvia de Castro cites both Frachetta's and Ammirato's definitions of reason of state, correcting them according to his view that the end must be the common good. Frachetta errs when he "pone por vltimo fin, la commodidad del Principe, no deuiendolo ser, sino el efecto que procede de lo honesto de la razon, equidad, y justicia."[50] Following the medieval distinc-

46 Ibid.

47 Fernando Alvia de Castro, *Verdadera razon de estado* (Lisbon: Pedro Craesbeeck, 1616), 1.

48 Ibid.

49 Ibid.

50 Ibid., 5.

tion between king and tyrant, his authorities are Aristotle as well as Saint Thomas: "Aristoteles en diuersos lugares de la Politica y Ethica, dize a boca llena: que es tyrano aquel Principe, que solo procura su bien."[51]

In two chapters entitled "Verdadera difinicion Christiana de la materia de estado"[52] and "En que consiste la verdadera razon de estado Christiana,"[53] Alvia de Castro offers his own definition. Throughout, human prudence is combined with divine wisdom: "es, en el Principe Christiano y bueno, vn discurso sabio, vna disposicion, y execucion ajustada a la ley diuina, y razon natural, con que, quanto alcança el saber humano, se dispongan las cosas para conseguirse buenos successos, pero justos, tocantes al Principe y sus estados."[54] True, Christian reason of state is a faculty of human knowledge that is adjusted to divine law and natural reason. Similarly, prudence, which deals with human affairs, is not sufficient for the Christian prince, who must also learn true, divine wisdom, which is founded on the fear of God.[55] Therefore, Alvia de Castro concludes, "la verdadera razon y materia de estado, sancta, justa, limpia, y prudente del Principe Christiano, es el amor y temor de Dios, porque con esto y hazer de su parte lo que pueda, segura, parece, tendrà la prudencia, y ayuda suya, necessaria para bien gouernar."[56] Like Ribadeneyra before him, Alvia de Castro shifts the focus of the prince from this world, where the prince will do the best that his limited, earthly prudence will allow, to God, who always provides for those who are faithful to him.

After presenting his definition, he follows the reason-of-state tradition of contrasting it with the evil, false reason of state of

> algunos malos Politicos, y en particular el peruerso impio e ignorante Machiauelo … Dize pues, que de tal manera tenga el Principe Christiano las virtudes, que sepa y pueda mudarse, y hazer al contrario dellas; y que por conseruar su Reyno estará obligado a obrar contra la fee, caridad, humanidad, y religion, lo que le conuenga; como mas en particular refiere el Padre Ribadeneyra; y en substancia dispone y forja vn Principe hypocrita, falso, dissimulador, y fingido.[57]

Citing Ribadeneyra by name, Alvia de Castro draws from his authority the characterization of Machiavelli and his fictional followers as evil hypocrites. A marginal note even provides readers with a citation: "P. Ribadeneyra l.2. del

51 Ibid.
52 Ibid., 15.
53 Ibid., 17.
54 Ibid., 15.
55 Ibid., 17–18.
56 Ibid., 18.
57 Ibid., 22.

Princip. Christ. c 2.,"[58] which is exactly where he derived this description from. From this careful citation it is reasonable to conclude that Alvia de Castro did not in fact consult Machiavelli directly, but instead relied on his authority and simply reiterated Ribadeneyra's characterization of the evil Florentine. Alvia de Castro uses the same examples as Ribadeneyra. For instance, in both authors Ludovico Maria Sforza, Duke of Milan, is portrayed as a tyrant who was punished by God for using the false reason of state. Alvia even includes the same marginal citation found in Ribadeneyra's text, referring readers to Francesco Guicciardini's *History of Italy*, books 3 and 4.

Later on in his treatise, Alvia de Castro repeats the distinction that we have already seen between simulation (acting as if something is true when it is false) and dissimulation (keeping hidden something that is true), condemning the former and allowing the latter. Before setting out to distinguish between what is permissible and what is not, he reiterates that he is writing against "Machiauelo, y los demas sus sequaces" who believe that "conuienendole [*sic*] al Principe dissimular en las cosas de religion y virtudes, lo puede y deue hazer."[59] Even though this precept is so evidently false and evil that even the gentiles did not follow it, he will nevertheless go on to refute it, because it is "el punto, que mas guerra les parece nos hazen."[60] As this passage makes clear, Alvia de Castro continues the tradition of characterizing Machiavelli and his followers as evildoers who wage war with good, Christian princes.

Nevertheless, in order to justify dissimulation, Alvia de Castro appropriates Machiavellian necessity, which most likely he borrowed from his authority, Ribadeneyra: "La dissimulacion, como diffini ariba, es callar, y encubrir aquello, que es, como sino fuesse: y digo, que si la simulacion en la forma, que la dexo significada, es impia y peligrosa: la dissimulacion vsada bien, es justa, prudente, y necessaria."[61] Alvia de Castro immediately follows this justification, however, with the familiar admonition to his readers to tread carefully in this matter, citing the authority of Ribadeneyra as well as Juan Marquéz: "pero aduierto y pido con particular afecto; se aduierta y entienda, que si el Principe dissimulare contra la religion y virtudes, injusto serà, mucho se arrimarà a impio o tyrano: y assi en ello hallarà su daño y castigo: Dios se le embiará."[62] If the prince dissimulates in matters of religion, he will become an impious Machiavellian tyrant, and God will punish him accordingly.

58 Ibid.
59 Ibid., 46.
60 Ibid.
61 Ibid., 51.
62 Ibid.

Jerónimo de Zeballos

Jerónimo de Zeballos, Alderman of Toledo, dedicated his *Arte real para el buen gouierno de los reyes y principes y de sus vasallos* (Toledo, 1623) to his recently crowned king, Philip IV. He begins his treatise with two dedicatory prefaces: one addressed to the king himself, and one "Al excelentissimo señor don Gaspar de Guzman, Conde de Oliuares, Sumiller de Corps del Rey don Felipe Quarto nuestro señor, y de su Consejo de Estado, y Guerra, y su Cauallerizo mayor."[63] To the king, he declares that he wishes to form "vn viuo retrato, en que se miren los Reyes, y sus vassallos (para que cada vno cumpla con sus obligaciones)."[64] On the other hand he tells Olivares that "me puse muchas vezes a considerar, a que Principe con mas justo titulo, y con mas obligaciones de seruirle, pudiesse elegir por maestro, y protector deste Arte Real, por hazer mejor empleo del … y luego V. Excelencia ocupò mi memoria."[65] As Philip IV's favorite, Olivares will best take advantage of his treatise, evidently even more so than the king himself.

Zeballos wishes to teach Philip, who lacks experience, the art of governing: "desseoso que lo que V. Magestad no puede alcançar en sus tiernos años, por la falta de experiencia, se alcance, y facilite con sus documentos."[66] Zeballos reiterates Philip's lack of experience: "Y V. Magestad (Dios nos le guarde) estando en su edad de diez y siete años, falto de experiencia de las materias del gouierno, es fuerça que tenga necessidad deste arte de gouernar, que es vn conocimiento vniuersal."[67] Art and reason are mutually dependent: "Concluyo, señor, con que todo el gouierno politico que se exercitare con arte, estarà sugeto a la razon, y toda buena razon se alcançarà con arte."[68] For Philip's benefit, Zeballos will summarize the art of governing in a series of "documents": "Y con este presupuesto referirè a V. Magestad los principales documentos del gouierno politico, porque todos no se pueden comprehender en tan breue suma."[69]

Zeballos is another example of a writer who does not reveal any direct knowledge of Machiavelli's works, relying instead on the portrait of Machiavelli found in previous contributions to the reason-of-state tradition. For example, in Document 7, entitled "*Que conuiene a los Reyes, y Principes pedir, y tomar consejo en los negocios graues, y que no pueden yr contra el,*"[70] Zeballos attacks

63 Jerónimo de Zeballos, *Arte real para el buen gouierno de los reyes y principes y de sus vasallos, en el qual se refieren las obligaciones de cada vno, con los principales documentos para el buen gouierno* (Toledo: Diego Rodriguez, 1623), n.p.

64 Ibid.

65 Ibid.

66 Ibid., 18.

67 Ibid., 19.

68 Ibid.

69 Ibid.

70 Ibid., 45.

Machiavelli for advising that the prince only allow his advisors to express their opinions when he asks for them: "Pero esta opinion està tan reprouada como su autor Maquiabelo."[71] He then quotes this idea in Latin: "*Qui malè Principi suasit, vt expreto alieno consilio, suae ipsius prudentiae innitatur*,"[72] citing Damian Colerio, who condemns this opinion. As his prologue to both Philip IV and the Duke of Olivares makes clear, Zeballos, aware of his monarch's youth and inexperience, knows that he will need help from his favorite. Zeballos uses this situation to attack Machiavelli, establishing himself as a member of the anti-Machiavellian tradition.

Nevertheless, in Document 11, entitled "*Que no conuiene que los Reyes, y Principes hagan mercedes en perjuyzio de su real patrimonio, y que las hechas se bueluan a incorporar en el*,"[73] Zeballos incorporates the Machiavellian reconsideration of the princely virtues in order to advise both Philip IV and his favorite to rein in the abusive system of patronage that had been put in place by their predecessors. He begins by conceding that: "La liberalidad en los Reyes (como dize santo Thomas) es la virtud mas heroica que pueden tener."[74] However, this is true only when the goal is the "gloria de Dios, y prouecho de las almas, y bien vniuersal de los pueblos."[75] Like both Machiavelli and Botero before him, Zeballos declares that liberality is good only when the common good is taken into account. When liberality only benefits individuals, "resulta vna grande necesidad, que obliga muchas vezes a los Principes, a vsar de malos medios, para sacar dineros a los vassallos, de donde nace hazerse odiosos en su Republica."[76] Here, Zeballos attempts to reason with his king by using the Machiavellian rhetoric of the avoidance of hatred. Interestingly, while Philip IV did not heed this advice, spending lavishly on *mercedes* through the greater part of his reign, the idea of the avoidance of hatred does seems to have made an impression on him, since he was always reluctant to impose new taxes on his subjects, despite his growing debt.

In Document 19, "*Adonde se aduierte a los Reyes el poder que tienen de justicia en sus vassallos, en casos de publica necessidad*,"[77] Zeballos takes advantage of Machiavellian necessity to allow for moral flexibility in the person of the king. Interestingly, Zeballos allows behavior that he himself labels as tyrannical, in case of necessity: "Todo este capitulo se entiende de la potencia de vn Rey tyrano, y que se quiere hazer señor de toda la hazienda de sus vassallos, lo qual no le es permitido, sino es que tuuiere necessidad, para causas

71 Ibid.
72 Ibid.
73 Ibid., 75.
74 Ibid.
75 Ibid.
76 Ibid.
77 Ibid., 105.

publicas de las personas, y vidas de sus subditos; entonces bien puede vsar de aquella amplia potestad, que es vna soberania justa, hipotecada a su cetro y corona."[78] In Machiavellian fashion, Zeballos confuses the behaviors traditionally divided between the figures of the tyrant and the prince, when necessity and the common good call for these measures. As he repeats throughout this section, necessity is the justification for practices that traditionally had been considered tyrannical. Later, in Document 21, Zeballos expands the flexibility permitted by necessity even further:

> y es de tanta fuerça la necessidad publica, que ni los Reyes pueden dexar de socorrer a sus subditos, conseruandolos en paz, y justicia, ni los vassallos pueden dexar de socorrer a su Rey con estipendios, y millones, aunque el patrimonio real le huuiesse disipado, y gastado en cosas superfluas, y en donaciones excesiuas, sacadas de su real hazienda.[79]

Even if the king has imprudently spent his patrimony on individuals, against Zeballos's own advice, necessity allows kings to demand that their subjects pay taxes, and necessity obliges them to do so:

> Y assi por estas razones, es cosa euidente que tan obligados estan los vassallos a remediar la necessidad de su reyno, que le sobreuino por excessos, y gastos superfluos, como la que le sucedio por natural disposicion, y accidentes del tiempo (que nunca tiene constancia) porque de otra suerte vendria todo el edificio al suelo, en daño vniuersal de la Republica.[80]

The necessity of the kingdom as a whole, it appears, outweighs that of its parts. Nevertheless, this proposition does not prevent Zeballos from giving more weight to one of its parts in particular, namely the head of the political body: "Y quando se trata de la conseruacion de la cabeça, todo lo demas es acessorio; cortese el pie, y la mano, y viua la cabeça: muera el vassallo (que es miembro) y viua el Rey: derribense los arrabales, y fortalezcase la ciudad, porque en lo vno ay causa particular, y en lo otro vniuersal, y publica, a que todos deuemos acudir."[81] In the end, for Zeballos, necessity justifies the sacrifice of the subjects for the "conservation" of the king. Just like in Machiavelli, the pursuit of the common good justifies the moral flexibility necessary in order for the king to conserve his state.

Zeballos begins his consideration of truthfulness with the traditional precept that a king, in imitation of God, must always keep his word: "Sabida cosa es en las diuinas, y humanas letras, la obligacion que tiene vn Principe Christiano de

78 Ibid., 106.
79 Ibid., 116.
80 Ibid., 117.
81 Ibid., 117.

cumplir su fè, y palabra, aunque la aya dado a vn enemigo; porque los Reyes siempre han de ser imitadores de Dios, que cumple sus promesas."[82] Nevertheless, the title of the document already announces the flexibility of this rule: "*Que conuiene que los Reyes guarden su fe, y palabra, quando de su obseruancia no ha de resultar ruina de su reyno, porque si la huuiere, no les obliga.*"[83] Sure enough, after stating the traditional precept, Zeballos practically dismisses it as not pertaining to the theme of this document: "Pero el Documento propuesto no depende desta resolucion, sino de la question ventilada en materia de razon Christiana de estado: si concurriendo la palabra real de vna parte, y la vtilidad publica de otra, se ha de atender mas al contrato, y palabra real, que a la conseruacion de su Republica, y a su quieto y pazifico estado."[84] On the one hand, if the king's promise agrees with the conservation of his state, then he should keep it, "conforme a buena razon de estado, y justicia."[85] On the other, citing the authority of Cicero and Aristotle, Zeballos responds to this question clearly: "que concurriendo de vna parte la palabra real, y de la otra, la vtilidad, y conseruacion de su Republica, que se ha de resoluer lo que fuere mas conuiniente para su conseruacion, y a esto se encamina el fin de todo el gouierno."[86] To make his opinion even more clear, he compares the king to a doctor:

> assi aunque el Medico dè su fè y palabra al enfermo, que no le sangrarà, o purgarà, en llegando la necessidad, no ay que reparar en las palabras, antes para conseguir la salud se han de aplicar todas las medicinas necessarias, variandolas, y mudandolas; y las mismas medicinas que al principio no se recetaron se puede al fin vsar de ellas. Esto mismo ha de hazer el que està elegido por Medico de la salud de la Republica, que todo su fin ha de yr enderezado a su vtilidad, y perpetuidad.[87]

In the end, necessity justifies moral flexibility when the king's aim is the common good of his kingdom.

Pedro Barbosa Homem

The full title of Pedro Barbosa Homem's treatise reveals that he is writing primarily against Machiavelli: "*Discursos de la iuridica, y verdadera razon de estado formados sobre la vida, y acciones del Rey don Iuan el II. de buena memoria, Rey de Portugal, llamado vulgarmente el Principe Perfecto. CONTRA MACHAVELO, Y bodino, y los demas politicos de nuestros tiempos, sus sequazes.*"

82 Ibid., 119.
83 Ibid.
84 Ibid.
85 Ibid., 119–20.
86 Ibid., 119.
87 Ibid., 120.

In his dedicatory preface to Philip IV, he declares that the purpose of his treatise is to show the world that: "sola la Christiana razon de Estado, que V.M.sigue: y de cuya sciencia, la Catolica, y Real casa de V.M. es, y fue siempre en el mundo la principal, escuela, y aula es la verdadera, y segura regla, no sola para la espiritual, y eterna salud; mas para la temporal, y puramente humana conseruacion."[88] Following the reason-of-state tradition, Barbosa Homem claims that it is necessary for the king to follow the Christian reason of state not only to save his soul in the next life, but also to conserve his state in this world.

Barbosa Homem begins his treatise by defining reason of state:

> Sea el primer presuppuesto, que la razon de Estado en commun, su [*sic*] puede diffinir que es vna doctrina especial, que por medio de varias reglas haze diestro a vn Principe o para mantener en su propria persona los Estados que possee, o para conseruar en los mismos Estados la forma, y grandeza original que tienen, o para con nueuos augmentos illustrar, o acrecentar la antigua massa de que ellos se forman.[89]

In this definition, the rules of reason of state allow the king to do three things. First, he will be able to maintain his person in the position of power in which he finds himself. Second and third, the king will be able to maintain and/or augment his possessions. Like Zeballos before him, Barbosa Homem's conception of reason of state is more than usually focussed on the person of the monarch.

Barbosa Homem provides a short history of the terms *político* and *razón de estado*. He explains that *político* was not always a derogatory word; recently, however, it has taken on that attribute because of "vna secta de hombres, o ya hereges, o a lo menos nada buenos Christianos: que haziendo particular sciencia, y escuela de la humana policia: vinieron a cobrar por ello titulo de politicos: en señal no de las policias que enseñaron, mas de las policias que deprabaron."[90] As such, today the *políticos* who follow reason of state are known as heretics or atheists: "Y no solamente ya las policias, y los politicos suenan por la dicha razon, oy en mala parte: mas aun el proprio vocablo de razon de Estado: a quien muchos Autores ya simplemente llaman abuso, o heregia, o ateismo."[91] For this reason, authors such as Juan de Santa María have recently seen fit to speak of two different kinds of reason of state in order to differentiate their Christian version from the false reason of state of Machiavelli and Bodin:

> Y para que este vocablo, segun la comun inteligencia destos tiempos, no brote de si aquel veneno, es forçoso adulçarlo, o corregirlo con el antidoto

88 Pedro Barbosa Homem, *Discursos de la iuridica, y verdadera razon de estado* (Coimbra, Portugal: Nicolao Caruallo, n.d.), n.p.

89 Ibid., 1.

90 Ibid., 2.

91 Ibid., 3.

> que en nuestro titulo le applicamos, diziendo, razon de Estado verdadera, o razon de Estado Catholica, y Christiana; como tambien el reberendo, y Religiosissimo padre fr. Iuan de santa Maria lo hizo en el suyo, llamandole, Policia Christiana, para que de otro modo no pareciesse que trataua de la razon de Estado, o Policia, aguisa de Machiauelo, o Bodino, cabeças de la venenosa, y falsa: como adelante meior se verá.[92]

Barbosa Homem repeats the metaphor of poison, found in both Gracián and Alvia de Castro's earlier contributions to the anti-Machiavellian tradition, to describe Machiavelli's false reason of state.

For Barbosa Homem, reason of state was created for princes with smaller states who were worried about being overwhelmed by their more powerful neighbors. In this short history of the rise of reason of state, Barbosa Homem paints a typical portrait of Machiavelli. First, he follows the tradition of characterizing Machiavelli and his followers as a school:

> se han descubierto en el mundo (como algunas Indias nueuas) de pocos años acá, vnas escuelas de ciencia, ó arte, a que vnos llaman dotrina politica: otros razon de Estado: assi como politicos, y Estadistas à los professores de sus preceptos. Por autor principal (ó bien copilador de la metodo desta ciencia) nombra el vulgo à Machauelo Florentino, por grande ilustrador de sus reglas à Bodino Frances.[93]

The principal method that this school teaches the less powerful princes is *astucia*, which they may use to defeat their more powerful enemies easily: "si desnudandose el tal Principe de qualesquiera consideraciones diuinas, y humanas, en vna sola cosa pusiere la mira (para que aquesta en todo, y por todo le sirua de vltimo, y preciso fin de sus acciones) es a saber la pura, y vnica conseruacion de su estado."[94] Barbosa Homem continues this portrait with the common medical metaphor: "Esta es la suma de los discursos de Machauelo, sobre este punto. Y este en efeto el salutifero remedio, que aquel grauisimo fisico de Estados aconseja à vn Principe, à quien, ni aun con esso dexa de llamar Christiano, assi como, ni à si mismo niega esse titulo, quando esparse por el mundo semejantes recetas."[95] By ironically calling Machiavelli a "very grave doctor of states" who provides princes with this "healthy remedy" and "similar prescriptions," Barbosa Homem anticipates his attack, using the popular figure of the *matasanos*: "Vease aora si huuo algun dia homicida por oficio, que tales yeruas buscasse para matar, como este halló para curar."[96]

92 Ibid.
93 Ibid., 244.
94 Ibid., 245.
95 Ibid.
96 Ibid.

If Machiavelli were to claim that he was addressing tyrants, it would be acceptable; but to call his princes, along with himself, Christian, is going too far: "Y si el en esta dotrina protestara luego, que solo á Principes infieles, y aun entre estos à los puros tyranos, la dirigia, pudiera passar; pero, que proceda Machauelo, tanto adelante, que esto, que tan contra Christo enseña, quiera, que sea dotrina para Christianos: esso ya passa de error, y es atreuimiento intolerable."[97] Here Barbosa Homem touches on an issue that had been on the minds of the earliest readers of Machiavelli, who compared him to Aristotle: indeed Machiavelli did mix the methods of the tyrant with those of the good king, which had been kept carefully separate by medieval writers. Barbosa Homem concludes this portrait by pointing out how many writers have refuted this "impio Ateista" point by point; however, he will abstain from doing so, because "el hazer caso dellas, para responderlas metodicamente, y muy de proposito: es en cierta manera darles brio, y autoridad: suponiendo, que á lo menos merecieron ser disputadas, y respondidas."[98] Instead, he is of the opinion that the best way of dealing with Machiavelli and similar writers is to throw both them and their books into a bonfire: "Y seria yo siempre de voto, que en semejantes puntos, dexados del todo los argumentos, el negocio se tomasse luego, con las personas de los argumentantes, preuiniendoles tan á tiempo; que si el primer vomito de sus heregias, fuesse dende alguna catedra, ó libro: el segundo, nunca ya mas pudiesse ser, sino de en medio de vna hogera."[99] In this way, Barbosa Homem positions himself within the authoritative institution of the Inquisition, agreeing not only with its condemnation of Machiavelli, but with its methods as well.

Barbosa Homem explains that many virtues contribute to the conservation of the king's state. Nevertheless, justice is the most important: "siendo la razon desso lo mucho que Dios suele darse por obligado a defender siempre las Republicas en que vee, que con algun particular cuydado se exercita esta virtud."[100] Here Barbosa Homem follows the reason-of-state tradition of attributing to God the ultimate power to decide the fate of the king's state in this world, and he goes on to claim that the best way for the prince to preserve his state is to follow God's precepts and trust in him: "El primero antidoto pues (que la experiencia por infinitos exemplos palpables, ha mostrado valer mas solo, que todos los otros juntos) es el que depende de saber vn Principe, bien negociar con Dios."[101] In this way Barbosa Homem characterizes the relationship between the good, Christian prince and God as a business deal or a contract: if the prince follows God's divine laws, he will allow him to conserve his state.

97 Ibid.
98 Ibid.
99 Ibid., 245–46.
100 Ibid., 54.
101 Ibid., 247.

After setting up don Nuño Álvarez as an example of bravery in a captain, Barbosa Homem attacks Machiavelli:

> la peruersa impiedad, ô por mejor dezir insania heretica de Machauelo, y sus sequazes; que no sin alguna Luceferina influencia, se atreuieron á dezir, y escriuir, que la Religion Christiana, el temor de Dios, y deuocion, auian en gran parte debilitado los animos, y enflaquecido el valor de los naturales de las naciones de Europa: y que desto se auia seguido, quedar el mundo dado, como á saco, à otras naciones desalmadas, que vsando solamente de las fuerças, y medios humanos, sin darseles algo por las reglas diuinas, acometian las empressas, como, quando, y por los modos que bien les venian.[102]

Infinite examples show the contrary: "en que Dios N.Señor, practicando el titulo, que el para si ha tomado de Dios de los exercitos, mostró assistir con particular prouidencia á las batallas, dando, y quitando las vitorias, casi con visible mano."[103] It is important to notice that Barbosa Homem explains that God never intended for his religion to make men weak. This does not contradict what Machiavelli says: that the Christian religion has been interpreted poorly by weak and lazy men. Instead, Barbosa Homem is working with the anti-Machiavellian mischaracterization of Machiavelli's thoughts on the Christian religion.

Following the reason-of-state tradition, Barbosa Homem declares that: "en la vnidad, y pureza de Religion Christiana, consiste el mas apropiado, y eficaz medio de Estado, para sustentar pacifica, y libre de inquietudes, y temores, à vna Republica."[104] On the contrary, the diversity of religion causes the destruction of "todos aquellos Reynos, y Prouincias, en que mas á los Euangelios de Machauelo, y Bodino, y á otros desta Massa, quisieron creer los Principes, que no al de Christo, verdadero Rey de los Reyes, y verdadero Señor, dispensador de los Estados."[105] Machiavelli, along with Bodin, is presented as the leader of a religious sect that is contrary to Christianity. False reason of state is practiced by any kingdom that does not strictly enforce Catholicism.

Nevertheless, Barbosa Homem does turn to the question of what human means a prince may use, "en licita, y Christiana razon de Estado,"[106] in order to deal with his more powerful neighbors. Agreeing tacitly with Machiavelli, Barbosa Homem's answer is that the prince must put the common good above all other considerations:

> el primero, y principal medio de todos, consiste en vna determinacion, y presupuesto heroyco; que el Principe deue hazer consigo mismo, de assi traer

102 Ibid., 89–90.
103 Ibid., 90.
104 Ibid., 241.
105 Ibid.
106 Ibid., 253.

> en todo, y por todo, puestos los ojos en el bien comun, de su Republica, y en la eficaz conseruacion della, que en ninguna materia humana, se acuerde mas de otra cosa, que de aquesta: y para esso, en lo que toca à ella, tan de veras se desnude de todos los humanos, y personales afetos, ó passiones, que à los hombres suelen sacar de sus racionales propositos.[107]

In this way, Barbosa Homem agrees with Machiavelli's placement of the common good above all other personal concerns for leaders who desire to conserve their states.

In an interesting chapter on "Medios humanos,"[108] Barbosa Homem declares that in fact he agrees with Machiavelli that princes should not only trust in divine providence, but should use "humana prudencia y licita astucia" as well:

> Y assi en lo que toca a la aprobacion de los humanos medios, en comun, y en lo que es ajuntar el diuino concurso, lo que el hombre puede hazer de su parte; no contradigo yo a Machiauelo; solo en los particulares desto, le contradigo. El con su acostumbrada largueza de consciencia, le permite al Principe Christiano, medios Turquescos: yo teniendo delante de los ojos, la limitacion Catholica, al Principe Christiano, no se conceder medios, que no sean Christianos; y en esto consiste nuestra contienda.[109]

He disagrees with Machiavelli not in general, but on the particulars: the Christian prince should limit himself to using Christian means. As we have seen, this is a rhetorical distinction, not a real one: Barbosa Homem approves of the same means using the same justifications. The only difference is that Barbosa Homem calls them Christian, thereby making them acceptable for his Christian prince.

When Barbosa Homem begins to treat the subject of lying, he mentions that Machiavelli says that "para reynar bien, no se pueden escusar los vicios."[110] Following this he continues the tradition of portraying Machiavelli as one of the leading heretics:

> Monstruosidades son estas, bien dignas, que en el Real de Lutero (despues de las esquadras de Caluino, Zuinglio, Carolstadio, y otros, que ocuparon las batallas de en medio) viniessen ellas ocupando la retaguardia, con vn tan buen Capitan, como Machauelo, que en la sustancia es vna misma cosa, con su General, y Comilitones: y solo diferente, en que los assaltos de aquellos, fueron al descubierto, y aun por esso no tanto para temer: y los deste, tanto mas perniciosos, quanto mas encubiertos, y dissimulados.[111]

107 Ibid., 253.
108 Ibid., 297.
109 Ibid.
110 Ibid., 264.
111 Ibid.

Here Machiavelli is portrayed anachronistically as a military captain, the rear-guard of the heretics of Luther's army. Machiavelli is even worse then the rest, however, because his corruption is less easy to perceive.

Barbosa Homem divides *mentira* into two kinds, by words or by acts. Lying by words is further divided into three: "vna se llama yocosa: otra oficiosa: otra perniciosa."[112] The first is not relevant to reasons of state. The second, defined as "quando la mentira no solo no haze daño à nayde, mas della se sigue alguna vtilidad al que la dize, ó à otro,"[113] is considered a venial sin for all individuals. The third, defined as "quando con daño considerable, ageno, ó propio, se dize la mentira,"[114] is condemned as a mortal sin. This division allows Barbosa Homem to give the Christian prince considerable leeway in the form of the second kind of lying:

> como no es mas, que venial, si á caso el Principe cayesse en ella por alguna razon de Estado, podriamos dezir, que assi como antes de auerla dicho, seria imperfecion de conciencia aconsejarsela, assi despues seria dureza, y austeridad, el mucho reprehenderla; pues por esso se llama culpa venial, para que luego se le dé la venia: y aun el mismo acto casi la trae consigo: como se ve del nombre.[115]

While it would be unscrupulous to advise the prince to lie for some utility, the very name *venial* implies that the prince will be forgiven if he does so. On the other hand, *mentira perniciosa* is not only illicit, like *mentira oficiosa*, but entirely unacceptable in practice for reasons of state: "Y assi por consequencia indubitable, no solo seria siempre, y en todo caso ilicita, como la oficiosa; mas del todo inhabil, y incapaz, para della poder formarse algun acomodado medio de razon de Estado, por mas que impia, y insensatamente ladren en esto Machauelo, y sus sequazes."[116] In this way, Barbosa Homem makes lying acceptable, as long as the prince lies for some benefit, not only for the common good but also for himself, as his definition of *mentira oficiosa* allows. Machiavelli and his followers are characterized as dogs who bark whatever Barbosa Homem and the other reason-of-state writers believe to be the opposite of what the good king should do.

As is the norm in the reason-of-state tradition, for Barbosa Homem also the reason the good, Christian king should not commit *mentira perniciosa* is because it goes against God, whose divine providence is the ultimate arbiter of the conservation of his state: "à todos los actos de general gouierno de su

112 Ibid.
113 Ibid.
114 Ibid., 264–65.
115 Ibid., 265.
116 Ibid.

Estado, y particularmente â los tocantes á la conseruacion del, le está assistiendo de continuo la diuina prouidencia."[117] Barbosa Homem concludes this discussion by reminding his readers that while both *mentira oficiosa* and *mentira perniciosa* should be considered illicit, the former is in reality allowable for reasons of state:

> De suerte, que en lo que toca á la mentira de palabra, la resolucion es, que las dos especies della, oficiosa, y perniciosa, nunca al Principe por caso alguno le serian licitas: y si la oficiosa en algun caso podria no le ser tan vituperada: ninguno aurá nunca en que la perniciosa, no solo no le sea ilicita; mas aun por la diuina prouidencia, muy punible.[118]

By declaring that *mentira perniciosa* is punishable by divine providence, Barbosa Homem implies by omission that *mentira oficiosa* is not.

Barbosa Homem then proceeds to distinguish between *mentira* and *engaño*: "engañar sin mentir, quando con palabras equiuocas, ambiguas, o amphibologicas, diziendose en la realidad vna cosa, se haze por la superficie dellas entender otra."[119] Barbosa Homem divides *engaño* into two kinds, good and bad: "el malo se llama propriamente fraude: el bueno se puede llamar virtuosa astucia."[120] Barbosa Homem concludes that while lying is illicit (although allowable, as we have seen), *engaño* is licit:

> con ser verdad, que nunca al Principe en verdadera razon de Estado, le seria licito el mentir, se pueden todauia dar casos, en que licitamente pueda engañar. Lo qual el, no solo podrà hazer por obra (en que ay menos duda, como adelante lo veremos) mas aun verbalmente, vsando de algun arteficio de equiuocacion, ambiguidad, ó amphibologia de palabras: como ya en diuersas ocasiones, lo practicaron muchos.[121]

Barbosa Homem clarifies further that *engaño* is not always licit, but only when the one who is tricked is unjust: "la circunstancia precisa, que para justificarlo, siempre deue concurrir es, que de parte del engañado, sea en aquella materia injusto el proceder."[122] In this way, Barbosa Homem allows his Christian prince to trick his enemies, just as long as he considers them to be unjust.

Unlike most reason-of-state writers, Barbosa Homem says that simulation, "que consiste toda en el arteficio, con que siendo vna la cosa, que se haze, se

117 Ibid.
118 Ibid., 266.
119 Ibid.
120 Ibid.
121 Ibid.
122 Ibid., 267.

muestra à la vista, ô al oido, y ser otra diferente,"[123] is licit. The best example is God himself: "y por lo que toca à exemplos, ninguno ay, ni pudo auer, que mejor probasse la bondad, y aun la necessidad deste genero de engaño bueno, que el que suele traerse de la inefable simulacion con que el propio Dios debaxo de la forma de pecador, que mostraua á la vista, encubrio vn tiempo la realidad de su diuina essencia."[124] Therefore, simulation is licit for reasons of state: "por indubitable conclusion podremos poner en este lugar, que del se puede seruir el Principe por razon de Estado, en qualquiera materia tocante á su conseruacion, y en las demas, siendo el negocio tal, que ni la naturaleza del, ni los medios, ni el fin, repugnen á la justicia."[125]

Barbosa Homem declares that the only exception to this rule is that the Catholic king may not act like a heretic.[126] Nevertheless, the "Simulacion de virtud, o santidad"[127] may be justified for reasons of state, and in order to demonstrate this, Barbosa Homem borrows from *Discourses* 1.11, where Machiavelli offers the example of the Roman emperor Numa, who pretended to communicate with a nymph in order to give himself divine authority. Barbosa Homem approves of the same example for the same reasons:

> Digo, que de vna semejante a esta vsó en tiempo antigo vn famoso Estadista gentil, que fue Numa Pompilio Rey de Romanos. El qual para facilmente hazer creer, y acetar, por buenas las traças de gouierno, que proponia a su Republica, simulaua tener particulares congressos, con la diosa Egeria; y alçandose desso vna fama, que della recebia el, los consejos que comunicaua al pueblo Romano; fomentaua Numa este general engaño, de manera que sus palabras, eran creidas, y respetadas, no ya como humanas, mas como diuinas. Y dello en razon de Estado, sacaua grandes vtilidades; porque siendo este Rey, como fue de suyo prudentissimo, y estando la dificuldad, solo en la dureça, con que aquel pueblo, aun entonces barbaro, se acomodaua a la policia, que Numa en el yua introduciendo; esta dificuldad se allanaua con la astucia, con que el hazia creer la diuinidad de sus consejos, y despues los efetos eran todos por la mayor parte buenos, porque en la realidad los hazia ser tales, la gran prudencia, y saber de Numa.[128]

If this is to be taken as a good example, the implication is that the Catholic prince also may simulate holiness for reasons of state.

123 Ibid., 268.
124 Ibid.
125 Ibid., 269.
126 Ibid., 272–74.
127 Ibid., 274.
128 Ibid.

As applied to "Christiana razon de Estado"[129] Barbosa Homem divides this kind of trickery into two kinds: first, when someone does not do anything in particular, but instead takes advantage of the misjudgment of others; second, "quando el simulante, realmente haze aquellas obras, con fin, y direcion, para que dellas se collija aquel engaño: en los quales terminos, se comete propriamente el vicio de la hypocresia."[130] The former is not only allowed but praised: "ninguna duda tengo que serà licita, y guallarda la simulacion."[131] Interestingly, the "vice of hypocrisy" is not condemned outright, but is also divided into different kinds:

> pero en esta ay diuersos grados; porque si los bienes se simulan para con ellos acreditar, y encubrir algunas culpas graues, que a sombras de aquella apariencia, a caso se cometen, o quieren cometer; es mortal crimen; si solamente se simulan a fin solo de alcançar vna vana nombradia de bueno, sin serlo, es solo venial. Y si ni se simulan por acreditar mortales culpas, ni por conseguir aquella vana fama; mas por occasionar alguna licita, y verdadera vtilidad (como en razon de Estado, se pueden dar muchas) a mi ver (aunque se que lo repugnan muchos) ni mortal, ni venial culpa seria.[132]

Here, by dividing hypocrisy into different categories according to the intention of the simulator, Barbosa Homem goes from mortal sin, to venial sin, as he did before when discussing lying, to no sin at all, thereby making hypocrisy acceptable for the Christian prince, just so long as he uses it for some "true utility," for reasons of state. To conclude, Barbosa Homem anticipates the objection that some have brought up by saying: "que no se han de hazer males, para que vengan bienes."[133] Barbosa Homem considers this to be false: "pues lo primero que negamos, es dezir, que aquella simulacion de bienes, hecha solo por la obra, con bueno, y vtil fin, sea mala: porque antes es vna buena astucia en todo, y por todo justificada con su fin bueno, y solicita materia y esto es lo que pienso."[134] Here, Barbosa Homem basically puts forth the opinion that the ends justify the means.

Juan Blázquez Mayoralgo

Juan Blázquez Mayoralgo, Contador of Veracruz, Mexico, dedicated his *Perfecta raçon de estado* to Philip IV. Published in Mexico City by Francisco Robledo in 1646, and approved by the Viceroy of New Spain, the Count of Salvatierra, its full title reads: *Perfecta raçon de estado. Deducida de los hechos de el señor*

129 Ibid., 275.
130 Ibid.
131 Ibid.
132 Ibid.
133 Ibid.
134 Ibid.

rey don Fernando el Catholico, Quinto de este nombre en Castilla, y Segundo en Aragon, contra los politicos atheistas. In his dedication, Blázquez Mayoralgo's definition of reason of state is traditional: "la prudencia para gouernar, y ampliar los Reynos, y conseruar la Corona."[135] Blázquez Mayoralgo clarifies that reason of state must not go against Catholicism, in contrast to the *políticos* and especially "su Capitan Machiauello," whose "preceptos barbaros" he goes on to enumerate, following the same list of Possevino and Ribadeneyra:

> que todas las cosas penden del hado y la fortuna: que el Principe debe fingir la Religion, y no ser Religioso; atendiendo siempre a la vtilidad propria, y a lo soberano del Imperio: que a las Republicas se a de conceder la Religion â arbitrio suyo para tener voluntarios los subditos: que la Religion Christiana enflaquece la virtud y el animo: que el vltimo fin de las Republicas es su misma conseruacion: que en el Principe no son forçosas las verdaderas virtudes para tenerlas, pues vasta para la raçon de estado que sepa fingirlas: que puede ir contra la fee jurada; negar lo piadoso; y apartarse de lo humano, para perpetuar su estado; porque no sabe Reynar quien no sabe disimular.[136]

Blázquez Mayoralgo then follows the tradition of characterizing the *políticos* as a religious sect, opposed to Catholicism: "leyes, que establecio la tirania con engaño, para disculpar en las ofensas la malicia, de los que debiendo confesar la verdadera fe por conocimiento, siguen la doctrina falsa por emulacion, conuertidos en etnicos adorando idolos y dejando la verdad para llamarse Politicos."[137] What the *políticos* call their science is misused by tyrants; on the other hand, Catholicism and its doctors teach Christian prudence and law: "siendo cierto que lo que ellos introducen por ciencia para gobernar con tirania, es lo que los sagrados Doctores hazen ley para regir con prudencia; y esta no se deduce de los caminos violentos que ellos atribuyen a la conseruacion, sino de las disposiciones que se encaminan a lo Catholico."[138] Interestingly, this last phrase seems to imply that what distinguishes tyranny from Catholic prudence is not the means but the ends: what the *políticos* teach tyrants is the same as what the doctors teach kings; the only difference is that the latter seek "Catholic" ends.

Ferdinand the Catholic was the first to make reason of state conform to Catholicism: "porque Cornelio Tacito Padre de los Politicos, escribiò como Ientil, enseñanças para perpetuar honores, pero no verdades en todo para afirmar merecimientos; siendo doctrina asentada, que lo mas dificultoso con que se

135 Juan Blázquez Mayoralgo, *Perfecta raçon de estado. Deducida de los hechos de el señor rey don Fernando el Catholico Quinto de este nombre en Castilla, y Segundo en Aragon. Contra los politicos atheistas* (Mexico City: Francisco Robledo, 1646), n.p.

136 Ibid.

137 Ibid.

138 Ibid.

conserua el Principado, es lo mas facil con que se introduce la tirania."[139] Again, there seems to be a fine line between tyranny and true Christian reason of state. Tacitus wrote about the conservation of state, the "honors" of government, while true reason of state teaches the Christian prince not only to conserve his state, but to deserve or be worthy of his position of power as well.

Blázquez Mayoralgo declares that he is writing against those who have said that Ferdinand could not have succeeded in his enterprises the way he did: "sin animar las acciones con los medios violentos que ofrecio la necessidad, y con el arte que introduxo en las discordias la ocasion."[140] In other words, some claim that Ferdinand used Machiavellian methods:

> enseñados de el impio Machiauelo que se arrojò a escribir que actualmente (como se a dicho) no es necessario al Principe ser Religioso, y que basta que lo parezca porque es imposible que exercite las verdaderas virtudes si ha de conseruar la grandeça de el estado, donde es forçoso violar la fee, negar la piedad, y oluidar la Religion, sujeto a los accidentes de la fortuna: Siendo bueno quando puede, y malo quando la necesidad le obliga.[141]

What they do not consider, Blázquez Mayoralgo objects, is that if we examine all of his actions, we will inevitably arrive at the conclusion that Ferdinand acted as a true Catholic: "pues de sus mismos hechos se prueba, que en la disposicion de los medios, obrò como Catholico, y en la fortuna de las armas executò como soldado, formando niuel, a los Reyes para la extension de la Corona, y a los gouiernos, para la conseruacion de las Prouincias."[142] Blázquez Mayoralgo begins with the premise that Ferdinand must have been a true Catholic prince, so that his life may be considered worthy of imitation by his descendants.

The rest of the book is structured around a narration of key political events in Ferdinand's life. The historical events, the actions and words of Ferdinand, serve as a point of departure for discourses on reason of state, which themselves are backed up by other examples from both ancient and modern history.

Like Barbosa Homem before him, Blázquez Mayoralgo draws from Machiavelli's *Discourses* 1.11, citing the example of Numa Pompilius, who pretended to be married to a nymph in order to gain a reputation for divine prudence. While for Barbosa Homem, Numa represents a good example of the simulation of virtue and holiness, as we have seen, for Blázquez Mayoralgo his example teaches us more about secrecy:

139 Ibid.
140 Ibid.
141 Ibid.
142 Ibid.

> No auia nacido Numa Pompilio leyendo las Ydeas de Platon, ni las eticas de Aristoteles; y la fama de su prudencia le hizo Rey de Romanos, subiendo desde la aguijada al Cetro; y para que el credito introducido se conseruase con la prouidencia exercitada; fingiò que de secreto estaua casado con la Ninfa Egeria, cuyo respeto pudo tanto, que gouernando en paz el Imperio, jamas se abriò en su tiempo el Templo de Iano. No es licito al Rey hazer comun a todos el secreto que está en su pecho, ni ha de ser tan facil en las palabras que por ellas le lean el coraçon.[143]

Later, like Botero before him, Blázquez Mayoralgo draws from Machiavellli's *Discourses* 1.6, where Machiavelli argues that it is necessary to make the plebs numerous and powerful if one wishes to expand into a great empire. Blázquez Mayoralgo refers to the same examples of Sparta and Rome:

> Pero los grandes Reynos, no tienen mas poderoso neruio que la multitud de la gente en quien está segura la fuerça para la defensa, ò las armas para las empressas, porque en los pocos, siempre es mayor la perdida, aunque se gane la vitoria, como sucedió a los de Esparta, vencidos en vna batalla de los Thebanos que con sola la muerte de mil y setecientos Ciudadanos perdieron el señorio de la grecia, y despues a los de Thebas por la misma causa, se le quitò Philipo Rey de Macedonia. Los Romanos sujetaron el mundo con el valor, y con la gente, por ser tanta que en vn mismo tiempo sustentauan la guerra en distantes, y remotas Prouincias, y jamas perdieron el animo por vno, ni por muchos rompimientos, antes fortalecian las armas con el estrago de los exercitos … Y assi el Principe deue mirar por la conseruacion de sus Reynos porque no haga la falta de gente lo que no pudiera el estrago de las armas.[144]

In conformity with the Counter-Reformation Catholic worldview, Blázquez Mayoralgo adds: "mas no por esto a de permitir que se pueblen de naciones en religion contrarias a la suya, que no siempre la multitud es muralla de la Corona."[145]

Blázquez Mayoralgo drew from the same chapter the idea that conquest is necessary: "Forçossas à los Reyes son las conquistas, porque mayor enemigo de los Imperios es el ocio, que la mas cruel guerra: la magestad de la Corona, no consiste en eredarla, sino en la capacidad de defenderla, y esta firmeça se conserua, teniendo valor para lo adquirido, y poniendo medios para lo estraño."[146] Like Machiavelli, Blázquez Mayoralgo refers to the example of Rome: "luego que el Imperio Romano dejò por la blandura de la paz la aspereça de las armas, comencò á caer."[147]

143 Ibid., 18–19.
144 Ibid., 43–44.
145 Ibid., 44.
146 Ibid., 86.
147 Ibid., 86.

For Blázquez Mayoralgo, necessity justifies fraud when the end is justice:

> No es engaño que haze el Rey, desmentir con apariencias lo que pueden destruir asechanças: forçoso es al Principe (y mas en tiempo de guerras) vsar de fraude en la necessidad, no para quebrantar la fé, sino para asegurar la justicia ... De suerte que el engaño que no induce ofensa, no solo es necessario al Rey, pero asiento de las puntas de la Corona.[148]

Interestingly, Blázquez Mayoralgo allows for simulation, agreeing with Barbosa Homem: "Forçosa es â los Reyes la simulacion, pues tan pocas vezes la verdad entra por sus vmbrales ... Y mas en la guerra donde cada vno viue en la fê de engañar al otro."[149] Like Machiavelli, Blázquez Mayoralgo explains that fraud is necessary, because the reality is that the truth is rarely seen by the many. In general, Blázquez Mayoralgo agrees with Machiavelli when he asserts that necessity often makes the prince break the laws in order to bring about justice: "No quiere animo encogido el reinar: no puede siempre el Principe atarse á la ley, necessidad tiene de variarla segun los accidentes; que muchas vezes los fraudes, no solo no se opponen á la justicia pero suelen dar fuerça à la raçon."[150]

Despite this agreement with Machiavelli, Blázquez Mayoralgo unsurprisingly differentiates himself rhetorically from the Florentine: "No ajustandose á la falsa dotrina de Machiauelo, que el Principe, al mismo tiempo que asienta la paz, puede quebrantar la fe: opinion mal entendida; porque solo podra con algun engaño disimular sus motiuos, no en vituperio ageno, sino en conueniencia propria."[151] Blázquez Mayoralgo attributes to Machiavelli the specific opinion that it is permissible to lie at the time of making peace, which he condemns. By presenting such a narrow understanding of Machiavellism, he gives himself ample room to incorporate Machiavelli's ideas in his own treatise.

Blázquez Mayoralgo deals with one of Ferdinand's actions that, according him, the *políticos* point to in order to justify their opinions: "al mismo tiempo que el Rey Catholico ofrece al Gran Capitan con juramento el maestrazgo de Santiago, embia a prenderle."[152] In defense of Ferdinand, Blázquez Mayoralgo observes that the decisions of good kings are unfathomable; the *arcana imperii* should therefore not be judged by the uninitiated: "accion, si se mira por los lejos de la apariencia, culpada; y si se mide con la raçon de estado de la Corona; aplaudida: no se reduce á las formas comunes introducir la duracion al Principado, y siendo varios los tiempos en los accidentes, no pueden resoluerse las

148 Ibid., 94.
149 Ibid.
150 Ibid., 94–95.
151 Ibid., 95.
152 Ibid., 146.

materias ò por las leyes que estableciò la sujecion, ò por las costumbres que consintió la necessidad."[153] In other words, the variation of accidents and necessity justifies an action that is traditionally considered bad. Essentially, Blázquez Mayoralgo simply repeats the same justifications as Machiavelli and includes them under the label of reason of state. Because Ferdinand earned the reputation of divinity, he cannot be considered a tyrant: "el que llega á ser venerado por diuino; en ningun caso que se ofrezca, se à de persuadir el Reyno que puede ser tirano: los secretos de el reinar; mas presto se ofrecen á los ojos de quien los mira sin entenderlos, que à los entendimientos de quien los censura sin alcançarlos."[154] Here, Blázquez Mayoralgo is repeating Machiavelli's explanation, in the *Prince* 18, for why fraud is used so frequently in reality: "E li uomini in universali iudicano piú alli occhi che alle mani; perché tocca a vedere a ognuno, a sentire a pochi: ognuno vede quello che tu pari, pochi sentono quello che tu se' … e nelle azioni di tutti li uomini, e massime de' principi, dove non è iudizio a chi reclamare, si guarda al fine."[155]

Blázquez Mayoralgo applies this lesson to the specific example of Ferdinand: because people will praise him for the great ends of his enterprises, they will not blame him for using means that traditionally are considered vices. Blázquez Mayoralgo concludes by repeating Machiavelli's idea that it is not necessary to say the truth if doing so puts your position of power at risk: "no siempre es forçossa la verdad, si de confessarla se grange el peligro, y de paliarla se consigue el remedio."[156]

153 Ibid.

154 Ibid.

155 Machiavelli, *Principe*, 119.

156 Blázquez Mayoralgo, *Perfecta raçon de estado*, 147.

5

Juan Pablo Mártir Rizo's Rereading of the *Prince*

Juan Pablo Mártir Rizo was a well-known intellectual and historian at court who favored the Count-Duke of Olivares. He dedicated his *Norte de principes*, published by Diego Flamenco in Madrid in 1626, to don Diego de Corral y Avellano, member of the Council of Castile and author of the famous *consulta* of 1619, which had proposed to Philip III remedies for the "illness" of his kingdoms toward the end of his reign. Later Mártir Rizo was a personal correspondent and advisor to the Count-Duke of Olivares himself.[1] In 1632, one "Pablo Riccio" was accused of keeping "libros políticos y en particular los machabellos, u otros prohibidos," and his home was searched.[2] Although the results of this search are now unknown, Mártir Rizo's *Norte de principes* constitutes a close rereading of the *Prince*, adapting Machiavelli's text, almost chapter by chapter, to his readers' Catholic, imperialist worldview.

At the very beginning of his treatise, Mártir Rizo offers his readers a warning: "En estos discursos Politicos, hallaran los ingenios maliciosos ocasion en que derramarse, yo los disculpo, con el conocimiento de mi propia ignorancia."[3] He also acknowledges that he has taken much from those who have written previously on politics: "Aquellos que hazen estimacion de los escritos agenos tendran razon de agradecer estos cuidados, por ser el alma de muchos varones que escriuieron Policia, ya sean Latinos, Franceses, Italianos, o Españoles, a quien he vsurpado los mejores conceptos."[4] As we shall see, in the case of one Italian, Machiavelli, this warning was an extreme understatement.

In the first four chapters of his treatise, Mártir Rizo takes directly from Jean Bodin's *Six livres de la République* (1576) the different forms of government and the distinction between three kinds of monarchy: seigniorial, royal and tyrannical. In his summary of Bodin's tyrannical monarchy, Mártir Rizo employs the traditional rhetoric of hatred:

1 Elliot, *Count-Duke of Olivares*, 98–100, 294, 299.

2 Juan Ignacio Pulido Serrano, *Injurias a Cristo: Religión, política y antijudaísmo en el siglo XVII (Análisis de las corrientes antijudías durante la Edad Moderna)* (Alcalá de Henares: Instituto Internacional de Estudios Sefardíes y Andalusíes, Universidad de Alcalá, 2002), 31. Many thanks to Javier Castro-Ibaseta for this reference and for pointing out to me that the "Pablo Riccio" named in the document referred to Mártir Rizo, who added the *Mártir* himself in order to claim kinship with the famous Italian humanist Pedro Mártir de Anglería.

3 Juan Pablo Mártir Rizo, *Norte de principes* (Madrid: Diego Flamenco, 1626), n.p.

4 Ibid.

> La Monarchia tiranica, es aquella, donde el señor despreciando las leyes naturales, vsa de la libertad de los subditos como de sus esclauos, oprimiendoles, molestandoles, vsurpandoles los bienes, y aprouechandose dellos como de los suyos propios, no vsando de su hazienda para las cosas licitas, decentes, y del aumento de la honra y Fè de Iesu Christo nuestro Señor, sino disipandolas en las delicias, superfluidades, y excessos que le hazen aborrecible a los subditos.[5]

Mártir Rizo distinguishes between the good king and the tyrant along traditional lines: "Que el Rey se conforma con las leyes de la naturaleza, y el tirano las huella y desprecia, aquel haze todo lo que puede ser en aumento del bien publico y defensa de sus subditos, este no haze cosa que no sea por su interes particular, vengança, o deleite: el vno haze profesion de Piedad, Iusticia, y Fè: el otro ni tiene Dios, Fè, ni Ley."[6] Here, Mártir Rizo differentiates between the good king and the tyrant in the same way in which the reason-of-state writers distinguish between true and false reason of state: first, the good king looks to the common good, while the tyrant looks to his own advantage; second, the good king takes into account God, while the tyrant does not. Despite this traditional beginning, from this point on Mártir Rizo will follow Machiavelli's blurring of the dividing lines between king and tyrant, virtue and vice.

Mártir Rizo's rereading of Machiavelli's text begins in chapter 5, "Distincion de los Principados,"[7] which is based on the *Prince* 1:

> Tutti gli stati, tutti e' dominii che hanno avuto e hanno imperio sopra gli uomini, sono stati e sono o republiche o principati. E' principati sono o ereditari, de' quali el sangue del loro signore ne sia suto lungo tempo principe, o sono nuovi. E' nuovi, o e' sono nuovi tutti, come fu Milano a Francesco Sforza, o sono come membri aggiunti allo stato ereditario del principe che gli acquista, come è el regno di Napoli al re di Spagna. Sono questi dominii cosí acquistati o consueti a vivere sotto uno principe o usi a essere liberi; e acquistonsi o con l'arme d'altri o con le proprie, o per fortuna o per virtú.[8]

Mártir Rizo ignores the first sentence, because he is not interested in republics, and adds his own examples relevant for the seventeenth-century Spanish readership:

> Los Principados, o son hereditarios como los de España, Francia, Inglaterra, o son nueuamente adquiridos: en estos ay vna distincion, que

5 Ibid., 11–12.
6 Ibid., 12–13.
7 Ibid., 14.
8 Machiavelli, *Principe*, 7.

> o en todo tienen principio, como en Florencia le tuuo la familia de los Medicis, o se vnen con alguna antigua Monarchia como Portugal a Castilla, Borgoña a Francia, Irlanda a Inglaterra, o estauan acostumbrados a viuir sujetos a alguno, como Borgoña a sus Duques (cuyos legitimos sucessores son nuestros Reyes Catolicos) o era Republica libre como Florencia, y la variedad del tiempo, la reduxo a seruidumbre. Estos señorios, o se adquieren con las armas propias, y justo Derecho, como Castilla a Portugal, o con las fuerças de otros, como los Duques de Florencia, que ascendieron a esta dignidad, por las de España gouernadas por nuestro inuictissimo Emperador Carlos Quinto, o por propia virtud, como Francisco Sforcia, que se hizo dueño de Milan, o por fortuna, como muchos de los Emperadores antiguos, que de humilde nacimiento fueron colocados a la grandeza del Imperio de los orbes, por elecion de los soldados.[9]

The examples that Mártir Rizo chooses to add to Machiavelli's text reveal his imperial ideology, typical of the first half of the seventeenth century. The entire hereditary history of Portugal is erased as it is considered an appendage to the "ancient" monarchy of Castile that Philip II acquired through his own arms and natural right. Likewise, the Dukes of Florence ascended to their power through the arms of others, namely those of the emperor Charles V. Finally, Burgundy is offered as an example of a realm that, before France acquired it, was accustomed to living subject to its own dukes, whose legitimate successors are the Spanish line of kings.

In the rhetorical terminology of his time, Mártir Rizo's chapter 6, "De los Principados hereditarios,"[10] would have been considered an *amplificatio* of Machiavelli's short chapter 2 of the *Prince*:

> nelli stati ereditari e assuefatti al sangue del loro principe, sono assai minore difficultà a mantenergli che ne' nuovi, perché basta solo non preterire gli ordini de' sua antinati e di poi temporeggiare con gli accidenti; in modo che, se tale principe è di ordinaria industria, sempre si manterrà nel suo stato, se non è una estraordinaria ed eccessiva forza che ne lo privi: e privato che ne fia, quantunque di sinistro abbi l'occupatore, lo riacquista … Perché el principe naturale ha minori cagioni e minori necessità di offendere, donde conviene che sia piú amato; e se estraordinari vizi non lo fanno odiare, è ragionevole che naturalmente sia benevoluto da' sua. E nella antiquità e continuazione del dominio sono spente le memorie e le cagioni delle innovazioni: perché sempre una mutazione lascia lo addentellato per la edificazione dell'altra.[11]

Mártir Rizo adds additional explanation for why an hereditary king will re-acquire his kingdom easily. Otherwise, his chapter is strikingly similar to Machiavelli's:

9 Mártir Rizo, *Norte*, 14–15.
10 Ibid., 16.
11 Machiavelli, *Principe*, 8–10.

> Los Principados hereditarios son mas faciles de conseruar, porque con el largo tiempo del gouierno, tienen ya los subditos oluidada la violencia del primer señor que los sujetò, y viuiendo y guardando las leyes de sus Reynos, conseruandolos en paz, en sosiego, son los vassallos leales y obedientes a sus Principes, y assi en este capitulo tendremos poco que discurrir, porque con que el Principe sea industrioso y prudente viuira con felicidad: y si alguna vez sucediere (que faltando a su obligacion) fuere despojado de otro señor y este ocupare sus Reynos, con facilidad los boluerà a restaurar; porque el nueuo Principe que le quitare sus Estados, para poderlos conseruar, ha de vsar de algunos rigores, ha de alterar las costumbres, las leyes, y distribuir las Dignidades en otros, para assegurarse de los enemigos, porque siempre en vn Reyno aurà algunos que sigan los designios del que quisiere ocuparle: y por el contrario, otros que permanezcan en la obediencia de su antiguo Principe, y con qualquiera mudança que haga resultan nueuas quexas, y en Principe que no tiene adquiridas las voluntades de sus subditos, son mayores, y disimulanse menos sus defectos, que los de aquellos que dominauan antiguamente, y assi aclaman los vassallos por el Principe desposeido, y como mejor pueden le introducen en su Imperio, despojando al que se le auia ocupado.[12]

At this point, in place of the example of Ferrara found in Machiavelli, Mártir Rizo offers the examples of Edward IV of England, who was temporarily usurped by his cousin, Richard Neville of Warwick, and of the civil war between the brothers Pedro I and Enrique II of Castile:

> auiendo el Rey don Pedro de Castilla salido de su Reyno (vencido de don Enrique su hermano) cuyos rigores le conduxeron a tal estado: no bien boluio a Castilla, quando muchos Señores y Ciudades se pusieron a su deuocion, y aclamaron su nombre, y si moderase su animo, sin duda que no huuiera muerto con violencia, porque es fuerça que el Principe hereditario sea amado de sus vassallos, si ya sus vicios y maldades no le hazen aborrecible a todos.[13]

In his narration of this example, Mártir Rizo incorporates Machiavelli's rhetoric of hatred: Pedro could have avoided the hatred of his subjects, and thereby conserved his state, if he had been able to control his vices and evil ways.

In chapter 7, Mártir Rizo combines the general considerations found in Machiavelli's chapters 3, 6, 7 and 9 into one long and overarching chapter on the "principado nueuo."[14] Machiavelli's "mixed" principality, "quando al antiguo se junta otro Reyno,"[15] is presented first. As Machiavelli states, it is possible to

12 Mártir Rizo, *Norte*, 16–17.
13 Ibid., 17.
14 Ibid., 18.
15 Ibid.

conquer these "member" states because, "li uomini mutano volentieri signore, credendo migliorare, e questa credenza li fa pigliare l'arme contro a quello."[16] Similarly, Mártir Rizo declares that when the conquering prince is powerful, it is easy to add other states:

> porque en qualquiera parte hay quexosos de su principe, y estos desean nouedades, presumiendo que en el nueuo gouierno mejoraran de fortuna, y assi se inclinan a la parte del que los quiere adquirir; y teniendo el Principe que los conquista, fabor en los naturales de la prouincia, con facilidad se haze señor della.[17]

Nevertheless, as both Machiavelli and Mártir Rizo go on to add, it is then very difficult to maintain these member states. For Machiavelli, after the rebellious subjects find themselves subjected to the new lord, they are disappointed: "s'ingannano, perché veggono poi per esperienza avere piggiorato … che sempre bisogni offendere quegli di chi si diventa nuovo principe, e con gente d'arme e con infinite altre ingiurie che si tira dreto il nuovo acquisto."[18]

Mártir Rizo offers a similar explanation:

> mas tambien se ha de entender, que es dificultoso conseruarse dueño, porque como los subditos se hallan engañados en lo que creyeron, y experimentan muchas incomodidades de las guerras y tributos, principalmente que se hallan en el mismo estado, sin otro premio mas que las grandes esperanças, porque es imposible que nadie pueda satisfacer a toda vna comunidad.[19]

Both Machiavelli and Mártir Rizo write that it is difficult if not impossible to maintain a principality gained with the arms or the fortune of others. For Machiavelli, the reason is that it is unlikely that this kind of prince will have the necessary virtue to keep something that he has not won on his own: "Questi stanno semplicemente in su la volontà e fortuna di chi lo ha concesso loro, che sono dua cose volubilissime e instabili, e non sanno e non possono tener quello grado."[20] Even in the rare case when he does show such virtue, it remains nearly impossible, as Machiavelli seems to imply throughout the rest of chapter 7 in the example of Cesare Borgia, who despite doing all that he could to become independent of his father, Pope Alexander VI, failed when the latter died. Mártir Rizo elaborates his explanation using the Machiavellian discourse of the avoidance of hatred:

16 Machiavelli, *Principe*, 10.
17 Mártir Rizo, *Norte*, 18.
18 Machiavelli, *Principe*, 10–11.
19 Mártir Rizo, *Norte*, 18.
20 Machiavelli, *Principe*, 39.

> porque se la ha adquirido con armas estrangeras ha de estar el Principe desvelandose en conseruar la amistad del que le fauorecio, tanto, que por tenerle contento acomete cosas que le hazen odioso a los que con violencia le obedecen, ya quitandoles las haziendas para acudir a la recompensa o necessidades del amigo, ya dando amparo a aquellos a quien sus subditos aborrecen por ser causa de su opresion.[21]

Machiavelli also offers a naturalistic explanation for the instability of this kind of principality: "Di poi gli stati che vengono subito, come tutte l'altre cose della natura che nascono e crescono presto, non possono avere le barbe e corrispondenzie loro in modo che il primo tempo avverso non le spenga."[22] Mártir Rizo utilizes the rhetoric of fortune to offer a similar explanation: "El Principado que se adquiere por fortuna, tan poco es durable, porque como ella no lo es, es fuerça ser mudables sus efetos, y los que ascendieren por esta razon a las grandes prosperidades tienen presto fin sus dichas."[23]

In order to complete his consideration of this kind of principality, Mártir Rizo goes on to borrow from Machiavelli's treatment of "civil principalities" in the *Prince* 9, where he declares that the prince who has reached his state with the help of the great maintains it only with difficulty: "perché si truova principe con di molti intorno che gli paiono essere sua equali, e per questo non gli può né comandare né maneggiare a suo modo."[24] Mártir Rizo applies this idea to principalities acquired through the virtue or fortune of others: "los hombres no permanecen en sus intentos, y quando consideran a los Principes iguales en nobleza, desprecian su Gouierno, y con dificultad se sujetan a sus preceptos y ordenes, porque les parece cosa indigna rendir la libre voluntad a los que comunicaron como a semejantes, y aun como a inferiores."[25]

When he arrives at his discussion of those who acquire a principality through their own arms and virtue, Mártir Rizo repeats Machiavelli's general statement: "Dico adunque che ne' principati tutti nuovi, dove sia uno nuovo principe, si truova a mantenergli piú o meno difficultà secondo che piú o meno è virtuoso colui che gli acquista."[26] In Mártir Rizo's words, "en los estados adquiridos por propia virtud, se hallarà mas o menos dificultad en conseruarlos, segun fuere mas o menos virtuoso el que los conquista."[27] Machiavelli goes on to explain that the prince who has acquired his principality through virtue maintains it more easily than the one who has relied on fortune: "E perché questo evento, di diventare di privato principe, presuppone o virtú o fortuna, pare che l'una o

21 Mártir Rizo, *Norte*, 20.
22 Machiavelli, *Principe*, 39.
23 Mártir Rizo, *Norte*, 39.
24 Machiavelli, *Principe*, 64.
25 Mártir Rizo, *Norte*, 21–22.
26 Machiavelli, *Principe*, 32–33.
27 Mártir Rizo, *Norte*, 22.

l'altra di queste dua cose mitighino in parte molte difficultà; nondimanco, colui che è stato meno in su la fortuna si è mantenuto piú."[28] Mártir Rizo elaborates on this same idea:

> porque aunque en estos Principados, y los que se grangean por fortuna, vna y otra facilitan muchas dificultades: con todo esso, si la virtud del que los possee no se aumenta, antes va en diminucion, es fuerça que los que obedecen viendo la mudança de costumbres del que merecio con ellas ascender a ser señor, aborrezcan su Imperio, y sacudan el yugo a que voluntariamente se inclinaron; mas si la aumenta, si la conserua, y en sus designios y acciones siempre la lleua por blanco, no ay duda que no solo se conseruarà, sino que harà vn señorio estable y dilatado para sus sucessores."[29]

Mártir Rizo again profits from the Machiavellian discourse on the avoidance of hatred in order to explain that the prince who shows the same or more virtue from the time he has acquired his principality will maintain it with ease. In addition, Mártir Rizo utilizes the gendered discourse of fortune to elaborate this point further: "y la inconstancia de la fortuna no desmaya, ni debilita el animo del buen Principe, porque el virtuoso no se ensoberuece con la buena dicha, antes los bienes exteriores son de vil y baxo precio, no se aflige y acobarda con la infelice suerte tanto, que venga a apartarse del camino de la razon que le conduxo al Principado."[30]

To conclude his treatment of this kind of principality, acquired with one's own arms and virtue, Mártir Rizo returns to Machiavelli's consideration of "member" principalities in order to borrow two more concepts. When these member states speak a similar language and observe similar customs, Machiavelli writes that the new prince should not make any changes to their laws: "non alterare né loro legge né loro dazi: talmente che in brevissimo tempo diventa con il loro principato antiquo tutto uno corpo."[31] Mártir Rizo, taking into account the importance of the new prince's reputation, offers a similar observation:

> Estos, que por propia virtud ascienden al Principado, si aspiran a su conseruacion, no alteran las antiguas constituciones del Reyno, antes las hazen obseruar inuiolablemente para acreditar su integridad y rectitud, que los subditos con razon justa hazen estimacion de las leyes y ordenes que les conserua en paz y justicia; y quando el Principe no inoua en ellas no le tienen por sospechoso, y assi se dexan gouernar voluntariamente de aquel que con la razon y antiguedad de sus costumbres los rige, los manda.[32]

28 Machiavelli, *Principe*, 33.
29 Mártir Rizo, *Norte*, 22–23.
30 Ibid., 23.
31 Machiavelli, *Principe*, 13.
32 Mártir Rizo, *Norte*, 25.

When the new member state does not have the same language and customs, Machiavelli believes that the best way to maintain it is to go there to live:

> Perché standovi si veggono nascere e' disordini e presto vi puoi rimediare: non vi stando, s'intendono quando sono grandi e che non vi è piú rimedio; non è oltre a questo la provincia spogliata da' tua offiziali; satisfannosi e' sudditi del ricorso propinquo al principe, donde hanno piú cagione di amarlo, volendo essere buoni, e, volendo essere altrimenti, di temerlo.[33]

Mártir Rizo repeats these same reasons for recommending that the new prince live in his acquired principality:

> No es de menor importancia (si al Principe le fuere possible) habitar en la misma Prouincia posseyda, porque su presencia acobarda los animos concitados, alienta a los amigos en la perseuerancia de su obediencia, y los vassallos viuen contentos quando veen a su Principe que le pueden hablar, quexarse del rigor de sus ministros.[34]

After a brief digression, in chapter 8, on the question of free will, Mártir Rizo's chapter 9, "De los que por maldad ascienden al Principado,"[35] corresponds to Machiavelli's infamous *Prince* 8. However, while Mártir Rizo's examples are similar to Machiavelli's, his evaluation of those who ascend to power through evil ways differs from his model's significantly: Dionysus of Syracuse and his son of the same name are here unequivocally labeled tyrants. Mártir Rizo ignores Machiavelli's reflections regarding "le crudeltà male usate o bene usate,"[36] focussing instead on the tragic and violent deaths that they suffered. At one point, Mártir Rizo appears to praise the virtues of Dionysus the Elder, such as his liberality, prudence and military acumen; nevertheless, he concludes that all of these virtues were not enough to make up for his extreme cruelty.

In chapter 10, Mártir Rizo adapts the general considerations found in Machiavelli's *Prince* 19, on avoiding hatred and contempt, to the Catholic worldview. There Machiavelli brings to a conclusion his reorganization of the traditional understanding of virtue and vice in politics: "Ma perché, circa le qualità di che di sopra si fa menzione, io ho parlato delle piú importanti, l'altre voglio discorrere brevemente sotto queste generalità: che el principe pensi, come in parte di sopra è detto, di fuggire quelle cose che lo faccino odioso o contennendo."[37] For Machiavelli, hatred is avoided when the prince does not steal men's property and women. On the other hand, several things make a prince worthy of contempt:

33 Machiavelli, *Principe*, 14.
34 Mártir Rizo, *Norte*, 25–26.
35 Ibid., 33–42.
36 Machiavelli, *Principe*, 61.
37 Machiavelli, *Principe*, 120.

"Contennendo lo fa essere tenuto vario, leggieri, effeminato, pusillanime, irresoluto: da che uno principe si debbe guardare come da uno scoglio … e si mantenga in tale opinione che alcuno non pensi né a ingannarlo né ad aggirarlo."[38] When considering "las primeras acciones del Principe,"[39] Mártir Rizo encourages the new prince to cultivate the reputation of a king who is both Catholic and prudent: "Religioso en las cosas diuinas, y prudente en las humanas."[40] At this point, making use of Machiavelli's language, he then urges the new prince to avoid superstition and simulation of religion:

> pero sepa el Principe que ha de huir mucho la superstición y simulacion, como dos escollos; en el vno suele herir la mucha astucia, y en el otro la poca prudencia; la supersticion le harà inhabil, despreciable, y despojo de quien quisiere engañarle; la Religion simulada a largo andar la confundira, y quanto el verdadero habito haze al Principe digno de veneracion, tanto la Religion vsada por mascara de sus designios, se haze odioso y sospechoso a todos, y le empeora todas las condiciones de sus manejos, por ser obra de prudencia y digna de alabança el proceder con verdad.[41]

Here Mártir Rizo differs greatly from Machiavelli regarding what makes his Catholic king *despreciable* and *odioso*: he must be a true Catholic who gives little heed to superstition. Nevertheless, Mártir Rizo has adapted Machiavelli's discourse on the avoidance of hatred and contempt, admonishing his king to avoid their causes like *escollos*.

Chapter 10 serves as an introduction to the general consideration of chapters 11, "Qual conuiene al Principe mas, ser piadoso, o seuero,"[42] and 12, "Como serà vn Principe amado y temido de los subditos, y de los que no lo son sin ofenderlos,"[43] both of which expand upon Machiavelli's *Prince* 17. Mártir Rizo begins on a traditional note, distinguishing between tyrants, who use cruelty and fear, and hereditary princes, who make good use of clemency and piety.[44] Nevertheless, this traditional approach is limited to this brief introduction; what follows in the bulk of these two chapters are Machiavellian considerations of the exceptions to these traditional rules. Like Santa María before him, Mártir Rizo reveals a keen familiarity with Machiavelli's ideas regarding the plebs and the great in both the *Prince* 9, on civil principalities, as well as *Discourses* 1.5, on where it is better to place the guard of freedom, in the people or in the great: "si tal vez quisiere hazer demostracion de su seueridad, no conuiene que sea en

38 Ibid., 120–21.
39 Mártir Rizo, *Norte*, 42.
40 Ibid., 44.
41 Ibid., 44–45.
42 Ibid., 45.
43 Ibid., 56.
44 Ibid., 45.

los pueblos y personas inferiores: contra las grandes cabeças ha de emplear su indignacion, si son culpadas."[45] Mártir Rizo makes this distinction for the same reasons as Machiavelli:

> Los poderosos son los que hazen maquinas contra las vidas de los Principes, inuidiosos de verlos en tanta alteza, ofendidos de que no aya distribuido con ellos de las dignidades y mercedes … Los pueblos viuen pacificamente quando no les roban sus bienes, apremiandolos con violencia, con tirania, o no veen que la justicia parece a las telas de las arañas, que solo se enredan y quedan presas en ellas los animales pequeños, y qualquiera grande las rompe y deshaze, sin que aya estoruo que le suspenda.[46]

Machiavelli argues in the *Prince* 17 that having a reputation for being cruel and the use of fear can be effective, so long as the prince avoids hatred. In the *Prince* 19, Machiavelli adds that contempt as well as hatred should be avoided at all costs. Like Botero, Mártir Rizo agrees with this analysis, although he presents it in a slightly different way: "Disputeremos aora, qual parte destas dista mas del medio para conseguir el amor de los vassallos, el desprecio, o el temor. Yo, a lo que puedo alcançar, juzgara, que esta mas apartado el desprecio."[47] While fear may be combined with love, contempt should absolutely be avoided. In the *Prince* 17, Machiavelli reorganizes the traditional distinction between cruelty and piety. For him cruelty to a few is justified when the end is peace, as the example of Cesare Borgia shows:

> Era tenuto Cesare Borgia crudele: nondimanco quella sua crudeltà aveva racconcia la Romagna, unitola, ridottola in pace e in fede … Debbe pertanto uno principe non si curare della infamia del crudele per tener e' sudditi sua uniti e in fede: perché con pochissimi esempli sarà piú pietoso che quelli e' quali per troppa pietà lasciono seguire e' disordini, di che nasca uccisioni o rapine; perché queste sogliono offendere una universalità intera, e quelle esecuzioni che vengono dal principe offendono uno particulare.[48]

Without referring to the specific example of Cesare Borgia, Mártir Rizo demonstrates that he has learned the general outline and vocabulary of Machiavelli's lesson when he similarly justifies the use of fear and punishment of the few when the end is peace for the entire kingdom:

> porque quando es el Principe oluidado en el castigo, y con mucha facilidad perdona los delitos, no puede auer seguridad en los vassallos, ni pueden

45 Ibid., 46.
46 Ibid., 47.
47 Ibid., 52.
48 Machiavelli, *Principe*, 108–9.

> viuir contentos: porque los buenos no estan seguros de los malos, y estos con la satisfacion que tienen de ser perdonados los ofenden: mas si conocen que despues de la maldad se les ha de seguir el castigo, temen, y procuran reprimir sus afectos; y los buenos viuen contentos debaxo del dominio que sabe conseruarlos en paz … Todos aman a quien los haze bien, y no lo es pequeño la seguridad de la hazienda, vida, honra: y por el contrario, aborrecen a los que son causa de sus daños, o permiten sus injurias.[49]

Mártir Rizo concludes chapter 11 by reiterating the importance of punishing the few for the benefit of the many, just as he had learned from the *Prince* 17: "Mas aunque es verdad, que es conueniente el castigo, la forma de hazerle es de mucha importancia, con la pena de pocos se puede escarmentar a muchos."[50]

In chapter 12, "Como serà vn Principe amado y temido de los subditos,"[51] Mártir Rizo follows Machiavelli's reconsideration of the traditional debate about whether it is better to be loved or feared, also found in the *Prince* 17. There, Machiavelli goes against the traditional view that the good prince is loved, while the tyrant is feared: "Nasce da questo una disputa, s'e' gli è meglio essere amato che temuto o e converso. Rispondesi che si vorrebbe essere l'uno e l'altro; ma perché e' gli è difficile accozarli insieme, è molto piú sicuro essere temuto che amato, quando si abbi a mancare dell' uno de' dua."[52] Mártir Rizo does not say outright that it is better to be feared than loved; nevertheless, he uses similar reasoning to conclude that the prince should not rely solely on love, but should seek to be both loved and feared: "porque no puede ser durable el amor, donde falta la estimacion del sujeto, digo que deue procurar igualmente ser amado y temido."[53]

At one point in this chapter, Mártir Rizo summarizes Machiavelli's *Prince* 14, where he declares that the prince should become a master of the art of war: "Perché, in tra le altre cagioni che ti arreca di male, lo essere disarmato ti fa contennendo, la quale è una di quelle infamie delle quali el principe si debbe guardare, come di sotto si dirà."[54] This reference to contempt anticipates his discussion in the *Prince* 19. Mártir Rizo, who began this series of chapters with a Machiavellian consideration of hatred and contempt, decides to emphasize the positive rewards of exercising the art of war: "La disciplina de la milicia, y tener sus Reynos guarnecidos de Soldados experimentados, dà grande reputacion a los que gouiernan, y les harà amados y temidos."[55] Here Mártir Rizo suggests that the king who is a master of the art of war will achieve the

49 Mártir Rizo, *Norte*, 52.
50 Ibid., 55–56.
51 Ibid., 56.
52 Machiavelli, *Principe*, 110.
53 Mártir Rizo, *Norte*, 57.
54 Machiavelli, *Principe*, 98.
55 Mártir Rizo, *Norte*, 62.

Machiavellian goal of being both loved and feared. As Machiavelli writes, war should be the prince's art in times of peace as well as war: "Debbe pertanto mai levare il pensiero da questo esercizio della guerra; e nella pace vi si debbe piú esercitare che nella guerra."[56] Similarly, Mártir Rizo declares that: "El arte de la Milicia, es propia de los Principes, en ella se deuen exercitar, assi en la paz, como en la guerra, haziendose capazes de los sucessos que pueden ocurrir."[57]

Both Machiavelli and Mártir Rizo conclude this discussion with a reference to the adversity inevitably brought to the prince by the fickle goddess Fortune. In Machiavelli's words: "Questi simili modi debbe osservare uno principe savio; e mai ne' pacifici stare ozioso, ma con industria farne capitale per potersene valere nelle avversità, acciò che la fortuna, quando si muta, lo truovi parato a resisterli."[58] Similarly Mártir Rizo states: "y si la fortuna se mostrare aduersa por sus continuas mudanças, siempre serà estimado su valor."[59] He concludes this chapter by arguing against those who might object that love and fear cannot go together:

> yo juzgo lo contrario, y digo que le haze mas espantoso a los enemigos, porque que Principe estrangero ha de auer que tome las armas contra otro, para quitarle sus estados que sea conocidamente amado de sus subditos? y quando lo emprendiere que empressa pretende conseguir que no le sea ruina? porque tantas Fortalezas tiene vn Señor inexpugnables, quanto subditos le asisten contentos con su dominio.[60]

This metaphor comes directly from the second half of the *Prince* 20, where Machiavelli considers whether or not it is a good idea for princes to construct fortresses, concluding that: "la migliore fortezza che sia è non essere odiato dal populo."[61]

In order to compose chapter 13, "De la liberalidad,"[62] Mártir Rizo took much from the *Prince* 16. He has already anticipated this discussion at the end of chapter 12, where he denounces excessive taxes as one of the causes that make a people hate their king:

> Vltimamente, si viuen los Soldados contentos debaxo del dominio de Principe prudente y virtuoso, adornado de las calidades que auemos dicho, serà la vltima y no menos excelente, el no oprimir a los vassallos con excessiuos

56 Machiavelli, *Principe*, 98.
57 Mártir Rizo, *Norte*, 62.
58 Machiavelli, *Principe*, 101.
59 Mártir Rizo, *Norte*, 62.
60 Ibid., 66.
61 Machiavelli, *Principe*, 145.
62 Mártir Rizo, *Norte*, 67.

> tributos, porque estos son la cosa mas aborrecible del pueblo: por esto se deue atender con sumo cuidado como serà menor este daño forçoso.[63]

This is in fact the essential point of Machiavelli's reorganization of the traditional consideration of liberality in previous political treatises. Machiavelli begins the *Prince* 16 by repeating the traditional opinion on liberality: "e' sarebbe bene essere tenuto liberale."[64] Nevertheless, he immediately adds that the danger of maintaining the reputation of being liberal is that eventually it forces the prince to tax his subjects excessively: "e sarà necesitato alla fine, se si vorrà mantenere el nome del liberale, gravare e' populi estraordinariamente ed essere fiscale e fare tutte quelle cose che si possono fare per avere danari; il che comincerà a farlo odioso a' sudditi, o poco stimare da ciascuno divenendo povero."[65] Thus, Machiavelli offers two alternatives for a prince who is too liberal: either he is forced to tax his subjects excessively, or he will become poor. While the former will produce hatred, the latter will result in contempt.

As is his practice, perhaps imitating the example of Machiavelli himself in these chapters 15–18, Mártir Rizo begins his chapter on liberality on a traditional note: "La liberalidad compra la libertad de las almas, haziendose el Principe con ella dueño de los vassallos."[66] Yet he immediately follows this statement by explaining that this traditional view does not always agree with reality and reason, and that prodigality, the excess of liberality, often does more harm than good:

> mas supuesto que en nuestro discurso vamos con animo de tratar la verdad, o a lo menos, lo que nuestro juizio nos dicta, que conforma mas con la razon, diremos, que siempre la prodigalidad fue muy dañosa a los Principes, porque derramando las riquezas y tesoros, vienen a quedar pobres; y el Principe que se halla con necessidad, es fuerça que oprima a los pueblos con tributos, de donde resulta el aborrecimiento.[67]

As is usual throughout the *Prince* 15–19, Machiavelli places the common good above all other considerations, pointing out that the prince who is liberal to the few and thus eventually greedy with respect to the many puts his own position of power in danger: "In modo che, con questa sua liberalità avendo offeso gli assai e premiato e' pochi, sente ogni primo disagio e periclita in qualunque primo periculo."[68] Mártir Rizo makes a similar argument: "La

63 Mártir Rizo, *Norte*, 65–66.
64 Machiavelli, *Principe*, 104.
65 Ibid., 105.
66 Mártir Rizo, *Norte*, 67.
67 Ibid., 67–68.
68 Machiavelli, *Principe*, 105.

liberalidad del Principe puede ser con algunos, y a este no le llamaria yo tan liberal como al que satisfaciendose con sus rentas no molesta a los vassallos con demandas o tributos."[69]

Machiavelli argues that the prince who uses parsimony will in the end be held more liberal than the one who gives excessively: "perché col tempo sarà tenuto sempre piú liberale veggendo che, con la sua parsimonia, le sue entrate gli bastano, può difendersi da chi gli fa guerra, può fare imprese sanza gravare e' populi."[70] Mártir Rizo offers a similar support for the same argument: "Quando los enemigos consideran a vn Principe rico y poderoso, temenle, porque veen que con facilidad puede juntar grandes exercitos, pagar sus Soldados, y defenderse de los que le quieren ofender."[71] Machiavelli essentially offers a new, negative definition of liberality as not taking, as well as of the contrary, miserliness, as not giving: "Talmente che viene a usare liberalità a tutti quelli a chi e' non toglie, che sono infiniti, e miseria a tutti coloro a chi e' non dà, che sono pochi."[72] Mártir Rizo offers a strikingly similar redefinition of liberality: "porque esta liberalidad es general, pues no pedir lo que le auian de dar, no es muy diferente de dar lo que tiene recebido, solo me parece que consiste la diferencia en auerlo recebido o no."[73]

Following this, Mártir Rizo concludes by pointing out the other alternative that Machiavelli offers for a prince who is too liberal, to become poor and therefore worthy of contempt:

> Siguese otro inconueniente, que el que es liberal gasta con facilidad sus rentas, y hallandose empeñado, y en estado que no puede vsar de su liberalidad, es fuerça reprimirse, y no dar, porque no tiene; y como passa del medio, que es la liberalidad al estremo que es no dar, viene a adquirir el nombre de misero, calidad que tambien le haze aborrecible.[74]

Machiavelli had said that becoming poor will result in contempt; Mártir Rizo instead points out that the prince who is too liberal and, rather than taxing his subjects, becomes poor will turn his liberality to the opposite extreme, miserliness, and thus will attract the hatred of his subjects. In this way, Mártir Rizo focusses Machiavelli's argument that excessive liberality will produce either hatred or contempt, suggesting instead that the result will inevitably be hatred.

Machiavelli anticipates and responds to an objection that some might put to him, saying that liberality is necessary in order to gain power:

69 Mártir Rizo, *Norte*, 68.
70 Machiavelli, *Principe*, 106.
71 Mártir Rizo, *Norte*, 68.
72 Machiavelli, *Principe*, 106.
73 Mártir Rizo, *Norte*, 68.
74 Ibid., 68–69.

E se alcuno dicessi: Cesare con la liberalità pervenne allo imperio, e molti altri, per essere stati ed essere tenuti liberali, sono venuti a gradi grandissimi; rispondo: o tu se' principe fatto o tu se' in via de acquistarlo. Nel primo caso questa liberalità è dannosa. Nel secondo, è bene necessario essere ed essere tenuto liberale; e Cesare era uno di quelli che voleva pervenire al principato di Roma: ma se, poi che vi fu pervenuto, fussi sopravvissuto e non si fussi temperato da quelle spese, arebbe destrutto quello imperio.[75]

Mártir Rizo, referring to the same example of Julius Caesar, makes the exact same argument:

Dirà otro, que por la liberalidad algunos han ascendido al Imperio. A esto respondo; que Cesar si fue liberal, era quando aspiraua ascender al Principado, y assi daua lo que tenia, y aun las rentas del Erario publico derramò entre la milicia, con cuyas alas leuantaua sus pensamientos; mas despues que arribò a ser supremo Emperador, anduuo mas limitado, porque conocio que entonces deuia mudar de calidad para no hazerse odioso a los pueblos, agrauandolos con tributos: que el Principe deue ser moderado en sus gastos por no obligarse gastando con excesso a poner tributos en los pueblos, o cobrar con rigor los ya puestos.[76]

At this point, Mártir Rizo draws from Machiavelli's portrait of human nature, found in the *Prince* 17, and transfers it to the context of his discussion of liberality. When Machiavelli says that it is better to be feared than loved, he justifies this radically new choice through a rather traditional, Judeo-Christian description of human nature:

Perché degli uomini si può dire questo, generalmente, che sieno ingrati, volubili, simulatori e dissimulatori, fuggitori de' pericoli, cupidi del guadagno; e mentre fai loro bene e' sono tutti tua, offeronti el sangue, la roba, la vita, e' figliuoli … quando el bisogno è discosto: ma quando ti si appressa, si rivoltono, e quello principe che si è tutto fondato in su le parole loro, trovandosi nudo di altre preparazioni, ruina.[77]

Mártir Rizo applies a very similar characterization of human nature, using the same terms as Machiavelli, to the context of excessive liberality:

Los hombres, en tanto que reciben el beneficio son agradecidos, y quando el que le haze no necessita de su amparo; mas luego que el bien hechor se halla en estado de auer menester, son ingratos, son desconocidos, todos quieren lo que es suyo, todos saben guardar, y assi el Principe ha de considerar, que es

75 Machiavelli, *Principe*, 107.

76 Mártir Rizo, *Norte*, 71–72.

77 Machiavelli, *Principe*, 110.

> mas conueniente tener bienes propios de que valerse, que Imperio para pedir los agenos; porque tal puede ser el estado en que se halle, que los subditos no le concedan lo que les pide, y vea entre la liberalidad y arrepentimiento su propia ruyna.[78]

After the brief chapter 14, on the institution of the *privado*, for chapter 15, "Como se ha de auer el Principe en la Prouincia donde es Protector y Arbitro,"[79] Mártir Rizo draws from the *Prince* 3, where Machiavelli treats mixed regimes, where one state is added as a member to another. Machiavelli advises the prince who desires to maintain his power over one such member to carefully manipulate its neighbors:

> Debbe ancora chi è in una provincia disforme … farsi capo e defensore de' vicini minori potenti, e ingegnarsi di indebolire e' potenti di quella, e guardarsi che per accidente alcuno non vi entri uno forestiere potente quanto lui: e sempre interverrà ch'e' vi sarà messo da coloro che saranno in quella malcontenti o per troppa ambizione o per paura … E l'ordine delle cose è che, subito che uno forestieri potente entra in una provincia, tutti quelli che sono in essa meno potenti gli aderiscano, mossi da una invidia hanno contro a chi è suto potente sopra di loro.[80]

Following this passage even more closely than Furió Ceriol before him, Mártir Rizo offers the same advice for the same reason:

> El Principe que es Protector de vna Prouincia, deue atender principalmente a que en ella no entre con armas otro que sea no solo mas poderoso, pero igual, ni con armas algunas, porque no ay Principe por felizmente que gouierne, que no tenga algunos quexosos, y estos procuran luego acomodarse con el tiempo, porque la presuncion desprecia la seguridad, y no ay animo tan modesto, que en viendo la ocasion de vengarse, o la esperança de su aumento, no se auenture a experimentar su dicha, y con qualquiera rumor de armas se arrima a los enemigos del Principe, los quales le pueden ser de mucho daño, porque quando en los naturales vassallos hallan los contrarios, amparo, cerca està la ruina del estado del Principe.[81]

The prince must make sure that another powerful prince does not come into the province, because then those who are unhappy will adhere to the new prince in order to free themselves from subjugation.

As its title declares, chapter 16 is ostensibly dedicated to refuting Machiavelli's *Prince* 18: "Como deue guardar la Fè el Principe, y cumplir su palabra.

78 Mártir Rizo, *Norte*, 72–73.
79 Ibid., 80.
80 Machiavelli, *Principe*, 16.
81 Mártir Rizo, *Norte*, 80–81.

Escriuese contra el Capitulo 18. del Principe, de Nicolao Machiauello."[82] Nevertheless, a close reading reveals that in this chapter and the next, Mártir Rizo attempts to refashion the negative image of Machiavelli so common in the reason-of-state tradition, while still remaining within the bounds of that same tradition. He begins by deflecting attention away from Machiavelli, declaring that he does not deserve the credit for inventing his "falsa doctrina."[83] Instead, Mártir Rizo gives this honor to Seneca, who in his *Thyestes* made the tyrant Atreus say: "Piedad, razon, y Fè, son priuados bienes; pero conuiene al que rige hazer lo que quisiere para el aumento de su Estado."[84] Seneca wrote his tragedy, Mártir Rizo clarifies, in order to make his audience hate tyranny, instead choosing to live content under the dominion of good, virtuous men. The problem is that Machiavelli has taken this idea out of the context of poetry and placed it in a treatise meant to educate princes. The result is that "Machiavello se valio de esta doctrina para formar vn Principe tirano, no para instituir vn Rey Catolico."[85] This digressive introduction employs the conventional, anti-Machiavellian characterization of Machiavelli as a writer of "false doctrine" and advisor for tyrants that was common in the reason-of-state tradition. On the other hand, Mártir Rizo subtly deflects blame away from Machiavelli himself, through a two-part operation: first, he goes against the same reason-of-state tradition by denying that he was the originator of the false doctrine; second, he indirectly suggests that Machiavelli's intention could have been the same as Seneca's, to make his republican readers hate tyranny when it appears under the guise of legitimate principalities.

Mártir Rizo goes on to attack the anti-Machiavellians themselves, such as Possevino, Ribadeneyra and Frachetta, pointing out that they do not answer Machiavelli on his own terms:

> no le arguyen con armas iguales, vno haze aparato de sus yerros, alguno alaba las virtudes, que ellas por si mismas lo estan tanto, y otros no dizen cosa de importancia; por esta causa me determinè escriuir contra este capitulo, por ser adonde el particularmente derramò su veneno, siendo mi intento reprouar su doctrina, no con sentencias de Santos, y Filosofos, pues no ha auido alguno en el mundo, que no alabe la Fè, la Religion, y las demas virtudes, de que deuen los Principes estar adornados: y hazerlo assi, no seria hazer prueua, sino amontonar sentencias, sin descubrir la verdad. Gran fuerça hazen las autoridades de los doctos, mas en esta ocasion nos auemos de deshazer de las opiniones, y oluidar el parecer de los que han tratado desto. La defensa e la

82 Ibid., 89.

83 Ibid.

84 Ibid., 91. Interestingly, Mártir Rizo adds "para el aumento de su Estado" to his translation of the original text: "Sanctitas pietas fides priuata bona sunt; qua iuuat reges eant" (vv. 217–18). In this way, he adapts Seneca's play to the language common in the reason-of-state tradition.

85 Ibid.

> verdad ha de ser con la razon natural, y con la historia supuesto que el Autor no prueua su opinion con mas autoridades, que con las razones y historias que hallò para ello.[86]

While situating himself within the anti-Machiavellian tradition, and employing the common poison metaphor, Mártir Rizo criticizes the anti-Machiavellians' method of repeating the traditional list of virtues described by the usual ecclesiastical and classical authorities. He is writing from the perspective of one who believes that once Machiavelli had reorganized these virtues in such a way as to permit the prince to maintain his state and bring about the common good in this life, a simple restatement of the virtues as they were conceived before Machiavelli is insufficient. In fact, in this critique of the anti-Machiavellians, Mártir Rizo draws heavily from the *Prince* 15, precisely the chapter where Machiavelli begins this reorganization. For example, when Mártir Rizo points out that no one has ever not praised these virtues, he is not only implying that Machiavelli should be included in this assertion; in fact, he is repeating Machiavelli's own idea, which he puts forth after enumerating the traditional virtues and vices: "E io so che ciascuno confesserà che sarebbe laudabilissima cosa uno principe trovarsi, di tutte le soprascritte qualità, quelle che sono tenute buone."[87] Later, when Mártir Rizo writes that we must forget the opinions of the authorities in order to use reason and the examples of history, he is not simply pointing out that these are Machiavelli's own methods of discourse; he is again repeating Machiavelli's own idea:

> E perché io so che molti di questo hanno scritto, dubito, scrivendone ancora io, non essere tenuto prosuntuoso, partendome massime, nel disputare questa materia, da li ordini delli altri. Ma sendo l'intenzione mia stata scrivere cosa che sia utile a chi la intende, mi è parso piú conveniente andare dreto alla verità effettuale della cosa che alla immaginazione di essa.[88]

Mártir Rizo follows the reason-of-state tradition when he claims that Machiavelli's historical analyses are inaccurate. He quotes the passage from the *Prince* 18 that he cannot accept:

> *En nuestros tiempos enseña la experiencia que aquellos Principes han conseguido grandes cosas, que han hecho poco caso de su palabra, y que han sabido con astucia traer engañados los juizios de los hombres, y en fin han vencido a los que se fundauan en la lealtad y fundamento de su palabra.*[89]

86 Ibid., 93–94.
87 Machiavelli, *Principe*, 104.
88 Ibid., 102.
89 Mártir Rizo, *Norte*, 94.

This translation, although not word-for-word, follows quite closely Machiavelli's opening remarks of that chapter: "si vede per esperienza ne' nostri tempi quelli principi avere fatto gran cose, che della fede hanno tenuto poco conto e che hanno saputo con l'astuzia aggirare e' cervelli delli uomini: e alla fine hanno superato quelli che si sono fondati in su la realtà."[90] According to Mártir Rizo, this statement is false: "Lo primero auemos de suponer, que en esto miente."[91] To prove its falsehood, Mártir Rizo imitates the reason-of-state writers who point out historical examples of evil princes who died violently.

Mártir Rizo repeats the idea commonly found in the reason-of-state tradition that lying is impractical, because from it a prince will gain a bad reputation: "Y dado caso que vn Principe pudiesse engañar a alguno, esto seria vna vez: y en otras ocasiones era fuerça que nadie se fiasse de Principe que carecia de palabra y Fè."[92] At the same time, if every prince followed the advice of Machiavelli, then international politics would be completely chaotic:

> El Machiavello escriuio su Politica, para que todos los Principes se valiessen della; pues como puede ser que ninguno consiga su intento? siendo forçoso que el vno pretenda engañar al otro, y que todos viuan desconfiados, temiendo no caer en el lazo del contrario, y esto era proceder en vn infinito de engaños, pues aquel compondria alguno para arruinar al otro, y este armaria otros, a aquel para que se despeñasse en ellos, y estarian continuamente en vna guerra interior sin poder jamas assegurarse.[93]

In addition, lying offends God: "pues el perjuro que jura para engañar, manifiesta que desprecia a Dios y que teme mas aquel a quien haze el juramento que al mismo Dios."[94]

At this point, not surprisingly, Mártir Rizo introduces an exception. If a prince promises something that goes against natural and/or divine law, then he is permitted not to keep his word: "porque fuera mayor maldad dar la Fè, o palabra de hazer vn hecho malo, y el que aqui faltasse de su palabra, no solo no es perjuro, antes merece premio … los Principes prudentes no deuen obligarse con Fè y juramento a los otros Principes, de cosa que de derecho natural es ilicita, o por el derecho de las gentes."[95] In this way, Mártir Rizo follows the reason-of-state tradition of allowing the Christian prince moral flexibility: as long as he determines that whatever he has promised goes against natural or divine law, he is allowed to go against his word.

90 Machiavelli, *Principe*, 115.
91 Mártir Rizo, *Norte*, 94.
92 Ibid., 97.
93 Ibid., 99–100.
94 Ibid., 100.
95 Ibid., 101.

In the following chapter 17, "En que se prosigue la materia,"[96] Mártir Rizo proceeds to comment on other passages found in the *Prince* 18 that he declares false. In the context of keeping one's faith, Machiavelli continues his reorganization of the traditional dichotomy between virtue and vice by making the point that while it is impossible for a prince to have all of the traditional virtues, it is necessary and useful to appear to have them:

> A uno principe adunque non è necessario avere in fatto tutte le soprascritte qualità, ma è bene necessario parere di averle; anzi ardirò di dire questo: che, avendole e osservandole sempre, sono dannose, e, parendo di averle, sono utili; come parere piatoso, fedele, umano, intero, religioso, ed essere: ma stare in modo edificato con lo animo che, bisognando non essere, tu possa e sappia diventare il contrario.[97]

Here Machiavelli applies to the subject of appearances an important theme that runs throughout these chapters: the prince should be "good," from the traditional perspective, when he can; but he must also know when it is necessary to be "bad." Although Mártir Rizo's Spanish rendering of this passage is presented in italics, giving the impression of a quotation, a comparison reveals that it may more accurately be described as a summary: "*A vn Principe no es necessario ser benigno, piadoso, deuoto, y verdadero; pero es prouechoso parecer que tiene estas calidades, y tener de tal manera dispuesto el animo, que siendo necessario, pueda y sepa passarse a las contrarias*."[98] His summary leaves out the idea that the prince should not only appear to be good, but should also actually be good whenever possible. In this subtly altered form, Mártir Rizo condemns this passage: "Las quales razones son escandalosas, y indignas de que alguno las execute, pues era totalmente arruinar la naturaleza."[99]

In this same discussion, found in the *Prince* 18, regarding the importance of maintaining appearances, Machiavelli argues that the majority of men will judge the prince by his appearance, not by his essence: "ognuno vede quello che tu pari, pochi sentono quello che tu se'."[100] Mártir Rizo's Spanish translation of this isolated phrase changes the second to the third person, giving the impression of a universal aphorism: "*Todos ven lo que el hombre parece, y pocos sienten lo que es*."[101] He then follows the anti-Machiavellian practice of taking an idea out of context and making it appear that Machiavelli suggests that evil princes are able to hide their malice: "No ay en la naturaleza cosa mas dificil, que reprimir los afectos, no solo para la execucion de ellos, ocultallos parece impos-

96 Ibid., 103.
97 Machiavelli, *Principe*, 118.
98 Mártir Rizo, *Norte*, 103.
99 Ibid.
100 Machiavelli, *Principe*, 119.
101 Mártir Rizo, *Norte*, 105.

sible, por los ojos se descubre el coraçon, y este las mas vezes se manifiesta en la lengua, en las acciones."[102] In the end, a prince who lies will acquire the reputation of a liar, which is exactly what Machiavelli advises against: "y vn Principe sabio, antes deue mirar a lo que es justo que a la fama; y adquirilla de simulador, cauteloso, y engañador, no conuiene para la conseruacion del estado."[103] In this regard, Mártir Rizo's arguments in this context follow closely the reason-of-state tradition: the prince must not only appear to be a good, Christian prince, he must actually be one. Nevertheless, his advice points to the advantages produced in this world of maintaining a public image of being a good Christian. Following the criteria he established at the beginning of the previous chapter, he meets Machiavelli on his own terms, focussing on the conservation of the prince's state in this world, rather than his salvation in the next.

To conclude chapter 17, Mártir Rizo declares that he will use Machiavelli's own words to refute the idea that the appearance of religion is sufficient. Revealing an extensive direct familiarity with Machiavelli's works, he cites three passages from *Discourses* 1.11, where Machiavelli points out the importance of religion in political life:

> *Hallando Numa Pompilio vn pueblo ferocissimo, y queriendo reduzirle a la obediencia ciuil, con las artes de la paz se valio de la Religion, como cosa la mas necessaria para conseruar la vida ciuil: y de tal modo la estableciò, que en muchos siglos no huuo en otra parte tanto temor de Dios como en aquella Republica, lo qual facilitò qualquiera empressa, que el Senado, o aquellos grandes hombres Romanos intentaron conseguir.* Y mas adelante prosigue diziendo. *Y el que considerare bien las Historias Romanas, conocerà quanto seruia la Religion no simulada, para que obedeciessen los exercitos, para mantener la plebe, para conseruar los hombres buenos y auergonçar a los malos, de suerte que si se viniese a disputar a qual Principe estaua Roma mas obligada, a Romulo o a Numa? tengo por cierto que Numa alcançaria el primer grado, porque donde ay Religion, facilmente se pueden introduzir las armas, y donde ay armas y no Religion, con dificultad se podrà introduzir esta.* Concluiremos nosotros este discurso, con exortar a los Principes, Que cumplan la Fè, Que sean Religiosos, no se valiendo dello para aumento de los Estados, pues les saldra al contrario de lo que juzgaron, como auemos prouado, y persuadiremoslos con otras razones del mismo Autor, para que la autoridad que los engañò los dissuada del yerro concebido, dize pues al fin del capitulo citado: *Concluyo, que la Religion introducida por Numa fue de las primeras ocasiones de su felicidad, porque aquella causò buenas ordenes, y estas hazen buena fortuna, y della nacen los buenos sucessos de las empressas: y como la obseruancia del Culto diuino es ocasion de la grandeza de la Republica, assi el desprecio dello es ocasion de su ruina,*

102 Ibid., 105–6.
103 Ibid., 106.

> *porque donde falta el temor de Dios, es fuerça, o que aquel Reyno se destruya, o que se sustente del temor de vn Principe, que supla los defectos de la Religion: y porque los Principes, como hombres, son de corta vida, aquel Reyno se ha de acabar presto al passo que falta su virtud, de donde procede que los Reynos, y los que dependen solo de la virtud de vn hombre, son poco durables porque la virtud falta con la vida de aquel, y raras vezes se ha visto que se renueue con la sucession de otro, como prudentemente lo dize el Dante.*
>
> *Raras vezes deciende por la ramas*
> *el humano valor, que assi lo ordena*
> *el que le dà, porque se llame suyo.*
>
> Digan nos aora sus discipulos, y los professores de aquella falsa doctrina, quando le auemos de dar credito? quando habla la verdad como Catolico? o quando sin Fè enseña mintiendo a que yerren los hombres?[104]

While Mártir Rizo's Spanish translation of these three passages is quite accurate on the whole, he introduces one significant alteration, replacing Machiavelli's "religione" with "*Religion no simulada.*"[105] In this way, Mártir Rizo subtly emends Machiavelli so that his text is more acceptable to the seventeenth-century Spanish readership.

When he introduces this passage, Mártir Rizo states that Machiavelli contradicts himself. Nevertheless, he also implies that Machiavelli was not entirely evil and that, in this case, he was writing like a true, pious Christian: "Mas por si las razones que auemos dicho, no concluyen las opiniones que estan propuestas, sirua el mismo Autor, de confutarse sus yerros, con lo que en otras partes dizen en fabor de la Religion, hablando entonces con tanta piedad Christiana, como aqui temerariamente."[106] After reproducing the three passages, he again implies that Machiavelli contradicts himself. In this same passage, however, he distinguishes between one Machiavelli who sometimes writes as a true Catholic and one who sometimes teaches falsehood. In addition, he goes on to differentiate between Machiavelli, on the one hand, and the teachers and students of "that false doctrine," on the other. By employing "aquella," the demonstrative adjective that implies distance, he grammatically distances that doctrine from what Machiavelli says in these passages. In this way Mártir Rizo's portrait of Machiavelli, while following the reason-of-state tradition in part, is much more nuanced than the picture of the evil mastermind behind tyrants put forth by the extreme self-proclaimed anti-Machiavellians.

104 Ibid., 106–9.
105 Ibid., 107.
106 Ibid., 106.

In chapter 18, "Del Consejo del Principe,"[107] Mártir Rizo draws his main ideas from the *Prince* 22 and 23. First, Machiavelli divides the intellectual capacity of the prince into three kinds: "e' sono di tre generazione cervelli, – l'uno intende da sé, l'altro discerne quello che altri intende, el terzo non intende né sé sé altri: quel primo è eccellentissimo, el secondo eccellente, el terzo inutile."[108] Mártir Rizo describes only the first two of these three: "es juzgado por excelente hombre ciuil el que por si mismo se sabe aconsejar en las ocurrencias propias, aunque esto es muy dificultoso, respeto de la pasion con que todos miramos las cosas que pretendemos; y serà tenido por mediano juizio, el que no sabiendo por si, se sabe reduzir al Consejo del que es tenido por sabio."[109] Perhaps Mártir Rizo did not wish to imply that his monarch could possibly be considered the third kind, he who displays total incompetence. In any case, the reference to the "mediano juizio" implies its existence. In the *Prince* 23, Machiavelli teaches the prince several measures to protect himself from flatterers. He should reduce his council to a small group of wise men; they should only be allowed to speak to him on subjects about which he asks for advice; he should listen patiently to the truth and insist that they leave nothing out; then he should make a decision on his own and act accordingly and consistently. As Machiavelli concludes the chapter: "e' buoni consigli, da qualunque venghino, conviene naschino da la prudenza del principe, e non la prudenza del principe da' buoni consigli."[110]

Likewise, Mártir Rizo insists that the prince be independent:

> pero deue el que gouierna alentarse a ser tal, que en su dominio sepa ser solo, y si quiere ser señor, trate las materias de Estado, manejando los instrumentos del gouierno … este Consejo por prudente y sagaz que sea, conuiene vencerle con la inteligencia y capacidad del Principe, de forma que a la conseruacion del estado le sea acessorio y no principal.[111]

Like Machiavelli, according to Mártir Rizo the council should be an "accessory." In the *Prince* 23, Machiavelli repeatedly insists that although the prince should be somewhat independent, he should still make good use of his council by asking them for advice frequently: "ma debbe domandargli d'ogni cosa."[112] And again: "ma lui debbe bene essere largo domandatore."[113] Similarly, Mártir Rizo urges the prince to make wise use of his council:

107 Ibid., 109.
108 Machiavelli, *Principe*, 154.
109 Mártir Rizo, *Norte*, 109.
110 Machiavelli, *Principe*, 159.
111 Mártir Rizo, *Norte*, 109–10.
112 Machiavelli, *Principe*, 157.
113 Ibid., 158.

> y no porque yo desee al Principe sabio, en si mismo, le pretendo quitar el Consejo cerca de si: antes digo, que vno de los mayores fundamentos de su reputacion serà la fama, de que ha juntado al juizio y inteligencia propia, vn fiel y prudente Consejo, teniendo gran cuidado en hazerle tal.[114]

In fact, this notion of acquiring fame through the prudent use of one's faithful council also comes from Machiavelli's opening remarks of the *Prince* 22: "E la prima coniettura, che si fa del cervello d'uno signore, è vedere li uomini che lui ha d'intorno: e quando sono sufficienti e fedeli, sempre si può reputarlo savio, perché ha saputo conoscerli sufficienti e sa mantenerli fedeli."[115]

For chapter 19, "De la Milicia,"[116] Mártir Rizo draws heavily from the *Prince* 12. There Machiavelli emphasizes the importance of military strength:

> E' principali fondamenti che abbino tutti li stati, cosí nuovi come vecchi o misti, sono le buone legge e le buone arme: e perché e' non può essere buone legge dove non sono buone arme, e dove sono buone arme conviene sieno buone legge, io lascerò indietro el ragionare delle legge e parlerò delle arme.[117]

Mártir Rizo's opening remarks are so similar that they may be considered an elaborated translation:

> La conseruacion del Estado de vn Principe, consiste en buenas leyes, y buenas armas, y donde estas faltan, no es possible que sea durable el Imperio, aquellas son las que a los subditos los hazen viuir conforme la razon, y estas las que los defienden; y porque donde ay buena Milicia se presume que aurà buenas leyes, pues estas las gouiernan, dexarè de tratar de las leyes; porque no conuienen a este discurso, y hablaremos de las armas.[118]

Machiavelli then distinguishes between several kinds of arms: "Dico adunque che le arme con le quali uno principe difende el suo stato o le sono proprie, o le sono mercennarie o ausiliarie o miste."[119] These reappear unchanged in Mártir Rizo's chapter: "Las armas con que los Principes se defienden, son mercenarias, auxiliares, mistas, o de soldados vassallos propios, que son las mejores."[120] Machiavelli explains why mercenary and auxiliary soldiers (*arme*) are useless: "le non hanno altro amore né altra cagione che le tenga in

114 Mártir Rizo, *Norte*, 110.
115 Machiavelli, *Principe*, 153–54.
116 Mártir Rizo, *Norte*, 117.
117 Machiavelli, *Principe*, 78.
118 Mártir Rizo, *Norte*, 117–18,
119 Machiavelli, *Principe*, 79.
120 Mártir Rizo, *Norte*, 118.

campo che un poco di stipendio, il quale non è sufficiente a fare che voglino morire per te."[121] In contrast, Mártir Rizo elects to cite the reasons why one's own soldiers are useful:

> porque los soldados vassallos del Principe, no solo pelean por el interes, sino por la Fè con que estan obligados a su Principe por su patria a quien aman y desean que se conserue, por sus mugeres, hijos y familia a quien desean guardar las vidas por su honra, pues consiste en vsar bien de las armas, la estimacion que hazen dellos, y por el premio que esperan (demas de su sueldo) quando han seruido valerosamente.[122]

While Machiavelli states the negative and Mártir Rizo the positive, both teach that one's own soldiers fight better out of love for their monarch and homeland, something a wage cannot replace.

***

Mártir Rizo's *Norte de principes* is a special case in the history of the reception of Machiavelli in Spain. Certain important Machiavellian discourses run throughout the reason-of-state tradition, even in those authors who do not demonstrate a direct familiarity with Machiavelli's writings, as we have seen. Mártir Rizo, on the other hand, engaged Machiavelli's political works directly, carrying out a close rereading of major sections of the *Prince*, and even including quotations from the *Discourses on Livy*, in an effort to attenuate the popular negative image of Machiavelli and adapt his texts to his Catholic readership. With this in mind, while we take for granted an attitude of general acceptance of Machiavelli on the part of Mártir Rizo, his expression of hostility toward the author of the text with which he is working and the ways he adapts that text reveal much about the context in which he is writing and his assumptions regarding his readers. What emerges is a rather clear picture of the extent to which Machiavelli's political discourse could be useful for the Spanish readership in the first half of the seventeenth century. Spaniards could accept Machiavelli's mixing of the traditional, Aristotelian division between king and tyrant, his reorganization of the princely virtues and vices, and the need, in many situations, to focus on the avoidance of hatred rather than the cultivation of love. They could accept his call for the prince to be morally flexible in the service of the common good. They could accept his insight into matters of war, with regard to having a policy of imperial expansion and using one's own soldiers. They could even accept, at least in part, his observations regarding the practical, political usefulness of institutionalized religion. What they could not accept, on the other hand, was a politics completely independent from religion, a Spain independent from the

121 Machiavelli, *Principe*, 79–80.
122 Mártir Rizo, *Norte*, 118.

Roman Catholic Church and its representatives, or a king who was not sincerely Catholic himself. Now, this separation between Church and state is not precisely, nor could it have been, what Machiavelli's texts express. However, for reasons that we have pinpointed, the figure of Machiavelli came to represent for the Spaniards exactly this idea. In this way, their attack on "Maquiavelo" should not be understood as an attack on Machiavellian discourse; on the contrary, as I hope this study makes clear, this discourse was pervasive in Spanish political thought throughout the early modern period.

Conclusion

In this study I offer a new method for determining to what extent Spanish political prose writers should be considered Machiavellian, based not on their own self-fashioning, but on the observable appropriation of Machiavelli's vocabulary and theoretical framework used to deal with the unpredictable and the contingent in political life. As such, this new method allows us to make historically valid judgments regarding the scope of Machiavelli's influence over the subsequent political discourse in Spain. This method reveals that Maravall, over half a century ago, was in part correct, because he recognized that many Spaniards incorporated important aspects of Machiavellian thought; his over-generalizations are explainable because he was writing before the ideological reading of Machiavelli, employed in this study, had fully developed. Maravall simply lacked the tools necessary to pinpoint not only the specific Machiavellian borrowings but a general acceptance of key changes to the tradition ushered in by Machiavelli that Spaniards would later incorporate into their own political discourse. On the other hand, I argue that more recently historians such as Fernández-Santamaría and Bireley essentially brought the Counter-Reformation anti-Machiavellian tradition up-to-date. They accepted the anti-Machiavellians' descriptions of the so-called "doctrine" or "school" of Machiavelli and his supposed followers and, as a result, their own self-characterization by contrast to this invented doctrine.

As I have demonstrated throughout this study, the breadth and depth of Machiavelli's impact in early modern Spain have been vastly underestimated until now. Machiavelli's texts changed the face of Spanish political thought. His general reorganization of the traditional dichotomies between virtue and vice, king and tyrant, controlled the parameters of the discussions found in the political essays written in Spain from around the middle of the sixteenth century to the end of the Baroque and beyond, both in and around the courts of the successive Hapsburg monarchs, but also abroad, in important centers of the Spanish empire such as the Netherlands, Portugal and Mexico. Many of the Spanish political writers of the early modern period demonstrate a direct familiarity with Machiavelli's *Prince* and *Discourses*. And this should come as no surprise, since Puigdomenech demonstrated the wide circulation of these texts in Spain in both manuscript and print, in the original Italian and in translation, as we have seen. Perhaps more importantly, the vast majority of these writers appropriated various of Machiavelli's key discourses and adapted them to their own Catholic imperialist ethos. Regardless of whether or not they silently cited Machiavelli directly or even characterized themselves as anti-Machiavellian, these writers should be considered Machiavellian, in a strictly historicized sense of this adjective. By demonstrating just how widely Machiavelli's discourses had spread among political treatises, this study constitutes the foundation for a general reconsideration of Machiavelli's impact in Spain in the sixteenth and seventeenth centuries.

What remains to be done in order realize fully such a reconsideration is to expand this inquiry beyond political treatises strictly speaking to other genres of texts. A perusal of the few literary studies of specific cases of Machiavellian reception in Spain reveals an uncritical use of the Spanish anti-Machiavellians' own misleading representations of Machiavelli. Critics have used the term *Machiavellian* in a wide variety of ways: pragmatic or utilitarian,[1] republican,[2] absolutist or autocratic,[3] unethical or amoral,[4] pagan or un-Christian,[5] tyrannical,[6] even demonic;[7] often two or more of these definitions coincide in the same author. One critic disregards chronology completely and labels *Celestina* as Machiavellian.[8] In some cases critics support their use of *Machiavellian* indirectly, through reference to one or more of the anti-Machiavellians;[9] others imitate the anti-Machiavellian method of taking passages out of the context of Machiavelli's works, usually the *Prince*.[10] In any case, the general trend among

1 Gonzalo Restrepo Jaramillo, "Maquiavelo-Saavedra Fajardo," *Universidad Pontificia Bolivariana* 21 (1957): 348; Ingrid Vindel, "Política y educación para príncipes en una comedia de 1615: *El mejor maestro, el tiempo*," *Anuario Lope de Vega* 6 (2000): 212.

2 Rupp, *Allegories of Kingship*, 20.

3 Restrepo Jaramillo, "Maquiavelo-Saavedra Fajardo," 349, who goes so far as to label Machiavelli "totalitarista" (352); Jorge Kattán Zablah, "Maquiavelo y el jesuita Gracián," *Káñina: Revista de Artes y Letras de la Universidad de Costa Rica* 5, no. 2 (1981): 91; Bernal Herrera Montero, "*Fuenteovejuna* de Lope de Vega y el maquiavelismo," *Criticon* 45 (1989): 141–42; Rupp, *Allegories of Kingship*, 20.

4 Restrepo Jaramillo, "Maquiavelo-Saavedra Fajardo," 348–49; S. I. Luis Sierra, "La moral política: El antimaquiavelismo en Suárez y Gracián," *Arbor: Revista General de Investigación y Cultura* 48, no. 183 (1961): 41.

5 Restrepo Jaramillo, "Maquiavelo-Saavedra Fajardo," 350; Sierra, "La moral política," 36–37; Rupp, *Allegories of Kingship*, 7–8.

6 Restrepo Jaramillo, "Maquiavelo-Saavedra Fajardo," 347; Rupp, *Allegories of Kingship*, 7.

7 Rupp, *Allegories of Kingship*, 8.

8 Barrio Olano, *La novela picaresca*, 51.

9 See, for example, Sierra, "La moral política," and Rupp, *Allegories of Kingship*.

10 Restrepo Jaramillo, "Maquiavelo-Saavedra Fajardo," 354–55; Kattán Zablah, "Maquiavelo y el jesuita Gracián"; Claudia Ruiz, "Apologistas de la manera y de la apariencia," *Anuario de Letras Modernas* 7 (1995–96): 125–41; Herrera Montero, "*Fuenteovejuna*"; Santiago García-Castañón, "Corrientes del pensamiento maquiavélico en una comedia inédita de Bances Candamo," *Cuadernos de Aldeeu* 7, no. 1 (1991): 19–29; Irene Mizrahi, "El maquiavelismo renacentista en *Las cartas de relación* de Hernán Cortés" *Dactylus* 12 (1993): 98–115.

these critics is to use the term *Machiavellian* without examining whether or not their implicit definitions of the term are valid for their discussion. Instead, they use the word as if it conveyed some universal point of view with respect to politics, regardless of any particular cultural context and moment in history in which their definition might have developed. Hopefully the diachronic vision of the reception of Machiavelli in Spain developed in this study may be used as a framework for making more accurate observations regarding the specific mechanisms by which Spanish authors of histories and *relaciones*, emblems, theatrical plays, epic and lyrical poems, and prose novels appropriated Machiavellian discourses throughout the early modern period.

Bibliography

Primary Sources

Alvia de Castro, Fernando. *Verdadera razon de estado*. Lisbon: Pedro Craesbeeck, 1616.

Aquinas, Thomas. *De regimine principum ad regem Cypri*. Ed. Joseph Mathis. Casali, Italy: Marietti, 1971.

Aristotle. *The Politics*. Trans. Carnes Lord. Chicago: University of Chicago Press, 1984.

Ayala, Balthazar. *De jure et officiis bellicis et disciplina militari libri III*. Ed. John Westlake. Trans. John Pawley Bate. 2 vols. Washington, D. C.: Carnegie Institution of Washington, 1912.

Barbosa Homem, Pedro. *Discursos de la iuridica, y verdadera razon de estado formados sobre la vida, y acciones del Rey don Iuan el II. de buena memoria, Rey de Portugal, llamado vulgarmente el Principe Perfecto. CONTRA MACHAVELO, Y bodino, y los demas politicos de nuestros tiempos, sus sequazes*. Coimbra, Portugal: Nicolao Caruallo, n.d.

Blázquez Mayoralgo, Juan. *Perfecta raçon de estado. Deducida de los hechos de el señor rey don Fernando el Catholico Quinto de este nombre en Castilla, y Segundo en Aragon. Contra los politicos atheistas*. Mexico City: Francisco Robledo, 1646.

Botero, Giovanni. *Della ragion di stato*. Ed. Chiara Continisio. Roma: Donzelli, 2009.

———. *Diez libros de la razon de estado. Con tres libros de las causas de la grandeza, y magnificencia de las ciudades de Iuan Botero. Tradvzido de Italiano en Castellano, por mandado del Rey nuestro señor, Por Antonio de Herrera su criado*. Madrid: Luys Sanchez, 1592.

Clemente, Claudio. *El machiavelismo degollado por la Christiana Sabiduria de España y Austria. Discurso cristiano-politico a la Católica Majestad de Philippo IV, rey de las Españas. Por el Padre Clavdio Clemente de la Compañia de Iesvs, natural de Ornans en el Condado de Borgoña, Cathedratico de Erudicion en los Estudios Reales de Madrid. Tradvcido de la segvnda edicion latina, añadida con cosas muy particulares, y del tiempo*. Alcalá de Henares: Antonio Vázquez, 1637.

Furió Ceriol, Fadrique. *El concejo y consejeros del príncipe*. Ed. Henry Méchoulan. Madrid: Tecnos, 1993.

García de Castrojeriz, Juan. *Glosa castellana al "Regimiento de príncipes" de Egidio Romano*. Ed. Juan Beneyto Pérez. 2nd. ed. Madrid: Centro de Estudios Políticos y Constitucionales, 2005.

Gentillet, Innocent. *Anti-Machiavel*. Ed. Edward Rathé. Geneva: Droz, 1968.

Gracián de la Madre de Dios, Jerónimo. *Diez lamentaciones del miserable estado de los Atheistas de nuestros tiempos*. Brussels: Roger Velpio & Huberto Antonio, 1611.

Guevara, Antonio de. *Menosprecio de corte y alabanza de aldea. Arte de marear*. Ed. Asunción Rallo Gruss. Madrid: Cátedra, 1987.

———. *Obras completas*. Madrid: Turner, 1994.

———. *Relox de príncipes*. Ed. Emilio Blanco. Madrid: ABL Editor, 1994.

Machiavelli, Niccolò. *Discorsi sopra la prima deca di Tito Livio*. Ed. Francesco Bausi. Roma: Salerno Editrice, 2001.

———. *Il Principe*. Ed. Giorgio Inglese. Torino: Einaudi, 1995.

Mártir Rizo, Juan Pablo. *Norte de principes*. Madrid: Diego Flamenco, 1626.

Ottevanti, Juan Lorenzo. *Discursos de Nicolao Machiaueli Dirigidos al muy alto y poderoso Señor don Philippe Principe de España nuestro Señor*. Medina del Campo: Guillermo de Millis, 1552.

———. *"Discursos de Nicolao Machiaueli": Juan Lorenzo Ottevanti's Spanish Translation of Machiavelli's Discourses on Livy (1552)*. Ed. Keith David Howard. Tempe: Arizona Center for Medieval and Renaissance Studies, forthcoming.

Penna, Mario, ed. *Prosistas castellanos del siglo XV*. Vol. 1. Madrid: Ediciones Atlas, 1959.

Ptolemy of Lucca. *On the Government of Rulers:* De regimine principum*; With Portions attributed to Thomas Aquinas*. Trans. James M. Blythe. Philadelphia: University of Pennsylvania Press, 1997.

Ribadeneyra, Pedro de. *Obras escogidas*. Biblioteca de Autores Españoles 60. Ed. D. Vicente de la Fuente. Madrid: Imprenta de Hernando y Compañía, 1899.

Salazar, Diego de. *Tratado de re militari*. Ed. Eva Botella Ordinas. Madrid: Ministerio de Defensa, 2000.

Sánchez de Arévalo, Rodrigo. *Suma de la política*. Ed. Juan Beneyto Pérez. Madrid: Consejo Superior de Investigaciones Científicas, 1944.

Santa María, Juan de. *Tratado de republica y policia christiana para reyes y principes y para los que en el gobierno tienen sus veces*. Madrid: Imprenta Real, 1615.

Sepúlveda, Juan Ginés de. *Demócrates segundo o de las justas causas de la guerra contra los indios*. Ed. Ángel Losada. 2nd ed. Madrid: Instituto Francisco de Vitoria, 1984.

Valdés, Alfonso de. *Diálogo de Mercurio y Carón*. Ed. Rosa Navarro Durán. Madrid: Cátedra, 1999.

Vitoria, Francisco de. *Political Writings*. Ed. Anthony Pagden and Jeremy Lawrance. Cambridge: Cambridge University Press, 1991.

Zeballos, Jerónimo de. *Arte real para el buen gouierno de los reyes y principes y de sus vasallos, en el qual se refieren las obligaciones de cada vno, con los principales documentos para el buen gouierno*. Toledo: Diego Rodriguez, 1623.

Secondary Sources

Anglo, Sydney. *Machiavelli: A Dissection*. New York: Harcourt, Brace & World, 1969.

———. *Machiavelli—The First Century: Studies in Enthusiasm, Hostility, and Irrelevance*. Oxford: Oxford University Press, 2005.

Arbulu Barturen, María Begoña. "La primera traducción española." in *The First Translations of Machiavelli's "Prince": From the Sixteenth to the First Half of the Nineteenth Century*, ed. Roberto De Pol, 117–69. Amsterdam: Rodopi, 2010.

Baron, Hans. *The Crisis of the Early Italian Renaissance: Civic Humanism and Republican Liberty in an Age of Classicism and Tyranny*. Princeton, NJ: Princeton University Press, 1955.

———. "Leonardo Bruni: 'Professional Rhetorician' or Civic Humanist?" *Past and Present* 36 (1967): 21–37.

Barrio Olano, José Ignacio. *La novela picaresca y el método maquiavélico*. Madrid: Editorial Pliegos, 1998.

Bataillon, Marcel. *Erasmo y España: Estudios sobre la historia espiritual del siglo XVI*. 2nd ed. México: Fondo de Cultura Económica, 1966.

Beame, Edmond M. "The Use and Abuse of Machiavelli: The Sixteenth-Century French Adaptation." *Journal of the History of Ideas* 43, no. 1 (1982): 33–54.

Bireley, Robert. *The Counter-Reformation Prince: Anti-Machiavellianism or Catholic Statecraft in Early Modern Europe*. Chapel Hill: University of North Carolina Press, 1990.

Bollard de Broce, Kathleen. "Authorizing Literary Propaganda: Alfonso de Valdés' *Diálogo de las cosas acaecidas en Roma*." *Hispanic Review* 68, no. 2 (2000): 131–45.

———. "The Rhetoric of Exemplarity in Two Spanish Sixteenth-Century *Specula Principis*." *Symposium* 53, no. 2 (1999): 83–91.

Bouza, Fernando. *Corre manuscrito: Una historia cultural del Siglo de Oro*. Madrid: Marcial Pons, 2001.

Braun, Harald E. "Baroque Constitution and Hybrid Political Language: The Case of Juan de Mariana (1535–1624) and Juan Márquez (1565–1621)." *Revista Canadiense de Estudios Hispánicos* 33, no. 1 (2008): 79–104.

Burke, Peter. "Tacitism, Scepticism, and Reason of State." In *The Cambridge History of Political Thought: 1450–1700*, ed. J. H. Burns, 479–98. Cambridge: Cambridge University Press, 1991.

Cardascia, G. "Machiavel et Jean Bodin." *Bibliothèque d'Humanisme et Renaissance* 3 (1943): 129–67.

Castilla Urbano, Francisco. "Rasgos maquiavélicos en un pensador antimaquiavélico: Juan Ginés de Sepúlveda." In Forte and López Álvarez, *Maquiavelo y España*, 111–33.

Cochrane, Eric W. *Historians and Historiography in the Italian Renaissance*. Chicago: University of Chicago Press, 1981.

Colish, Marcia L. "The Idea of Liberty in Machiavelli." *Journal of the History of Ideas* 32 (1971): 323–50.

———. "Republicanism, Religion, and Machiavelli's Savonarolan Moment." *Journal of the History of Ideas* 60, no. 4 (1999): 597–616.

Cutinelli-Rèndina, Emanuele. *Chiesa e religione in Machiavelli*. Pisa: Istituti editoriali e poligrafici internazionali, 1998.

De Mattei, Rodolfo. *Dal premachiavellismo all'antimachiavellismo*. Florence: Sansoni, 1969.

———. *Il problema della "ragion di stato" nell'età della Controriforma*. Milan: Riccardo Ricciardi Editore, 1979.

Di Camillo, Ottavio. *El humanismo castellano del siglo XV*. Valencia: F. Torres, 1976.

Donaldson, Peter S. *Machiavelli and Mystery of State*. Cambridge: Cambridge University Press, 1988.

Edwards, John. *Ferdinand and Isabella*. New York: Pearson, 2005.

Elliot, J. H. *The Count-Duke of Olivares: The Statesman in an Age of Decline*. New Haven, CT: Yale University Press, 1986.

Fernández de la Mora, Gonzalo. "Maquiavelo, visto por los tratadistas políticos españoles de la Contrarreforma." *Arbor: Revista General de Investigación y Cultura* 13, no. 43–44 (1949): 417–49.

Fernández-Santamaría, J. A. *Natural Law, Constitutionalism, Reason of State, and War*. 2 vols. New York: Peter Lang, 2006.

———. *Razón de estado y política en el pensamiento español del barroco (1595–1640)*. Madrid: Centro de Estudios Constitucionales, 1986.

———. *The State, War and Peace: Spanish Political Thought in the Renaissance, 1516–1559*. Cambridge: Cambridge University Press, 1977.

Feros, Antonio. *Kingship and Favoritism in the Spain of Philip III, 1598–1621*. Cambridge: Cambridge University Press, 2000.

Fontana, Benedetto. "Love of Country and Love of God: The Political Uses of Religion in Machiavelli." *Journal of the History of Ideas* 60, no. 4 (1999): 639–58.

Forte, Juan Manuel, and Pablo López Álvarez, eds. *Maquiavelo y España: Maquiavelismo y antimaquiavelismo en la cultura española de los siglos XVI y XVII*. Madrid: Biblioteca Nueva, 2008.

García-Castañón, Santiago. "Corrientes del pensamiento maquiavélico en una comedia inédita de Bances Candamo." *Cuadernos de Aldeeu* 7, no. 1 (1991): 19–29.

Geerken, John H. "Machiavelli's Moses and Renaissance Politics." *Journal of the History of Ideas* 60, no. 4 (1999): 579–95.

Gerli, E. Michael. "Performing Nobility: Mosén Diego de Valera and the Poetics of Converso Identity." *La Coronica: A Journal of Medieval Spanish Language and Literature* 25, no. 1 (1996): 19–36.

Gilbert, Allan H. *Machiavelli's Prince and Its Forerunners:* The Prince *as a Typical Book* De Regimine Principum. New York: Barnes & Noble, 1968.

Gilbert, Felix. *Machiavelli and Guicciardini: Politics and History in Sixteenth Century Florence*. Princeton, NJ: Princeton University Press, 1965.

———. *Niccolò Machiavelli e la vita culturale del suo tempo*. Bologna: Mulino, 1964.

Hafter, Monroe Z. *Gracián and Perfection: Spanish Moralists of the Seventeenth Century*. Cambridge, MA: Harvard University Press, 1966.

Herrera Montero, Bernal. "*Fuenteovejuna* de Lope de Vega y el maquiavelismo." *Criticon* 45 (1989): 131–53.

Hörnqvist, Mikael. *Machiavelli and Empire*. Cambridge: Cambridge University Press, 2004.

Iñurritegui Rodríguez, José María. *La gracia y la república: El lenguaje político de la teología católica y "El príncipe cristiano" de Pedro de Ribadeneyra*. Madrid: Universidad Nacional de Educación a Distancia, 1998.

Kahn, Victoria. *Rhetoric, Prudence, and Skepticism in the Renaissance*. Ithaca, NY: Cornell University Press, 1985.

Kamen, Henry. *Philip of Spain*. New Haven, CT: Yale University Press, 1997.

Kantorowicz, Ernst H. *The King's Two Bodies: A Study of Mediaeval Political Theology*. Princeton, NJ: Princeton University Press, 1957.

Kattán Zablah, Jorge. "Maquiavelo y el jesuita Gracián." *Káñina: Revista de Artes y Letras de la Universidad de Costa Rica* 5, no. 2 (1981): 91–94.

Kelley, Donald R. "Murd'rous Machiavel in France: A Post Mortem." *Political Science Quarterly* 85, no. 4 (1970): 545–59.

Kohut, Karl. "Sánchez de Arévalo (1404–1470) frente al humanismo italiano." *Actas del VI Congreso de la Asociación Internacional de Hispanistas* (1980): 431–34.

Kristeller, Paul Oskar. "Studies on Renaissance Humanism During the Last Twenty Years." *Studies in the Renaissance* 9 (1962): 7–30.

Lawrance, Jeremy. "Humanism in the Iberian Peninsula." In *The Impact of Humanism on Western Europe*, ed. Anthony Goodman and Angus MacKay, 220–58. London: Longman, 1990.

———. "On Fifteenth-Century Spanish Vernacular Humanism." In *Medieval and Renaissance Studies in Honour of Robert Brian Tate*, ed. Ian Michael and Richard A. Cardwell, 63–79. Oxford: Dolphin, 1986.

———. "The Spread of Lay Literacy in Late Medieval Castile." *Bulletin of Hispanic Studies* 62, no. 1 (1985): 79–94.

———. *Un tratado de Alonso de Cartagena sobre la educación y los estudios literarios*. Barcelona: Universidad Autónoma de Barcelona, Facultad de Letras Bellaterra, 1979.

Lupher, David A. *Romans in a New World: Classical Models in Sixteenth-Century Spanish America*. Ann Arbor: University of Michigan Press, 2003.

Lynch, John. *The Hispanic World in Crisis and Change*. Oxford: Blackwell, 1992.

Maravall, José Antonio. *Carlos V y el pensamiento político del Renacimiento*. Madrid: Instituto de Estudios Políticos, 1960.

———. "Maquiavelo y maquiavelismo en España." In *Estudios de historia del pensamiento español*, 39–72. Madrid: Ediciones Cultura Hispánica, 1983.

———. *La teoría española del Estado en el siglo XVII*. Madrid: Instituto de Estudios Políticos, 1944.

Martin, John. "Inventing Sincerity, Refashioning Prudence: The Discovery of the Individual in Renaissance Europe." *The American Historical Review* 102, no. 5 (1997): 1309–42.

Meinecke, Friedrich. *Machiavellism: The Doctrine of Raison d'État and its Place in Modern History*. Trans. Douglas Scott. New Haven, CT: Yale University Press, 1957.

Mizrahi, Irene. "El maquiavelismo renacentista en *Las cartas de relación* de Hernán Cortés." *Dactylus* 12 (1993): 98–115.

Muldoon, James. *Empire and Order: The Concept of Empire, 800–1800*. London: Macmillan, 1999.

Najemy, John M. "Papirius and the Chickens, or Machiavelli on the Necessity of Interpreting Religion." *Journal of the History of Ideas* 60, no. 4 (1999): 659–81.

Nederman, Cary J. "Amazing Grace: Fortune, God, and Free Will in Machiavelli's Thought." *Journal of the History of Ideas* 60, no. 4 (1999): 617–38.

Nieto Soria, José Manuel. *Fundamentos ideológicos del poder real en Castilla (siglos XIII–XVI)*. Madrid: Eudema, 1988.

Patch, Howard Rollin. *The Goddess Fortuna in Mediaeval Literature*. New York: Octagon Books, 1967.

Pitkin, Hanna Fenichel. *Fortune Is a Woman*. Berkeley and Los Angeles: University of California Press, 1984.

Pocock, J. G. A. *The Machiavellian Moment: Florentine Political Thought and the Atlantic Republican Tradition*. 2nd ed. Princeton, NJ: Princeton University Press, 2003.

Preus, J. Samuel. "Machiavelli's Functional Analysis of Religion: Context and Object." *Journal of the History of Ideas* 40 (1979): 171–90.

Procacci, Giuliano. *Machiavelli nella cultura europea dell'età moderna*. Roma: Editori Laterza, 1995.

Puigdomenech Forcada, Helena. *Maquiavelo en España: Presencia de sus obras en los siglos XVI y XVII*. Madrid: Fundación Universitaria Española, 1988.

Pulido Serrano, Juan Ignacio. *Injurias a Cristo: Religión, política y antijudaísmo en el siglo XVII (Análisis de las corrientes antijudías durante la Edad Moderna)*. Alcalá de Henares: Instituto Internacional de Estudios Sefardíes y Andalusíes, Universidad de Alcalá, 2002.

Rabil, Albert Jr., ed. *Renaissance Humanism: Foundations, Forms, and Legacy*. 3 vols. Philadelphia: University of Pennsylvania Press, 1988.

———. "The Significance of 'Civic Humanism' in the Interpretation of the Italian Renaissance." In Rabil, ed., *Renaissance Humanism*, 1: 141–74.

Restrepo Jaramillo, Gonzalo. "Maquiavelo-Saavedra Fajardo." *Universidad Pontificia Bolivariana* 21 (1957): 347–55.

Rico, Francisco. *Nebrija frente a los bárbaros: El canon de gramáticos nefastos en las polémicas del humanismo*. Salamanca: Universidad de Salamanca, 1978.

Risco, Antonio. "El empirismo político de Fadrique Furió Ceriol." *Cahiers du Monde Hispanique et Luso-Bresilien* 29 (1977): 123–55.

Ruiz, Claudia. "Apologistas de la manera y de la apariencia." *Anuario de Letras Modernas* 7 (1995–1996): 125–41.

Rupp, Stephen. *Allegories of Kingship: Calderón and the Anti-Machiavellian Tradition*. University Park: Pennsylvania State University Press, 1996.

Santoro, Mario. *Fortuna, ragione e prudenza nella civiltà letteraria del Cinquecento*. Naples: Liguori, 1967.

———. "Humanism in Naples." In Rabil, ed., *Renaissance Humanism*, 1: 296–331.

Schellhase, Kenneth C. "Botero, Reason of State, and Tacitus." In *Botero e la "ragion di stato": Atti del convengo in memoria di Luigi Firpo (Torino 8-10 marzo 1990)*, ed. A. Enzo Baldini, 243–59. Florence: L. S. Olschki, 1992.

Seigel, Jerrold E. "'Civic Humanism' or Ciceronian Rhetoric?" *Past and Present* 34 (1966): 3–48.

———. *Rhetoric and Philosophy in Renaissance Humanism: The Union of Eloquence and Wisdom, Petrarch to Valla*. Princeton, NJ: Princeton University Press, 1968.

Seznec, Jean. *The Survival of the Pagan Gods: The Mythological Tradition and its Place in Renaissance Humanism and Art*. Trans. Barbara F. Sessions. Princeton, NJ: Princeton University Press, 1972.

Sierra, S. I. Luis. "La moral política: El antimaquiavelismo en Suárez y Gracián." *Arbor: Revista General de Investigación y Cultura* 48, no. 183 (1961): 281–301.

Skinner, Quentin. *The Foundations of Modern Political Thought*. 2 vols. Cambridge: Cambridge University Press, 1978.

———. *Machiavelli*. New York: Hill and Wang, 1981.

Strauss, Leo. *Thoughts on Machiavelli*. Chicago: University of Chicago Press, 1984.

Sullivan, Vickie B. *Machiavelli's Three Romes: Religion, Human Liberty, and Politics Reformed*. DeKalb: Northern Illinois University Press, 1996.

Tate, Robert Brian. "The Civic Humanism of Alfonso de Palencia." *Renaissance & Modern Studies* 23 (1979): 25–44.

———. *Ensayos sobre la historiografía peninsular del siglo XV*. Madrid: Editorial Gredos, 1970.

———. "Political Allegory in Fifteenth-Century Spain: A Study of the *Batalla campal de los perros contra los lobos* by Alfonso de Palencia (1423–92)." *Journal of Hispanic Philology* 1, no. 3 (1977): 169–86.

———. "*El tratado de la perfección militar* de Alfonso de Palencia (1459): la Villa de Discreción y la arquitectura humanista." In *Essays on Narrative Fiction in the Iberian Peninsula in Honour of Frank Pierce*, ed. Robert Brian Tate, 163–76. Oxford: Dolphin, 1982.

Tate, Robert Brian, and Anscari M. Mundo. "The *Compendiolum* of Alfonso de Palencia: A Humanist Treatise on the Geography of the Iberian Peninsula." *Journal of Medieval and Renaissance Studies* 5 (1975): 253–78.

Tenenti, Alberto. "La religione di Machiavelli." *Studi storici* 10 (1969): 709–48.

Tierno Galván, Enrique. *Escritos (1950–1960)*. Madrid: Editorial Tecnos, 1971.

Truman, R. W. *Spanish Treatises on Government, Society, and Religion in the Time of Philip II: The* De regimine principum *and Associated Traditions*. Leiden: Brill, 1999.

Ullman, B. L. *Studies in the Italian Renaissance*. Rome: Edizioni di storia e letteratura, 1955.

Vindel, Ingrid. "Política y educación para príncipes en una comedia de 1615: *El mejor maestro, el tiempo*." *Anuario Lope de Vega* 6 (2000): 209–18.

Viroli, Maurizio. *From Politics to Reason of State*. Cambridge: Cambridge University Press, 1992.

———. *Machiavelli's God*. Princeton, NJ: Princeton University Press, 2010.

Weber, Alison. *Teresa of Avila and the Rhetoric of Femininity*. Princeton, NJ: Princeton University Press, 1990.

Zagorin, Perez. *Ways of Lying: Dissimulation, Persecution, and Conformity in Early Modern Europe*. Cambridge, MA: Harvard University Press, 1990.

Index

Alba, Duke Fernando Álvarez de Toledo 59-60, 63
Alvia de Castro, Fernando 108-10, 116
anti-Machiavellians 9, 13-14, 39, 47-50, 54, 72, 85, 86, 155
  in France 69-71
  in Spain 1-4, 10-11, 54, 71-95, 97-128, 145-6, 148, 150, 156
arcana imperii 1, 39, 127
Aristotle 5-7, 15, 17, 20-1, 27, 29, 36, 38-9, 52-3, 109, 114, 117
  The Politics 15
Ayala, Balthazar 8, 63-7
  De iure et officiis bellicis et disciplina militari 63-7
Azpilcueta, Martín de 92-3

Barbosa Homem, Pedro 114-23, 125, 127
  Discursos de la iuridica, y verdadera razon de estado 114-23
Baroque 5, 8, 10, 13, 50, 99, 155
Blázquez Mayoralgo, Juan 123-28
  Perfect raçon de estado 123-28
Boccaccio 26
  Comento sopra Dante 26
Bodin, Jean 2, 69, 71, 84, 99-100, 114-6, 118, 129
  Methodus 69
  République 69, 129
Boethius 26, 31
Botero, Giovanni 8-10, 71-83, 85, 87, 95, 98, 112, 126, 138
  Della ragion di stato libri dieci 8, 71-83
Bruni, Leonardo 18-19, 20, 36

Cardano, Girolamo 6
Cartagena, Alfonso de, Bishop of Burgos 20, 23
Cerdán de Tallada, Tomás 8
Charles V, Holy Roman Emperor 7, 41-46, 50, 56, 131
Charles VIII of France 25, 33, 34, 90
Cicero 18, 27, 31, 66, 114
  De officiis 27
civic humanism 18-19, 26-7, 46-8
  influence in Spain 20, 22, 23-5
Clemente, Claudio 1-4, 5, 11, 98
  Machiavelismo degollado 1-4
common good 2, 15-25, 27, 29-30, 33, 45, 49, 54, 55-8, 63, 74, 85, 90, 92, 108, 112-14, 118-19, 120, 130, 146, 153. *See also under* Machiavelli.
contingency 18, 20, 22, 24-5, 28, 29-32, 34, 37, 42, 55-6, 59, 63, 65, 94, 155. *See also under* Machiavelli.
corpus mysticum 15, 16-17, 22-3, 24, 30, 55, 89, 103, 113
Cortés, Hernán 86, 156n10
Counter-Reformation 5, 8-9, 13, 39, 54, 71-2, 95, 98n2, 126, 155

Dante 19, 26, 150
Inferno 26
dissimulation 30, 50, 77, 91-3, 106, 109, 110, 119, 124, 127, 132, 143. *See also* simulation; *see also* mendacity.

empire. *See also under* Machiavelli.
in Spain 41-6, 50-52, 55-63, 83, 97, 131, 155-6
Erasmus 43-4, 44-5
Institutio principis christiani 43, 45

favorite *See valido*
fortune 6, 40, 42-3, 55-8, 78-9, 87, 90, 95, 124, 125, 131, 133-5, 140. *See also under* Machiavelli.
and virtue 25-9, 31-2, 33, 34, 43, 56-8
Fox Morcillo, Sebastián 8
fraud. *See* mendacity.
Furió Ceriol, Fadrique 8, 52-63, 67, 87, 144
El concejo y consejeros de príncipes 52-9, 60
Remedios 59-63

García de Castrojeriz, Juan 16-17, 22
Glosa castellana al "Regimiento de príncipes" de Egidio Romano (*see* Giles of Rome: *De regimine principum*)
Gentillet, Innocent 70-71, 84, 95, 98, 100, 101, 102
Discours sur les moyens de bien gouverner ... contre Nicolas Machiavel 70, 71
Giles of Rome 16-17, 21, 22, 37, 38-9
De regimine principum 16-17, 22, 37, 38-9
Gracián de la Madre de Dios, Jerónimo 99-102, 103, 108, 116, 156n3
Diez lamentaciones del miserable estado de los Atheistas de nuestros tiempos 99-102
Guevara, Antonio de 42-44, 45
Marco Aurelio con el Relox de príncipes 43-44
Menosprecio de corte y alabanza de aldea 42-43

Herrera, Antonio de 71-2, 74, 76, 77, 83
Diez libros de la razon de estado (*see* Botero, Giovanni: *Della ragion di stato libri dieci*)
hypocrisy *See* mendacity; dissimulation.

kingship
councillors in 52-4, 56-9, 60, 107, 111-12, 151-2
divine origins of 15, 17, 20, 22, 29-30, 45, 89
hatred and/or contempt in 39, 44, 58-60, 63, 65, 73-6, 94, 105, 112, 129-30, 132, 133-5, 136-44, 153 (*see also under* Machiavelli)
love and/or fear associated with 6, 28, 39-40, 44, 49, 59, 60, 63, 66, 73-5, 79, 94, 103-4, 105, 137-44, 153 (*see also under* Machiavelli)
medieval 15-17
religion and 1-4, 6, 15-18, 19-23, 29-32, 41-6, 63-4 69-71, 72, 76-9, 82, 84-95, 100-2, 103, 106-8, 108-10, 115-18, 124-5, 126, 137, 145, 147, 149-50, 153 (*see also under* Machiavelli)

reputation of king 28, 53, 57, 74-5, 79, 82, 93-4, 100, 128, 135, 137, 139, 147, 149, 152 (*see also under* Machiavelli)
in Spain 19-20, 21-3, 29-32, 41-42, 55-6, 59, 85, 97, 153-4
tyranny and 3, 6, 15, 17, 22, 28, 29-30, 36, 38-9, 44, 45, 59, 70-71, 73, 84, 89-90, 105-6, 109-10, 112-13, 117, 124-5, 128, 129-30, 136-9, 145, 150, 153, 155 (*see also under* Machiavelli)
virtues associated with 15, 16, 17-18, 21, 22, 30-2, 42-43, 55, 73, 76, 85-8, 91-5, 101-2, 108-10, 112, 117, 122, 124-5, 127-8, 130, 133-44, 144-50, 153, 155 (*see also* Machiavelli: virtues and vices)

Las Casas, Bartolomé de 50
Le Roy, Louis 7, 69
Lerma, Francisco Gómez de Sandoval y Rojas, Duke of 97, 102-5
lying *See* mendacity.

Machiavelli, Niccolò
Art of War 7
circulation of works in Spain 7, 155
common good in 36-40, 48, 55, 85, 93, 141
conspiracies in 39-40, 58-9
contingency in 14, 35-40, 65-6
councillors in 53-4, 151-2
Discourses on Livy 6, 7, 8, 10, 35, 36, 37, 46, 48, 49, 50, 51, 56, 58-9, 63-67, 77-82, 84, 85-7, 102, 104, 122, 125, 126, 149-50, 153, 155
empire in 35-6, 50-52, 56, 57, 61-3, 79-83, 126
Florentine Histories 90
fortune in 34-6, 56, 66, 80, 91, 95, 130, 133-5, 140, 149
hatred and/or contempt in 39-40, 50, 58-9, 63, 65-6, 73-6, 93, 136-44
ideological reading of 14, 33-40, 155
love and/or fear in 6, 39-40, 66, 73-5, 137-44
mischaracterizations of 1-4, 11, 13, 69-71, 72, 84-6, 91-3, 95, 98, 99-102, 109-10, 111-12, 115-20, 124-5, 127, 145-50
necessity in 35-6, 39-40, 54, 56, 64, 67, 75, 80, 91, 131, 141-3, 148, 149
plebs and/or great in 57, 79, 104-5, 126, 134, 137-8, 149
Prince 5-6, 7, 8, 10, 14, 34, 35, 38, 39-40, 48, 49-50, 53-54, 55, 58-9, 59-63, 64, 70, 71, 73-6, 82-3, 84, 90-1, 93, 94-5, 100, 102, 104, 128, 129-48, 151-53, 155, 156
principalities, kinds of, in 130-36, 144
prohibition of 7, 48, 63, 67, 84, 129
prudence in 35, 38, 40, 87, 94, 150, 151-2
reception of in Europe 5-11, 69-71, 97-8, 153-4, 155-7
religion in 10-11, 13, 46-50, 64, 77-8, 85-7, 102, 122, 149-50
reputation in 37, 39, 82, 93, 125, 138, 141, 152
tyranny in 36, 37, 38-40, 52, 66
virtues and vices in 35-40, 47, 52, 55, 75-6, 91, 93, 128, 133-44, 146-50
war in 64-7, 139-40, 152-3

Machiavellism 4-5, 7-8, 10-11, 13, 14, 50, 54, 71, 127, 155-7
Mártir Rizo, Juan Pablo 129-53
Norte de principes 129-53
mendacity 54, 61, 71, 92-3, 105-8, 113-14, 119-23, 127-8, 144-50
Mexico 123, 155

necessity 4, 28, 35, 54, 61, 79, 92-4, 103, 106, 110, 112-14, 122, 125, 126-8, 141. *See also under* Machiavelli.
Netherlands 42, 53, 59-64, 67, 155
Nifo da Sessa, Agostino 5-6
De regnandi peritia 5-6
Noue, François de la 71, 84, 99

Olivares, Gaspar de Guzmán, Count-Duke of 97, 111-12, 129
Osorio da Fonseca, Jeronimo 47, 48, 49-50, 64, 71, 85
De nobilitate civile et christiana 48, 49, 71
De regis institutione 49
Ottevanti, Juan Lorenzo 50
Discursos de Nicolao Machiaueli 50

Palencia, Alfonso de 20, 23-5
Batalla campal de los perros contra los lobos 23
Tratado de la perfección del triunfo militar 23, 24-5
Petrarch 18, 26
De remediis utriusque fortunae, 26
Philip II of Spain 7, 8, 42, 52, 55, 56, 58-63, 63-4, 67, 72, 97, 131
Philip III of Spain 72-3, 97, 99, 102-5, 108, 129
Philip IV of Spain 97, 111-12, 115, 123
Plessis Mornay, Philippe du 2, 71, 84, 99-100
Pole, Reginald 47, 48, 49-50
Apologia ad Carolum Quintum 48, 49-50
políticos 1-4, 84-90, 99-100, 103, 105-7, 108-9, 114-16, 124, 127
politiques 69-70, 84, 87. *See also políticos.*
Pontano, Giovanni 25, 27, 28-9, 34, 35
De fortuna 28
De Principe 28
De prudentia 28, 34
Portugal 108, 114, 131, 155
Possevino, Antonio 71, 84, 93, 100, 101, 124, 145
Judicium 71
providence 26, 27, 31-2, 43, 44, 57, 86-7, 90, 93, 94, 95, 118, 119, 120-1
prudence 3, 25, 27-9, 31-2, 34, 35, 55-7, 60, 62, 72, 75, 82, 89, 92-3, 94-5, 103, 104, 108, 109, 110, 112, 119, 122, 124, 125-6, 132, 136, 137, 140, 147, 151-2. *See also under* Machiavelli.

reason of state 1, 5, 8-10, 47, 67, 71-3, 76, 83, 85, 89-90, 92-3, 95, 97-100, 101, 102, 103, 105-7, 108-10, 111, 114-18, 120-3, 123-5, 127-8, 130, 145-7, 149-50, 153
Ribadeneyra, Pedro de 10, 54, 71-2, 76, 83-95, 98, 100, 101, 102, 105-6, 107, 109-10, 124, 145
Tratado de la Religion y Virtudes que deue tener el Principe Christiano 10, 71-2, 84-95, 110
Rucellai, Bernardo 34
De bello italico 34

Saint Bartholomew's Day Massacre, 60, 69-70

Salutati, Coluccio 18, 27-8, 36
De nobilitate legum et medicine, 27-8
Sánchez de Arévalo, Rodrigo 20-3, 24
Suma de la política 21-3
Sansovino, Francesco 6
Santa María, Juan de 102-8, 115-16, 137
Tratado de republica y policia christiana 102-8
Segni, Bernardo 6-7
Seneca 2, 31-2, 145
Thyestes 145
Sepúlveda, Juan Ginés de 8, 47, 48, 50-52
Democrates primus 48
Demócrates segundo 51-52
simulation 92-3, 106, 110, 121-3, 125, 127, 137, 143, 149, 150. *See also* dissimulation; *see also* mendacity.

Thomas Aquinas, Saint 15-16, 17, 21, 29, 109, 112
tyranny. *See under* kingship; *see under* Machiavelli.

Valdés, Alfonso de 44-46
Diálogo de las cosas acaecidas en Roma 45
Diálogo de Mercurio y Carón 45-46
Valera, Diego de 29-32, 37
Doctrinal de príncipes 29-31
Exortación de la pas 31, 32
Tratado de providencia contra fortuna 31-2
valido 29, 97, 102, 104-5, 111-12
vernacular humansim 20
virtue. *See under* fortune; *see under* kingship; *see under* Machiavelli.
Vitoria, Francisco 58
De potestate ciuili 58

Wars of Religion, French 69-70, 85

Zeballos, Jerónimo de 111-14, 115
Arte real para el buen gouierno de los reyes y principes y de sus vasallos 111-14